NETWORK

How does a telecommunications company function when its right hand often doesn't know what its left hand is doing? How do rapidly expanding, interdisciplinary organizations hold together and perform their knowledge work? In this book, Clay Spinuzzi draws on two warring theories of work activity – activity theory and actor–network theory – to examine the networks of activity that make a telecommunications company work and thrive. In doing so, Spinuzzi calls a truce between the two theories, bringing them to the negotiating table to parley about work. Specifically, about *net work*: the work that connects, coordinates, and stabilizes polycontextual work activities.

To develop this uneasy dialogue, Spinuzzi examines the texts, trades, and technologies at play at Telecorp, both historically and empirically. Drawing on both theories, Spinuzzi provides new insights into how network actually *works* and how our theories and research methods can be extended to better understand it.

After receiving a BA in computer science and an MA in English at the University of North Texas, Clay Spinuzzi earned his PhD in rhetoric and professional communication at Iowa State University. He served as assistant professor of technical communication and rhetoric at Texas Tech University for two years before accepting a position at the University of Texas (UT) at Austin. From 2004 to 2008, he directed UT's Computer Writing and Research Lab.

Spinuzzi's work has appeared in the *Journal of Business and Technical Communication, Technical Communication Quarterly,* and *Technical Communication*. His previous book, *Tracing Genres through Organizations,* was named the National Council of Teachers of English 2004 Best Book in Technical or Scientific Communication, one of four national awards the author has received.

Network

THEORIZING KNOWLEDGE WORK IN TELECOMMUNICATIONS

Clay Spinuzzi
University of Texas at Austin

CAMBRIDGE
UNIVERSITY PRESS

CAMBRIDGE
UNIVERSITY PRESS

32 Avenue of the Americas, New York NY 10013-2473, USA

Cambridge University Press is part of the University of Cambridge.

It furthers the University's mission by disseminating knowledge in the pursuit of education, learning and research at the highest international levels of excellence.

www.cambridge.org
Information on this title: www.cambridge.org/9781107564862

First published 2008
Reprinted 2013
First paperback edition 2015

A catalogue record for this publication is available from the British Library

Library of Congress Cataloguing in Publication data
Spinuzzi, Clay.
Network : theorizing knowledge work in telecommunications / Clay Spinuzzi.
  p. cm.
Includes bibliographical references and index.
ISBN 978-0-521-89504-0 (hardback)
1. Telecommunication.   2. Communication in organizations.
3. Knowledge management.   4. Information theory.   I. Title.
HE7661.S66   2008
384.068'4 – dc22   2008011283

ISBN 978-0-521-89504-0 Hardback
ISBN 978-1-107-56486-2 Paperback

CONTENTS

ACKNOWLEDGMENTS

Finally it's done. I wrote this book in waiting rooms and lobbies, on buses and at bus stops, on airplanes, in coffee shops, and sometimes even in my office; I wrote it on sticky notes and notepads, on scrap paper, on printouts from rudimentary drafts, and in pieces on my blog. I absorbed more literature from activity theory, actor–network theory, and knowledge work than I would have thought possible. And after seven years, I'm very proud of the result – and very relieved to be done with it.

This book would have gone nowhere without the deep support offered by many, many people. At the top of the list, the managers at Telecorp generously agreed to let me study the organization, and its workers let me observe and interview them. I hope I have represented them well.

This research project was also supported by internal grants, both at Texas Tech University and the University of Texas at Austin. Thanks especially to Bill Wolff, a research assistant supported by a TLC Curriculum Development Grant at the University of Texas. Bill helped compile historical information on the Texas telecommunications market for Chapter 4.

Many of my colleagues generously gave their time to review the book manuscript and/or the articles that fed into it. Bonnie Nardi, Mark Zachry, and Bill Hart-Davidson in particular gave great critical feedback. Bonnie in particular had some rousing discussions – and disagreements – with me about actor–network theory. That dialogue, like the one in the book itself, did not come to a dialectical resolution, but it did improve the book considerably.

I'm profoundly grateful to Cambridge University Press, which accepted the manuscript after two thorough and intelligent anonymous reviews. Eric Schwartz, my editor at Cambridge, expertly shepherded the project through the process, aided by his assistant, April Potenciano.

Thanks to Gail Bayeta and Bella Bayeta-Spinuzzi, my wife and daughter, for their patience and moral support.

Most important, thanks to my parents, John and Kitty Spinuzzi. Dad taught me teamwork, strategy, and tactics; Mom taught me critique, skepticism, and reverence; and both taught me hard work and persistence. This book is dedicated to them.

1

Networks, Genres, and Four Little Disruptions

It's mid-spring in 2001 and you've just moved to Midsize City, Texas. You order telephone service from a company we'll call Telecorp. You pick up a phone – not your own, of course, but one that you borrow from a friend or even one that is thoughtfully provided in the offices of the telecommunications company itself. You speak at some length with a Customer Service representative. Several days later the phone jacks in your new place are turned on. You plug in your phone line and begin dialing. What could be simpler?

Within Telecorp, however, your information has to undergo an extended series of transformations. In Customer Service, the information is written up in a file order confirmation (FOC), a form based on a word processor template. It is e-mailed to a supervisor, who forwards it to a data entry worker. That worker prints it out, highlights particular pieces of information, and enters data into the centralized database. The FOC also gets forwarded to other places: Credit & Collections, where workers make sure that you're creditworthy; CLEC Provisioning, where you're assigned a phone number from the database used by all telecommunications companies in the area, and your physical address is keyed into the 911 database; CLEC Design, where your personal circuit is designed and associated with the number you've been assigned. And just as the FOC is transformed in different ways to meet the needs of those different groups, the transformations themselves engender more transformations. Your new record in the centralized company database becomes hooked up with the billing system, ensuring that you get your bill on time; your new number is put in the switch, ensuring that you actually receive calls; a complete history of every interaction you have with the company is maintained in the central database by Customer Service, the Network Operations Center, Sales, and others with whom you may have contact throughout your relationship with the company. When

1

Accounts Payable	Data Network Products
Administration (including Accounts Receivable)	Human Resources
Alarm Management System	Information Services
Bill Verification	Internet Help Desk
CLEC Local Operations	Network Coordination
CLEC Network Administration	Network Design & Inventory
CLEC Provisioning	Network Operations
Computer Services	Network Operations Center
Credit & Collections	Sales
Customer Service	Wholesale Markets

FIGURE 1.1. Functional groups at Telecorp, 2001.

you place calls, those calls will go through a patchwork of lines, switches, and fiber owned by several different companies. If you make a call regularly (say, to your mother in Ohio), it will rarely follow the same pathway twice. Each company leases lines from the others and reconfigures its long distance routes each month on the basis of fluctuations in lease prices.

What's more, during your relationship with the company, the list of features available to you will continue to grow. Telecorp began by *reselling* long distance service – that is, it offered only long distance service, and even that service was actually provided by another company and simply rebranded as Telecorp's – but now it offered its own local and long distance service, calling cards, long distance pagers, DSL, Internet dial-up, mobile service, conference calling, and on and on. That increasing complexity is accompanied by an increasingly complex division of labor. From a handful of people in the 1980s, Telecorp grew to over 300 in 2001, grouped into about 20 heterogeneous functional groups (depending on how you count them). See Figure 1.1.

Few of these groups actually understand each other's work. When I began researching Telecorp, my research question was: How do genres circulate in a complex organization? By the end of the project, I inflected the question somewhat differently: How on earth does this company function when its right hand often doesn't know what its left hand is doing? How do such knowledge work organizations function and thrive, and how can we develop a better theoretical and empirical account of this sort of work? Like many knowledge work organizations, Telecorp was surprisingly heterogeneous and multiply linked, and those characteristics are not especially conducive to the centralized control that we associate with traditional, hierarchical, modular work.

Here are four ways in which the right hand doesn't know what the left is doing – four minor, quotidian disruptions that occurred regularly in Telecorp's ongoing knowledge work.

Disruption 1: Anita Thinks Geraldine Is Slacking. At the Internet Help Desk, Anita receives a note from Geraldine in Sales to call a customer who has a technical problem. It turns out that the customer has no technical problems, he just wants to sign up for Telecorp's dial-up Internet service – something that, according to Anita, Sales should handle. After transferring the customer back to Sales, Anita angrily logs the incident; later she tells me that she hopes upper management will see a pattern of this sort of behavior in the logs. Although she is convinced that Sales should have taken responsibility for the customer in the first place, Anita confesses that she doesn't really understand what Sales does.

Disruption 2: Darrel Thinks Gil Is Being Unreasonable. Darrel, a sales representative who has only been on the job for a few weeks, is happy to take a rather large service order from a company. Darrel sends the order to Credit & Collections for approval. Soon, he receives a terse e-mail from Gil in Collections saying that this customer is not a good bet and that this kind of customer should be avoided – but no explanation of why the customer is rejected. Incensed that his customer is treated so shabbily and (more to the point) dismayed that his large commission is about to disappear, Darrel enlists the help of more experienced workers as he writes an e-mail urging the vice president of Sales to intervene.

Disruption 3: Abraham Threatens to Fire Workers. Telecorp's database of customer accounts includes time-stamped notes, called "F1 notes," that Customer Service workers enter to record changes to each account. (They're called up by pressing the F1 key.) In Telecorp's early days, F1 notes were rarely used and tended to be only a couple of words when they were. Since Telecorp was much smaller then – just a handful of people – knowledge likely circulated through conversations and paper files. But as the company grew larger and the division of labor grew more complex, documentation became more important and workers were asked to use the F1 notes more thoroughly. Several months before my study began, the crisis came to a head in Customer Service and Abraham, the manager, threatened to fire workers who did not use F1 notes as prescribed; later, he introduced a script for workers to use.

Disruption 4: Jeannie Talks Past Local Provisioners. Long distance provisioners such as Jeannie periodically place orders with local (CLEC) provisioners. But they grow increasingly frustrated with each other because certain orders don't seem to be filled correctly. Eventually, they realize that they have been using the same terms to mean very different things. As Jeannie puts it: "Their prem to prem is just different from what we consider a prem to prem. So we were talking back and forth a long time about prem to prem, until we figured out, 'Oh, *your* prem to prem is not the same as *our* prem to prem.'"

These four little disruptions are by no means major or crippling, but they are surprising in their character and frequency. Telecorp is not an anomaly: it's not poorly managed or run. On the contrary, it's very successful and these disruptions result in part because of its rapid expansion. They are emblematic of the disruptions I saw over a 10-month period at Telecorp – and the sorts of disruptions that we are increasingly seeing in knowledge work. All involve people from different functional areas collaborating to solve problems, connecting in *networks* that include different tools, objectives, rules, and divisions of labor, tools, and artifacts. And all involve types of texts in one form or another, *genres* that are circulated, transformed, displaced, hybridized, and developed to meet the needs of particular, localized work.

In this chapter, I'll discuss these two commonalities, drawing on two major schools of thought based in two rather different understandings of activity that are currently competing to represent and explain knowledge work: activity theory and actor–network theory. These two approaches have strong similarities that make both strong candidates for theorizing knowledge work. But they also have sharp disagreements, and in airing those disagreements we can productively examine many of our assumptions about work organization and structure. The two commonalities of network and genre are a good place to start. So in this chapter, I'll discuss these two commonalities and how they structure the rest of this book, which is all about how genres circulate through and help build networks of activity in knowledge work and how we can trace those genres to better understand their networks. Then I'll discuss the Telecorp research study itself.

NETWORKS

Let's start with networks, the source of our first two disruptions. What is a network?

The term *network*[1] in the way I'm using it here – heavily influenced by actor–network theory and activity theory – is being abandoned right and left. In 1999, some of the guiding lights of actor–network theory wrote in the pages of *Actor–Network Theory and After* that actor–network theory was, well, over. Bruno Latour declares that the term *network* has "lost its cutting edge" and in the process has lost its meaning as "a series of *transformations* – translations, transductions – which could not be captured by any of the traditional terms of social theory" (1999a, p. 15). He agrees with Michael Lynch that "actor–network theory" should instead be called "actant–rhizome ontology" (p. 19), though to his credit he agrees that the new appellation is monstrous and nobody should actually use it.[2] Similarly, John Law argues that actor–network theory, by becoming an object of study, has lost its essential charm: "The act of naming suggests that its centre has been fixed, pinned down, rendered definite" (1999, p. 2). He declares that the purpose of the collection "is to escape the multinational monster, 'actor–network theory,' not because it is 'wrong' but because labeling doesn't help" (1999, p. 2). Like Latour, Law believes that the term *network* has worked against itself, providing the illusion that complexity can be managed and simplified, implying that "*an assemblage of relations would occupy a homogeneous, conformable and singularly tellable space*" (p. 8, his italics). In response, these scholars and others have attempted to add supplemental metaphors such as fluids, modes of coordination, regimes of delegation, rhizomes (see Latour, 1995), ecologies (Star, 1995; Star & Griesemer, 1989), gels (Sheller, 2004), and plasma (Latour, 2006). These get messy rather quickly, and although that's the point – to provide a nonfragmentary, amodern way to follow continually fluxing transformations, one that is not "a return either to essences or to structures" – it's still not much fun to wade through them.

For activity theorists, on the other hand, structure is a desirable aspect of a network. In an exchange in the pages of *Mind, Culture, and Activity*, Yrjö Engeström (1996b) complains that "Latour's actants [in actor–networks] seem to have no analyzable inner structure; they are like monads or amoebas. Instead of jumping directly from actants to networks, I suggest stopping to discover the intermediate institutional anatomy of each central

---

[1] Note that the term is used differently here than it is generally used in sociology (Polodny & Page, 1998), economics (Castells, 1996), or warfare studies (Arquilla & Ronfeldt, 2001b). I draw insight from some of this literature in later chapters, but my main focus is on examining networks as they are understood in actor–network theory and activity theory: as translations or transformations that tie together mediated activities.

[2] In *Reassembling the Social* (2006), Latour (characteristically) reverses himself and reclaims the term *actor–network–theory*, even adding a hyphen (p. 9).

actant – that is, the historically accumulated durability, the interactive dynamics, and the inner contradictions of local activity systems. And I recommend keeping one's eyes open for both vertical and horizontal relations in activity systems and their networks" (p. 263; see Engeström & Escalante, 1996, for an illustration). Latour (1996c) replies that Engeström has missed the point, as indeed he has: actor–network theory and its postvariants are *supposed* to have no inner structure, no scale or hierarchy. That doesn't stop Engeström and other activity theorists from cherry-picking elements of actor–network theory for their own use, envisioning *activity networks* in which relatively stable (though never static) cultural–historical activities become interlinked (e.g., Bazerman, 2003; Engeström, 1992; Korpela, Soriyan, & Olifokunbi, 2000; Russell & Yañez, 2003; Spasser, 2000).

Yet Engeström's own later work leads him away from stable structures and toward "work that requires active construction of constantly changing combinations of people and artifacts over lengthy trajectories of time and widely distributed in space" (Engeström, Engeström, & Vähäaho, 1999, p. 345), work that has no center or stable configuration (p. 346). That description sounds suspiciously like Latour's description of networks, but the authors argue that "networks are typically understood as relatively stable structures" and thus do not provide a sufficient explanation (p. 346)! Engeström et al. (1999) invent the term *knotworking* to describe this phenomenon. Elsewhere, Nardi, Whittaker, and Schwarz similarly accuse actor–network theory of being too reliant on structures. They favorably contrast *intensional networks* (or *netWORKing*) with actor–network theory, saying of the latter that it assumes "firm footings in institutional structures inhabited by Machiavellian 'Princes'" as opposed to the "incessant buzz of small but crucial communications and reflections [that] shaped people's worklives and consciousness" in their study (2002, p. 235).

In this gloss, some of the many subtleties of Engeström et al.'s (1999) and Nardi et al.'s (2002) arguments get lost; I'll take these up more thoroughly later in the book. But what I want to emphasize here is that just as actor–network theorists have more or less jettisoned the term *network* because it had come to imply static structures, activity theorists are now beginning to question the term for the same reasons – and imputing its structural connotations to actor–network theory itself![3]

---

[3] But see Reijo Miettinen's (1999) incisive comparison of actor–network theory and activity theory. Miettinen, more than other activity theorists, understands actor–network theory and provides an even-handed critique.

I think much of this confusion has to do with slippage in the term *network*. In actor–network theory, actor–networks are *assemblages of humans and nonhumans*; any person, artifact, practice, or assemblage of these is considered a node in the network and indeed can be an actor–network in itself. Links are made across and among these nodes in fairly unpredictable ways. Since there is no hierarchy or "analyzable inner structure," the only restrictions to linking are relational or associational. Will this link advance the agenda by enlisting more allies, enrolling more actants to accomplish one's agenda? Will an alliance with this person, this text, this practice, be productive? One can see why actor–network theory is considered *political* and *rhetorical*: it is in effect a politics and a rhetoric of symmetry, one in which no Cartesian lines are drawn between humans and nonhumans (see Latour, 1999b). One can also see why actor–network theorists have turned of late to the notion of *rhizome*. As Deleuze and Guattari (1987) lay out the concept, "any point in the rhizome can be connected to anything other, and must be." And "a rhizome may be broken, shattered at a given spot, but it will start up again on one of its old lines, or on new lines" (p. 9). Rhizomes are made up of diverse, heterogeneous acts and materials that cannot and should not be categorized, placed in subject–object distinctions, or otherwise separated to generate strong explanations of their workings (cf. Callon 1986a, 1986b, 1991; Law, 1986a, 1986b, 2002a). Among those strong explanations is cognition, and in fact Latour and Woolgar (1979) famously called for a moratorium on cognitive explanations.

As Engeström's quote suggests, activity theorists don't buy this freewheeling notion of network. Activity networks are *linked activity systems* – human beings laboring cyclically to transform the object of their labor, drawing on tools and practices to do so. These activities themselves are the nodes, nodes that are constituted by, but transcend, the humans and nonhumans who participate in them. The links in the nodes of an activity network are often portrayed as supply lines: Activity A labors to produce an artifact that then serves as a tool for Activity B; Activity C labors to develop practices that then serve as rules for Activity B; and so on. Activities do indeed *interpenetrate* or overlap (Russell, 1997a; Spinuzzi, 2003b), but they can still be pulled out and examined separately. And – most importantly – activity systems and the networks in which they operate *develop* and *change*. Activity theory incubated in the field of educational psychology; its central concern is not politics or rhetoric or alliances, but *cultural–historical development* of individuals and groups. Such a focus demands the foregrounding of human beings and their labor and requires ways to account for change-in-stability that aren't demanded in the political–rhetorical orientation of actor–network theory. At the same time, due partially to criticisms from other perspectives, activity theorists are beginning to examine how activity networks have often been conceived too rigidly to explore impromptu collaborative performances, and in response they have begun to turn to "knotworking," "netWORKing," and similar concepts adapted for knowledge work. Activity theorists do not reject cognition per se, but they lean toward a distributed understanding of cognition in which people mediate their cognition with physical and psychological tools (Cole & Engeström, 1993).

So with scholars turning away from networks in different directions – to rhizomes, ecologies, gels, plasmas, knotworking, netWORKing, and so forth – why should we stick with the tired old notion of networks? Simply, I think that this disagreement over networks can be useful. And rather than throwing up my hands and abandoning the whole mess, I want to exploit the tensions among these different understandings of network, and I want to apply them to a third understanding of network: a physical telecommunications network made of wires, wood, plastic, and glass. Let's move from this academic discussion into some concrete examples.

Disruption 1: Anita Thinks Geraldine Is Slacking

On one floor of the Telecorp Center, Anita and her colleagues at the Internet Help Desk answer calls from customers using Telecorp's dial-up Internet access. Since Anita works the day shift, she mostly fields calls from retirees. Their questions tend to be along the same lines: I can't log into my account today; I tried to connect to the Internet but nothing happened; I'm not getting my e-mail. These problems and their fixes are so routine that much of the time Anita can walk the customers through the fixes while simultaneously surfing Web sites. Anita becomes frustrated when her customers don't follow her instructions or try to improvise: "Older people are the worst," she says truculently after one particularly difficult call.

Anita, like her colleagues, is young: she celebrated her 21st birthday during one of my observations. Some of the other Internet Help Desk workers are in their teens. Many are college students, and a couple are high school students. Like Anita, they have deeply internalized routine problems and fixes: as they walk customers through their problems, they simultaneously play multiplayer computer games, download MP3s, or check www.hotornot.com to discover whether other visitors to the site found their photos to be sexually attractive. They do this without any apparent loss in effectiveness.

Calls are answered by whoever is available, and individual customers do not call in regularly, so workers cannot develop – and certainly do not seek to develop – bonds with their customers. The Internet Help Desk workers inhabit a relatively insulated work world, one in which they rarely interact with other teams and interact in very limited terms with customers.

On another floor in the same building, Sales is a very different place. Sales representatives tend to be older, and some are a *lot* older, nearing retirement. They have difficulty absorbing the ever-increasing number of features and services that they can sell to customers, and most don't really understand the architecture that underlies such features; when new sales representatives learn about ATM/frame relay or Internet accounts, they do so by attending training sessions by technical employees rather than by learning from their fellow sales reps. Sales reps actively compete for sales, and in fact the Sales office has something that is not found anywhere else in Telecorp: a prominently displayed markerboard on which workers' performances are summarized, showing who has sold the most – and the least – that week. Their main focus is commercial telephone service because businesses order many lines, use them heavily, and tend to commit for long periods of time to their telecommunications providers. Residential customers are usually forwarded to Customer Service, unless a sales rep is having trouble making quota for that month. Commercial customers are wooed, assigned permanent sales reps who periodically check on them, discuss new service options, and find new opportunities to save them money. Whereas Internet Help Desk workers are paid by the hour, sales reps are paid commission, providing a powerful incentive to forge and maintain relationships with customers.

These two teams are composed of very different people with different motives, tools, training, expectations, and so forth. But sometimes these teams' separate worlds touch, and when they do, disruptions often occur. In one instance, Anita received a message from Sales via her IHD co-worker Damon: call this customer who is having trouble with his Internet account. She called the customer and found that he didn't have an Internet account with Telecorp after all. He wanted to register a domain name – something that, according to Anita, was Sales's job. So she transferred him to Sales.

These teams' worlds touch others as well. For instance, when residential customers call Sales to get phone service, they are passed to Customer Service: residential commissions are too small for sales reps to deal with and distract from the important work of building relationships with the more stable and profitable corporate accounts. Customer Service expects this division of labor as a matter of course. It's hardly surprising, then, that Sales applies a similar model to its Internet dealings, off-loading new customers to the Internet Help Desk, which is seen as a sort of Customer Service for Internet services. And since we're on the subject of how groups perceive each other, let's talk about another important and multiply perceived group: management. Although this group is diverse, that diversity is rarely recognized in how managers are perceived by workers. Anita's acid notes on the above incident illustrate this point (typos are hers):

> GERALDINE CALLED DAMON TO OPEN UP SOME TICKET FOR CUSTS HWHO ARE NOT ABLE TO GET THROUGH TO THE HELP DESK. WHEN WE CALLED THE CUST BACK HE WAS NOT HAVING ANY PROBLESMS WITH HIS INTERNET, HE HAD QWUESTIONS ABOUT US HOSTING A DOMAIN FOR HIM.

> THIS HAS NOTHING TO DO WITH THE HELPDESK. THIS IS A ***SALES*** CALL.

> THE PERSON DAMON WAS TO CALL WAS NOT EVEN AVAILABLE. IMAGINE THAT...

As she was finishing up these notes on the trouble ticket, Damon called to her: "Hey, I have him on the line, and guess what. He wants to register a domain name!" Sales had transferred the customer right back to the Internet Help Desk! No wonder Anita's note is so acid and no wonder she chooses to surround the word "Sales" with so many asterisks. As she remarked after closing the ticket, this sort of incident happens a lot; she blames it on Sales pushing job responsibilities to others so they won't have so much to do. The majority of people who need our number have it, she says. According to Anita, when customers call Sales, they say: "I have a technical question," and Sales immediately routes the call to the Internet Help Desk – and the IHD workers have to open a trouble ticket for each one. That's why they write sarcastic notes, she explains – so that when "Corporate" reads through them, they'll see a pattern. The trouble ticket is not just an accounting of the problem or a way to cover one's bases; in Anita's hands, it becomes a rhetorical appeal to management, a way to enact change in the organization. By making this inscription – an account of the incident that she had to write anyway – Anita hijacked an existing sociotechnical network to protest how the division of labor was being enacted in the organization.

I saw no evidence that Anita's appeals were even read. It's not that management was uncaring, but who's going to read through the several dozen trouble tickets generated each day when there's so much other pressing work? As Latour argues (1986), power is best understood as a *consequence* rather than as a *cause*: not as something that is projected but rather as a token that others can choose to pick up and translate. Anita hopes that management (vaguely conceived) will pick up her tokens, her multiple accounts of encounters with Sales, and translate them into rebukes or new policies, but the people who read these notes are typically the other workers at the Internet Help Desk.

I'll talk about genres in a moment, but for now let's look at how many genres, how many varied types of texts are circulating and being transformed in order to sustain this uneasy collaboration between Sales and the IHD. Geraldine receives a customer's voice mail, a summary of the customer's needs, and in turn calls Damon with her own summary ("Wasn't nice about it either!" Damon remarked to Anita). Damon turns Geraldine's summary into his own one-line summary for the "face" of the trouble ticket: "CALL ASAP. GERALDINE FROM SALES REQUIRES WE CALL." Anita inherits the ticket, reads Damon's summary, calls the customer, and discusses his problem. She pulls up another text, a Web page detailing Telecorp's Web hosting information, and reads it to him. She explains that she can transfer him to a sales rep, and after trying his normal rep (she gets voice mail and concludes that that rep is out of the office), she transfers him to the main Sales number. Finally, she summarizes the interaction in the ticket, even as Damon reports that the customer has been transferred back to the IHD. What a cloud[4] of different texts, an ecology of genres, each with their own genealogies and circulating paths, and I've only catalogued a fraction of them here. With each inscription, accounts and narratives are materially instantiated, circulated, and translated to do particular work. To return to the example above, the trouble ticket has been translated in Anita's hands to become an indignant protest and an attempt to recruit powerful allies to remake her work.

Latour argues that to build a network, one should find ways to cover one's world in a parsimonious fashion, "[tying] as many settings as possible to as few elements as possible through as few intermediaries as possible" (1988b, p. 160). Telecorp's telecommunications network is a good example. Wherever you are in the network, you pick up the phone and dial, and your voice is thrown to the other end of the line, traveling the thin bits of metal and glass and sometimes the electromagnetic spectrum. Where the line travels – through neighborhoods, fields, and deserts, or up to geosynchronous satellites, or even from one cubicle to the next – isn't important.

---

[4] Johndan Johnson-Eilola (2001) uses the apt term *datacloud* to describe the saturation of texts in postmodern environments.

Technical networks, Latour says, are nets thrown over spaces; they embrace surfaces without covering them (1993b, p. 118). Those networks are used to link actants, make distance irrelevant, and circulate texts as "immutable mobiles," inscriptions that can withstand the trip and be presentable, readable, and combinable (1990, p. 26). *Knowing in* the network involves transforming these inscriptions appropriately at each node (1990, p. 40). The disruption that Anita and Geraldine encounter involves a fundamental disagreement about how inscriptions should be transformed and where in the network this transformation should occur. How are such disruptions dealt with? In this case, as in most cases, the answer is to enroll more allies to bolster one's position. In a political–rhetorical actor–network, the winner of a conflict is the one who can muster on the spot the largest number of allies (1990, p. 23), and Anita's notes are aimed at doing exactly that.

But this understanding of network doesn't do much to explore the cultural–historical development of these interlinked activities. Anita and Geraldine are after quite different things; their work has different objects, different objectives; they understand their own and each other's work in quite different ways. Part of the disagreement has to do with the newness of their division of labor: the Internet Help Desk is a very new group supporting a very new service, while Sales has been with the company since the beginning and has had difficulty developing ways to relate to this new group. The IHD and Sales can be seen as activity systems, each developmentally linked to their own trades and craft traditions, and each constantly changing in multiple attempts to keep Telecorp coherent through its constant technical, organizational, economic, and regulative changes. The two activity systems have developed a *contradiction* (Engeström, 1992), a fundamental disagreement about how they should relate, and that contradiction motivates both individual innovations (such as Anita's note) and, eventually, broader changes in the activities if the link is to survive.

Networks are relatively stable assemblages of humans and nonhumans that collectively form standing sets of transformations: the network represents and rerepresents phenomena in various areas. These phenomena include information such as orders but also people such as customers and co-workers. As we'll see below, these necessary rerepresentations introduce plenty of dissonance.

Disruption 2: Darrel Thinks Gil Is Being Unreasonable

The second little disruption, like the first, involves Sales. There's an inherent tension between Sales and another department with which Sales interacts frequently: Credit & Collections. Sales reps see themselves as the engine of prosperity in the company. But at Credit & Collections, the watchword is fiscal responsibility, and that sometimes means turning away customers that Sales has lined up.

This counterbalance relationship generates other tensions. Sales reps are paid on commission and have a strong interest in adding customers. Furthermore, their job is to build relationships, and they resent obstacles to that goal. On the other hand, Credit & Collections workers are paid by the hour and have no incentive to bring in new business. To the contrary, their job is to weed out the bad risks. They see Sales as underinformed or overeager. "Sometimes they get confused as to what needs to go through. Either that or – some people look at it, they don't want to take the time to go through Credit," one Credit & Collections worker told me.

In this situation, sales reps and Credit & Collections workers look at the same customer and see very different things – and each is put out that the other doesn't see the "obvious." This phenomenon is what Mol (2002) calls "multiplicity" (cf. Deleuze & Guattari, 1987; see also Haraway, 1991; Law, 2002a, 2004a; Law & Mol, 2002; Mol & Law, 1994) and what activity theorists call "polycontextuality" (Engeström, Engeström, & Kärkkäinen, 1995): people with different sets of expertise tend to use different frameworks, techniques, and tools, apprehend shared phenomena quite differently, and still manage to discuss these phenomena as more or less coherent. But sometimes that coherence is lost and people are startled to realize that they seem to be seeing entirely different things.

In the case outlined above, Darrel is having a hard time making the customer cohere as a single entity that he and Gil can discuss. Darrel could understand it if the customer were a borderline case, but to Darrel this customer is clearly a good risk. To Gil, the customer is just as clearly a bad risk, and he can't understand why Darrel would see it differently. It is as if they are talking about entirely different customers who happen to share the same name. Livid, Darrel discusses the problem with the local sales manager and the sales assistant, and they speculate on reasons why Gil has rejected the customer. (The manager suggests that it has to do with credit problems related to the customer's real estate; Darrel uncharitably suggests that Gil holds a personal grudge.) Darrel and the sales assistant collaborate on an e-mail to the vice president of Sales that attempts to stabilize the customer and make him coherent (typos are Darrel's):

> George, I have a customer that is needing to get 12 lines to be approved for credit. We have sent this order over to credit and Gil Brown had

denied this order for reasons I do not understand. I have informed the customer on the process of being approved for credit with Telecorp. My customer replied that his company has good credit and there must be some kind of mistake. However, the customer has told me that he would give me a $500.00 deposit to get these lines approoved and turned on in our switch, also, the customer wanted to know if Telecorp could try him. I have tried talking, and I have also sent email's to Gil Brown but he will not call me back, nor in his emails explain why this customer cannot be approved by Telecorp for credit. The customer is about to go back to BIGTEL [Telecorp's major competitor]. George I really need some hlep here and I would really appreciate an assistants on this matter. Thanks, Darrel Smith.

Who has it right, Darrel or Gil? Both and neither. The two employees and the parts of the network in which they labor use very different tools, rules, and techniques to evaluate their customers. In an important sense, the customer in one part of the network is not the same as the customer in another part; the trustworthy guy who is willing to put up a deposit as a good-faith gesture and the shady fellow with a spotty credit history are irreconcilable. But what that tells us is that the parts of the network differ radically. Sales and Credit & Collections seek to transform the same object in very different ways, and those differing aims represent what activity theorists call a "contradiction," a point at which the two activities pull in different directions. As they pull, they pull apart the coherent customer into noble and sinister figures, like Captain Kirk in a *Star Trek* episode. Darrel tries through his e-mail to put Captain Kirk back together again in a way that favors Darrel's own activity.

This example is not unique to Darrel, nor is it unique to Telecorp. In her book *The Body Multiple* (2002), Annemarie Mol persuasively argues that the things we take as settled, scientifically quantifiable, and observable phenomena are not really just objects-in-the-world; rather, they always multiply. Reality, she says, multiplies when we focus on artifacts or practices.

How could that be? Mol manages to take a very mystical-sounding concept and ground it through material, pragmatically gathered and analyzed data. She asks: What is the disease called "atherosclerosis"? And the best illustration comes from one of her informants who shows her a slide under the microscope and demonstrates how the veins have calcified and narrowed, restricting blood flow and causing great pain in the legs of the person who had the disease. This calcification, he tells her, is atherosclerosis. And after a pause, he qualifies: *under the microscope.*

It's an important qualification. The pathologist can make these slides only after the leg has been amputated (since the veins are otherwise occupied until that point, you see), so *his* version of atherosclerosis comes rather late in the game. Other people's versions of atherosclerosis are enacted differently (and Mol selects the term *enacted* carefully, to indicate the complex practices in which they are embedded). To the patient, atherosclerosis is great pain in the legs; to the general practitioner, one possible explanation for that pain and for the weak pulse in the legs; to the radiologist, a cloudy smear in the X-rays after a radioactive dye has been injected; to a surgeon, "pipes" that have to be cleaned; to an occupational therapist, a malady that can be abated with exercise. Mol points out that usually these multiple enactments of the disease cohere – that is, there's enough correspondence among them that people can be said to be talking about the same object, the same disease. But for Mol's doctors, as for Darrel and Gil, sometimes these enactments don't cohere. At those points, actors have to find ways to break the impasse by enrolling more human and nonhuman allies: Mol's doctors run more and different tests while Darrel appeals to a higher authority. In both cases, culturally and historically different activities[5] are brought to bear on the same object. They pull it in contradictory directions and negotiate[6] a bearable settlement. As Engeström remarks (1992), contradictions are the engine of change in activities, causing those activities to incessantly reconstruct themselves.

The customer Darrel and Gil are fighting over may be many things: a devoted husband, a lousy tipper, an expert golfer, a Baptist, an Irish American, a Republican. These designations all have meanings in other networks and other activities, and I won't deny that some of them may have reverberations in this one. But though networks claim large areas, in practice they are vanishingly small; their claim to power is that they transform the world so that things outside the network don't matter (Bowker, 1987; Latour, 1993b, pp. 117–118). In the Telecorp network, what matters about the customer is whether he will be a good customer or not, and the definition of "good" depends on the location within the network. In Sales, "good" is tacitly defined by a range of qualities such as the number of lines the customer wants, the set of features on those lines, the willingness to put cash up front, and the tendency the customer has to avoid arguing with salespeople. At Credit & Collections, "good" is explicitly defined by the credit report, and 5 percent to 10 percent of applicants are rejected.

---

[5] Elsewhere I have called them "interpenetrating activity systems"; see Spinuzzi, 2003b.

[6] The term *negotiate* has been used quite a bit in various literatures and has consequently lost some of its precision. Here I use it to refer to ongoing political–rhetorical interactions that typically result in compromise, leading to relatively stable but open-ended settlements. This use is roughly equivalent to *bargain* or *haggle*, as Latour uses these terms in *Pandora's Hope* (1999b).

Net Working

Let's leave the examples for a minute and talk about this notion of network a bit more. When I use the term *network* I mean an assemblage that makes up Telecorp: Internet Help Desk workers, computers, fibers, sales reps, telephones, software, vice presidents, routines, credit reports, wires, hallway conversations, servers, folders, Credit & Collections workers, cubicles, and so on. All are material, all are linked in complex and shifting ways, and all are brought to bear on the business of extending and developing the network, that is, bringing more elements into the assemblage and relating them in different ways. And how that network had expanded in the years before this study! At the time of the study in 2001, Telecorp was associated with approximately three times as many Internet Help Desk workers, sales reps, vice presidents, and other workers as it had been a few years earlier. It had acquired far more wires, fiber, customers, servers, corporate partners, features, and practices. Its vocabulary continued to grow, differentiate, and mingle with those of others. It had connected to new trades and disciplines. The network changed so rapidly that any description of it – even a description as long as this book – could only be a snapshot. And that's fine, because what interests me is not the network so much as the *net work*: the ways in which the assemblage is enacted, maintained, extended, and transformed; the ways in which knowledge work is strategically and tactically performed in a heavily networked organization.

As I mentioned earlier, I'll draw mainly on two understandings of networks when investigating Telecorp. *Activity theory* provides a cultural–historical, developmental view of networks grounded in the orientation of particular activities toward particular objects. It foregrounds the development of competence and expertise as workers labor to make Telecorp a success. (Of course, success means different things in different parts of the network, as we saw in Disruption 2.) *Actor–network theory* provides a political and rhetorical view of networks and foregrounds the continual recruiting of new allies – both human and nonhuman – to strengthen the Telecorp network. The two frameworks are very different, even contradictory, and can lead to very different conclusions. As I explain in the next chapter, rather than try to reconcile them, I will attempt to keep them in productive tension, yielding a productive dialogue.

To investigate the net work at Telecorp, I will follow the actors and texts (Callon, Law, & Rip, 1986), disruptions (Deleuze & Guattari, 1987), and genres (Spinuzzi, 2003b) wherever they lead. That is, I will examine the ways in which textual knowledge circulates through Telecorp and pay particular attention to how those texts and their genres are developed, adapted, transformed, translated, displaced, relinked, and added as they circulate. I will look closely at how certain texts mediate, regulate, and discipline the activities in which they are used. I'll investigate how they play a role in the competence and expertise of the workers who author, read, and use them. And finally, I'll examine how they serve to stabilize, lengthen, and strengthen the network.

So let's turn to the second half of this chapter, which is all about those circulating genres.

GENRES

Genres – which can be glossed as typified rhetorical responses to recurring social situations (Miller, 1984) – do much of the enacting that holds a network together. They do this work not by virtue of being simply text types or forms but because they are tools-in-use. That is, in this analysis, I stress genre as a behavioral descriptor rather than as a formal one (cf. Spinuzzi, 2003b; Voloshinov, 1973). Genres typically function in assemblages, as I've discussed elsewhere (Spinuzzi, 2004), and their compound mediation enables complex activities such as the ones we've seen in this chapter. As we saw in the first two disruptions, workers mobilized various genres to enroll allies for change as well as to support their routine, stable work. As relatively stable ways of producing and interpreting texts, genres impart some measure of stability (cf. Schryer, 1993) to the networks in which they circulate. But at the same time, genres develop, hybridize, interconnect, intermediate, and proliferate to support developments in those networks, providing the flexibility that networks need if they are to extend further and enroll other allies or activities (Spinuzzi, 2003b).

The word *text* comes from the root word *textere*, to weave together, and I suggest that's exactly what texts do: weave together these networks. In actor–network theory, *inscriptions* (texts, broadly speaking, though we'll tease out the subtleties of this term in Chapter 5) play a vital role in constructing networks. They transform complex, unmanageable, immobile phenomena into manageable, transformable, combinable, mobile texts (Latour, 1990). To recall our previous example, Darrel would have a hard time bringing the customer's business to Gil or vice versa, but he can *inscribe* the customer, turning him into the specific properties that he wants to examine. Similarly, Gil can hook into a different network – the financial network in which credit reports are generated – to obtain his own inscriptions of the customer, and he finds that these inscriptions are much better suited for his work. Gil can scale down a multitude of customers by simply looking at the flat, spare reports in a stack on his desk. No matter how large or small the customers' organizations are, they are turned into reports that are approximately the same size, and those reports' uniform categories allow Gil to easily compare the customers' properties, or at least the ones he's interested in. These reports are *immutable mobiles,* inscriptions that are presentable, readable, and combinable at multiple points in the network (Latour, 1990, p. 26). By aligning himself with the vast financial network and the inscriptions it provides, Gil is in a politically and rhetorically stronger position than Darrel. Gil's colleague in Credit & Collections can even quantify the rejection rate of applications! Naturally, Darrel attempts to do some enrolling of his own by producing and circulating his own inscriptions highlighting the properties he believes to be most important: "The customer is about to go back to BIGTEL," he warns, emphasizing the competitive aspect of his team's work.

Such inscriptions are produced and interpreted regularly, as genres, and that regularity lends them much of their usefulness. Without the genre of the credit report, Gil would have a hard time presenting, reading, and combining the reports. Genres impart regularity and stability to their networks, making and strengthening connections (cf. Devitt, 1991). To examine how genres help perform net work, let's turn to Disruptions 3 and 4.

Disruption 3: Abraham Threatens to Fire Workers

F1 notes – time-stamped annotations to the Customer Service database, so called because they were accessed by pressing a function key – were used by many groups across Telecorp.[7] As one Network Operations Center (NOC) worker remarked, every time you sneeze, you want to record it. But it was not always so. In Telecorp's early days, F1 notes were rarely used and tended to be only a couple of words when they were. Since Telecorp was much smaller then – just a handful of people in Customer Service, for instance – knowledge likely circulated through conversations and paper files. But the company grew quickly, especially after it entered the local phone service market in the wake of the Telecommunications Act of 1996. (During 2000, the year this study began, the Competitive Local Exchange Carrier [CLEC] market in Texas grew 60 percent.) As the company grew larger and the division of labor grew more complex, documentation became more important and workers were asked to use the F1 notes more thoroughly. As one worker recalled, the crisis came to a head in Customer Service:

[7] For a more detailed discussion, see Spinuzzi, 2003a, on which parts of this section are based.

But Abraham [manager of Customer Service] one time, people weren't being real good about putting their notes in, and you could be completely lost. And so he sent out a memo: "If you aren't putting in your F1 notes, you're gonna be fired!" . . . for four months he had been telling us F1 notes were important, and finally he threatened our jobs, and we started putting them in. (Sheila, Sales and formerly Customer Service)

Under this threat, workers in Customer Service began using the F1 notes in earnest, and they began recognizing value in them:

Anytime we do something to an account, we have to put it in the F1 notes. 'Cause we're not the only ones looking at these accounts. Sometimes Credit will look it up, a different department may have to get in there and see what's going on, and so the F1 notes are kind of like a diary. You know, what's going on with the account. So anytime we do something to it, we have to put what we've done. And who told us to. (Priscilla, Customer Service)

What goes into the F1 notes? Priscilla reports that her notes are just detailed enough "to let other people know . . . no use writing a book unless you have to." They were a "diary." Another Customer Service worker adds that the F1 notes' "rules" were to provide a detailed description of the worker's actions with the worker's name at the end. A third worker mentions that the F1 notes are also a way to record the experience with the customer – "this customer was not nice" – so that others will know how to handle the customer and how to interpret later interactions.

But guidelines such as these were apparently not enough. Workers were later told to be more explanatory in F1 notes, including date, action, and codes based on function keys. For instance, if the product was a calling card, the worker would press F5 to get to the calling card screen. So in the F1 notes, the worker would create a list: "F5, F7" to indicate the screens she or he filled out.

Furthermore, Customer Service's F1 note has become more rigid and more regulated with the help of another training genre. One newly trained worker reported that for new orders

You try to make them as brief as possible but as informative as possible. Abraham just recently, you'll see it on – I think it's on most people's monitor, a little white slip [with instructions and a model entry]. That is so everybody uniformly enters them instead of everybody having their own style and you not being able to read it real quick, you know. . . . And it's just to help out if you have to go back and review the customer's history. (Susan, Customer Service data entry)

So in Customer Service, F1 notes became more enforced, more rigidly defined and scripted – more *official*, to use a term I have used elsewhere (Spinuzzi, 2003b) – and more focused on helping other workers interact with the system and the customers. They have also become more focused on providing documentation to protect the company. For instance, one customer called and complained that she had been "slammed" by Telecorp – illegally switched to Telecorp's dial tone without her knowledge. This is a serious accusation attached to a substantial regulatory penalty. Fortunately, the F1 notes provided the documentation necessary to prove that the customer's husband had switched the service without telling her.

In the terms we have used, F1 notes are inscriptions that circulate through Telecorp's networks, creating and strengthening those networks. But the networks have become larger, farther reaching, and more attenuated, so more inscriptions are necessary to hold those networks together. And moreover, those inscriptions had to become more regularized, more oriented to common recurrent problems, and more easily interpretable. They had to become *genres.*

I say "genres" and not "a genre" because even though workers across Telecorp think of F1 notes as plainly written accounts of what happened, these notes have developed differently at particular nodes in the network. F1 notes in Customer Service, for instance, are much more scripted and differently oriented than in the Network Operations Center (NOC). In the NOC, workers were aware that their notes might have multiple audiences: their co-workers, who might be trying to follow the problem's history and determine whether the problem is chronic; upper management, especially on trouble tickets that turned out to be problematic for the company; and lawyers in possible lawsuits. So workers learned to "make them as detailed as possible but also as simple as possible," as one worker put it. That entailed using a looser narrative structure than is used in Customer Service, drawing on plain language and terminology that others would recognize rather than the specialized terminology used in the NOC, and noting contacts that the workers made with customers and other vendors. At the Internet Help Desk, as we saw, workers use F1 notes to lodge complaints against workers in other areas. At CLEC Provisioning, workers shun F1 notes in favor of their own Access database and paper documentation.

In other words, a note is not just a note. Telecorp employees talk about the F1 note as if it were a single type of text, an invariant form, but it has evolved into a variety of genetically related text types or "tools-in-use" (Russell, 1997a) that are routinely produced and interpreted to mediate cyclical activities. These genres continue to develop and adapt as the activities in which they are engaged develop and as other genres brought to bear on the activity develop. They (stabilize) the activity. The more official they are, the more widely they can circulate, but the less flexible they become. Despite developing for a particular activity, they can serve as *boundary objects*, "objects which are both plastic enough to adapt to local needs and the constraints of the several parties employing them, yet robust enough to maintain a constant identity across sites" (Star & Griesemer, 1989, p. 393). For instance, Customer Service's F1 notes have developed to mediate a particular activity in a particular node of the network, but they can circulate into other nodes (the NOC, Sales, and even the Legal department), where they serve quite different purposes and mediate quite different activities.

In activity theory, genres have been theorized extensively (e.g., Engeström, 1995; Russell, 1997a, 1997b; Spinuzzi, 2003b). We'll get into some of this theoretical work later in the book, but at this point I want to stress the question of *mediation.* As I've used it in the paragraph above, mediation involves controlling one's own behavior "from the outside," as it were, through physical and psychological tools (Vygotsky, 1978, p. 40). This self-regulative work is transformative: by mediating their own work, human beings transform themselves, finding that they can do things that they could not do in an unmediated way (Cole, 1996). For instance, workers in Customer Service use F1 notes to mediate their work, and these notes allow them to make better judgments about customers' complaints, solve problems more effectively and consistently, and make better guesses about which parts of the database to examine than would be possible otherwise. In turn, other artifacts such as the printed scripts mediate workers' writing, helping (or constraining) them write F1 notes more regularly. Checklists, sticky notes, annotations, highlighters, e-mails, sorted paper stacks, and other artifacts also play their part in mediating the work. And as workers mediate their work with these artifacts, they *internalize* the work. After a while, a Customer Service worker will not need to even glance at the F1 script before writing an F1 note that conforms closely to it. To that worker, the prescribed way of writing and reading F1 notes begins to seem natural and obvious – or, as is often the case, routine and regularized deviations from the script become unofficial parts of the genre.

In this example, the F1 note is actually occupying two different positions in the activity. As a tool, the F1 note *mediates* the activity by helping workers cyclically transform an *object*,[8] a customer's account. Over and over,

---

[8] Russell (1997a) uses the term *object(ive)* rather than the more widely used *object* to clarify activity theory's use of the term. When we hear the term *object*, we often think of an inanimate object ("that object is a telephone") or of detachment ("look at things objectively"). But in activity theory, *object* refers to the cyclically shaped material focus of an activity ("the object of the game is to solve the puzzle").

Customer Service workers read F1 notes and use them to guide changes and problem-solving actions related to their accounts. But the F1 note can itself become an object, a focus of activity that is *transformed* through the mediation of other artifacts such as scripts and sticky notes. Cheryl Geisler (2001) points out this double positioning of texts; Susanne Bødker (1991) touches on it as well in her discussion of focus shifts. This oscillation between *mediation* and *transformation* is tricky to capture in activity theory's triangular diagrams, but it is nonetheless an important point to understand if we're going to make sense of genres in activity theory.

Actor–network theory, on the other hand, finds this separation between mediation and transformation to be *unnecessarily* tricky, and not just in diagrams. In actor–network theory, mediation and transformation (translation)[9] are one and the same. All actants in the network – both human and nonhuman – simultaneously mediate each other. This mediation is carried out partially[10] through translation, the way in which actants in a network delegate actions to each other and how that delegation changes the shared action of the actor–network (Latour, 1992b; cf. Latour, 1996a). There is no analytical oscillation between mediator and object because actor–network theory's focus is on intermediation itself, resulting in what one observer has complained is "ultimately directionless motion" (Berg, 1996, p. 254).

Directionless indeed. While activity theorists use genre to trace and explore historical development, using mediation as a way to conceptualize the impetus for such changes, actor–network theorists have avoided developmental examinations of artifacts in favor of examinations that emphasize relentless and infinitely interconnected intermediations. "In AT [activity theory], the subject–object relation is a historical phenomenon that came into existence as a result of the biological and cultural evolution," Reijo Miettinen points out. "ANT [actor–network theory] postulates a general theory of association of forces, regardless of what they are" (1999, p. 178). Despite the historical examinations of developing technologies common in actor–network studies (Akrich, 1992; Callon, 1986a; Law, 1986b, 2002a; Law & Callon, 1992), the emphasis inexorably turns to rhizomatic actor–networks in which all actants are connected to each other and intermediate each other more or less equally. As the root word indicates, *genres* imply genealogies, but the rhizome is an antigenealogy (Deleuze & Guattari, 1987, p. 11).

---

[9] I oversimplify here by using *translation* and *transformation* interchangeably. In later chapters, I discuss the differences more thoroughly.

[10] In actor–network theory, mediation is carried out through translation, composition, black-boxing, and delegation (Latour, 1999b). We'll explore these concepts more thoroughly later in the book.

No wonder actor–network theory has a problem accounting for the stability of networks! Latour ruefully points this out:

> Rhyzomes and heterogeneous networks are thus powerful ways of avoiding essences, arbitrary dichotomies, and to fight structures. But . . . their limit is to define entities only through association. . . . they become empty when asked to provide policy, pass judgement or explain stable features. . . . Their dissolving power is so great that after having dissolved the illusions of critical postures, there is not much that is left and they even may turn into a somewhat perverse enjoyment of the diversity, perversity, heterogeneity, and multiplicity of the unexpected associations they deploy so well. (1995, p. 304)

Latour goes on to catalogue various attempts to stabilize actor–networks: Mol and Law's *fluids*, Callon's *modes of coordination*, and his own *regimes of delegation* (p. 304). At the same time that these scholars are attempting to shore up the stability of actor–networks, as I noted earlier in the chapter, Engeström et al. (1999) and Nardi et al. (2002) are grappling with the problem of *too much stability* in activity networks. I won't promise a tertium quid or a "just right" solution, but I turn to genre as a way to frame the stability/instability dialogue more productively. Genre supplies an account of stability-with-flexibility that is more fleshed out than fluids, modes of coordination, and regimes and at the same time leverages the notion of inscription that is so important to actor–network theory.

Genres are stable, then, but as boundary objects they mean different things and act differently at different nodes in a network. This has much to do with the different *activities* going on in the different nodes, the different trades and fields and disciplines to which they connect – the different logics (in the sense of *logos*, or "word"), the different social languages in play at each node. To illustrate, let's turn to the last disruption.

Disruption 4: Jeannie Talks Past Local Provisioners

Our last stop in this tour of Telecorp is at the third floor of Telecorp's corporate building. In an open-plan room, network coordinators such as Jeannie work in cubicles. Their offices don't look so different from their counterparts, the CLEC provisioners who work in the Telecorp Center a few miles away. On the surface, their work looks quite similar too: both receive, place, and coordinate orders for phone service, one for local (CLEC) orders, the other for long distance orders. And since business customers in particular often buy their local and long distance service from the same vendor, the two groups often coordinate with each other.

I say that the groups are *counterparts*, and in fact network coordinators are often called "LD provisioners" to reflect one important aspect of their work. But the groups are not exact analogs any more than the Internet Help Desk is the exact analog of Customer Service (see Disruption 1). The local and long distance markets are very different activities economically, regulatively, and technically. For instance, network coordinators lease lines from many different regional carriers and renegotiate those leases each month; CLEC provisioners either provide service through Telecorp's lines or resell the service of Telecorp's dominant competitor (a relationship we'll examine in Chapter 2). The differences are not only in activity but also in development. Telecorp has offered long distance service almost since it became legal in 1983 (through the antitrust suit settlement agreement between the U.S. Department of Justice and AT&T). The local service market was not opened until the Telecommunications Act of 1996, and Telecorp did not start offering its own dial tone until later, so CLEC Provisioning was still new at the time of this study (2000–2001).

But those differences tend to be masked by the similarities both in the work and in the terms used by the two groups. Until, of course, the differences are brought to the forefront through incidents such as the one described in Disruption 4. As Jeannie, a network coordinator, recounts:

> **Jeannie:** CLEC's lingo is different from ours. Their terminology for things are different from ours. And that was in course of, we wanted to choke them, they wanted to choke us because we thought we would talk the same lingo, and it turned out we weren't.... One of the problems is, we were placing an order with them for say a prem to prem. And to us, a prem to prem – when I place a prem to prem order with BigTel [the dominant regional company], that's from one customer directly to another customer and it's not really going through Telecorp. And I place one order with them. Well, it's different on CLEC. CLEC, they have to place two orders. Their prem to prem is just different from what we consider a prem to prem. So we were talking back and forth a long time about prem to prem, until we figured out, 'Oh, your prem to prem is not the same as our prem to prem.'
>
> **CS:** Why did that happen?
>
> **Jeannie:** [Draws diagram] Since we have a CLEC here in Midsize City, if we have them order it we'll get better pricing. So we have them order it for us. So there are three portions. The two ends are CLEC, the middle part is our department.

Let's unpack this explanation a bit so that we don't have the same problem the CLEC provisioners did. When Jeannie talks about a *prem to prem*, she means direct service from a customer's premises to other premises. For instance, suppose you want to connect your stores in Midsize City (Point A) and Hills City (Point B) with a dedicated data line; you're not going to be dialing anyone else with that line, just the other premises. You want a premises to premises (prem to prem) line. So you order that line through Telecorp. Since it's a long distance line, Telecorp selects an appropriate long distance vendor that can connect the two points – in this case, BigTel – and places an order.

If it were a local call, though – for instance, if you were to hook a cash machine's data line directly to the bank that owned it, and both were in Midsize City – it would normally be handled by CLEC Provisioning. And, as Jeannie found out, CLEC Provisioning places *two* orders: one at each end. "Their prem to prem is not the same." Yet this difference had been hidden successfully for months until exposed by the rupture Jeannie describes. It turns out that sometimes a long distance prem to prem can be handled more cheaply by CLEC Provisioning: they order one end through Telecorp and connect *locally* to whatever company is handling the long distance and the other end. This move, though handled by CLEC Provisioning, was coordinated by the LD provisioners (network coordination). And of course that's where the trouble started, because what had always seemed like a single order to the LD provisioners (because they had always placed it with another company) was exposed as not one, not two, but *three* orders: the local Points A and B and the long distance service in the middle.[11] When I say "exposed," I don't mean a sudden epiphany available to all, like Christ descending from the skies in the Revelation of St. John. I mean a more quotidian, gradual understanding gained only after painful, acrimonious argument. No wonder network coordinators had begun to have meetings in which they discuss differences in terms used by them and by CLEC Provisioning! They have discovered that they were speaking the same words but different social languages.

And how bitter that discovery is: workers have worked hard to learn their own social language, and now they have to learn another. "We are taken right off the streets with zero experience in this field," Jeannie told me, "and it was like walking into a language course of Greek and it was taught all in Greek and you didn't have a clue what they were saying. . . . They would plop you

---

[11] Three orders in *this* instance, anyway. Jeannie told me that when network coordinators handle these orders themselves rather than rely on other companies, sometimes they have to coordinate and place orders with several different companies, each of which owns a different piece of the network.

down with a book this big and say 'read it' but you can't even understand the lingo and can't even understand what you're reading." Jeannie eventually learned this Greek, then discovered that CLEC Provisioning had learned an entirely different Greek in which the same words and phrases meant quite different things.

The problem isn't simply one of identical words meaning different things. After all, one CLEC provisioner had previously been a youth pastor, laboring to convert people to Christ; now he labored to convert customers to Telecorp's dial tone. Yes, the word *convert* was the same, but he did not become confused by it, apply strategies from pastoring to provisioning, or promise everlasting life to customers. The two activities were sufficiently distanced that no confusion was likely. That's not the case with the term *prem to prem* or for that matter with the term *provisioning*; both terms are enacted differently depending on where you are in the network.

Alert readers may detect some affinity with the notions of multiplicity and polycontextuality I discussed earlier, and yes, we're skirting that territory again. But whereas my examples of multiplicity earlier referred to how different nodes in a network enact a shared phenomenon and strive to make it cohere as a unitary entity, in this example the nodes are trying to enact *different* phenomena using different social languages. The term *social languages* is drawn from the work of language philosopher Mikhail Bakhtin, whose work has often been paired with activity theory. Social languages develop around particular activities enacted by particular groups of people. They are not simply lists of terms; they are actually different *logics* (again, in the sense of *logos*, or word). "A social language," Bakhtin says, "is a concrete sociolinguistic belief system that defines a distinct identity for itself within the boundaries of a language [such as English, in this case] that is unitary only in the abstract" (1981, p. 356). No words are neutral: "Language has been completely taken over, shot through with intentions and accents. For any individual consciousness living in it, language is not an abstract system of normative forms but rather a concrete heteroglot conception of the world. All words," as Jeannie found out, "have the 'taste' of a profession, a genre, a tendency, a party, a particular work, a particular person, a generation, an age group, the day and hour" (p. 293). Social languages are not just acquired; they are enacted: "The word in language is half someone else's. It becomes 'one's own' only when the speaker populates it with his own intention, his own accent, when he appropriates the word, adapting it to his own semantic and expressive intention" (p. 293). A social language continually changes and develops through the work of all its speakers, even the ones who are busily acquiring it; language is "a process of heteroglot development" (pp. 356–357).

Acquisition, appropriation, development, and enactment imply each other, and the only time they stop is when the language is a "dead" language, studied rather than lived.[12] That's not the case here: Jeannie is learning "Greek," not Latin. And that means she and the other long distance provisioners are also enacting and developing their language, differentiating it from the newer and more rapidly developing language of the CLEC provisioners.

Activity theorists have often been intrigued by Bakhtin's work and have attempted to synthesize it with activity theory's concepts. For instance, Ritva Engeström (1995) ties social language to the level of cyclical activity, stating that a social language provides a "referentially semantic context" (p. 200) that ties communities to the mediating artifacts of words. James Wertsch (1998) makes a slightly different argument, suggesting that social languages are tied to classes of speakers. Both make some sense, but I think they miss the *logos*, the "sociolinguistic belief system" that Bakhtin says a social language implies. As David R. Russell once observed to me, some evolutionary biologists go to church; and as we've seen above, some pastors go to work for telecommunications companies. When these people talk about origins, when they discuss conversions, we have to understand that a change in social language can mean a change in logic, assumptions, ideology, standards of proof, rules, tools, and so forth. Learning a social language means joining, sharing, and coconstructing the *logos* constituted by it; it means joining a community and learning (if not necessarily accepting) that community's ideology or ideologies. And, as Bakhtin says, it also means differentiating oneself from others who have not learned the social language.

We see plenty of the latter at Telecorp. Perhaps Jeannie and the other long distance provisioners had to learn through trial and error how to differentiate their social language from that of CLEC Provisioning, but workers generally could identify several social languages that were active in different nodes of their network. These social languages – and the logics implied in them – seeped in from many places: disciplinary languages came from sustained work contact with other telecommunications companies (especially BigTel); from training sessions and education offered at telecommunications companies, universities, and equipment makers; from previous work at other companies (especially in the case of Sales, where sales reps usually had learned their trade somewhere else); and so forth. And they seeped out in the same way: just as workers learned social languages from contact with others outside the company, they also taught these social languages to

---

[12] This is true even for programming languages, as I have argued elsewhere (Spinuzzi, 2002b).

other companies' neophytes. In a practical sense, *Telecorp has no interior* – a phenomenon we'll discuss in detail in Chapters 4 and 5.

Many social languages can be at play at any given node or across nodes, and some of these social languages are not particularly germane to work. (For instance, when two CLEC provisioners discussed the possibility of Israel building a new temple in Jerusalem, and whether it meant Christ's return was near, they were using an evangelical social language that is really outside the scope of this study. But the logic of this social language did not overwhelm them: after a brief conversation, they returned to their work and its social language rather than putting on white robes and heading to the rooftop.) The social languages that are germane are the ones that tell us about how these nodes are constructed and stabilized. When workers talked about how "technically" they had to speak to different groups (least "technically" to Sales, most "technically" to the NOC), they were delineating boundaries in social languages and boundaries in networks.

These social languages were instantiated primarily through the ecologies or assemblages of genres deployed by workers, genres such as types of e-mail, phone calls, training, manuals, literature (Telecorp's and that of particular trades), instant messages, and dozens of others. These genres circulated through Telecorp but also through other entities, building networks to and through them. For instance, in Alarm Management Systems, workers labored to sensitize Telecorp's fiber to problems in fiber connected to it, fiber owned by small local providers, but they also introduced new local providers to the field, teaching them Telecorp's terms and its logic! They simultaneously built the telecommunications network, the political–rhetorical network, and the developing social–cultural–historical network. Or rather, they built a single sociotechnical network, for though there is an *abstract* difference between these two sorts of networks, there is no *practical* difference.

I've sketched out an understanding of how genres circulate through and help build sociotechnical networks, rendering them stable and constituting the social languages that provide coherent understandings of shared phenomena. Now here's how the rest of the book will unfold.

THE BOOK'S TRAJECTORY

We've gone on a whirlwind tour of Telecorp, the networks that can be said to constitute it, and the genres that circulate through it. We've laid out some issues to explore. We've asked the following:

- How does Telecorp function when its right hand often doesn't know what its left hand is doing – when constant disruptions rock its ever-expanding, ever-changing networks?
- How are these networks developed, repaired, and stabilized through the constant circulation of genres?
- How can we better account for net work at Telecorp and, more broadly, in knowledge work organizations?
- How can we use the dialogue between activity theory and actor–network theory to develop that account?

I'll break down these broad questions with short swipes that focus on particular theoretical and methodological issues, illustrated with incidents (particularly disruptions) at Telecorp. In doing so, my aim is to answer Kaptelinin and Nardi's (2006) call for activity theorists to develop a deeper account of how activity theory deals with the interplay among multiple activities. To do that, I extend activity theory's account of networks and texts through sustained contact with actor–network theory. I say "contact," not "conflict": dialogue, not simply grafting the most desirable aspects of actor–network theory onto activity theory. I won't resolve the contradictions between the two frameworks, but I will examine them and use the tension between them to develop activity theory in a useful manner. (After all, though actor–network theory intrigues me, I favor activity theory for reasons that will become evident throughout this book.)

What is a network? In Chapter 2, I'll trace a message as it makes its way through the three overlapping networks we'll study: a technical network made of glass, metal, and plastic; a political–rhetorical actor–network; and a developmental activity network. In doing so, I'll compare the three networks and set up what I hope will be a productive tension among them. In the process, I'll discuss a key difference between activity theory and actor–network theory, the difference between woven and spliced networks. And I ask the question: how did Telecorp come to be organized the way it is, with every worker massed on the company's border? We'll defer that question for a chapter while we delve into theory.

How are networks theorized? In Chapter 3, we'll back off from the empirical case and instead explore the theoretical and methodological differences between activity theory and actor–network theory. By the end, we'll understand how and why the two projects differ and we'll have a basis for a further dialogue between the two approaches. And we'll be prepared to compare their accounts of historical change.

How are networks historicized? In this chapter, we'll examine how Telecorp's workers came to be massed at the border. Using the principle of universal service as a focus, we'll examine the social, economic, regulative, and legislative environment in which Telecorp operates. We'll review the history of the telecommunications industry in the United States and particularly in Texas, and we'll examine it in terms of activity theory's contradictions and actor–network theory's translations. This work should prepare us for examining the present-day network.

How are networks enacted? In Chapter 5, we'll examine Telecorp in terms of the literature on knowledge work. We'll see how Telecorp's workers collaborate within and across teams, how they build new associations within and without the company, how they are (or are not) informed about each other's activities, and how they jointly enact and sustain Telecorp's net work. In particular, we'll trace genres, money, substitutions, and workers as they circulate through the network and examine how their circulation helps to sustain it. Finally, we'll discuss the implications for understanding knowledge work in distributed organizations.

How do networks learn? In Chapter 6, we'll see how new workers – of which there were many, given Telecorp's rapid expansion during the study – learned how to be workers. We'll discuss formal training but also the more important informal ways of learning, and we'll see how genres help support learning. During this discussion, we'll compare how activity theory and actor–network theory examine competence. We'll also talk about the implications for training and learning in distributed organizations.

In Chapter 7, we return to the question that drives this book: How does Telecorp function when the right hand doesn't know what the left hand is doing? Chapter 7 concludes with thoughts on net work, particularly in terms of how workers, managers, researchers, and theorists can better address it. Activity theory is well positioned to study knowledge work, probably better positioned than actor–network theory for reasons that will become clear in Chapter 6. But in its present "third-generation" stage, it needs to develop in specific ways to reach its potential. It could learn more from actor–network theory than it has. Here I'll make the case for further developing activity theory's account of networks in specific ways.

2

What Is a Network?

"In the past," Nardi, Whittaker, and Schwarz tell us, "much work took place in relatively stable settings" (2002, p. 205). In these settings, long-term relationships flourished; workers held long-term or lifelong jobs, maintained steady contacts with other organizations and with the public, and built up considerable expertise (cf. Braverman, 1974). They fulfilled clearly defined roles and developed strong working relationships. They "shared considerable social, cultural, and organizational knowledge that served as a backdrop for work and interaction" (Nardi et al., 2002, p. 205). But recent changes in work, particularly knowledge work, have destabilized these settings: downsizing, automation, flattening of work hierarchies, increasing numbers of relationships between companies, and continual reorganization (p. 206; cf. Deleuze, 1995; Engeström, Engeström, & Vähääho, 1999). One result, Nardi et al. say, is that "many corporations operate in an increasingly distributed manner, with workers, contractors, consultants, and important contacts such as those in the press located in different parts of the country or across the globe" (p. 206; cf. Zuboff & Maxmin, 2004).

This description certainly fits Telecorp in 2000–2001, during my observations. Telecorp was undergoing rapid and sometimes chaotic changes: rapid growth, rapid acquisitions, rapid turnover in workers, rapid adoption of new technologies and new features, all in the rapidly changing landscape of the telecommunications industry. The industry by its nature involves constant collaboration among companies and frequent contact with customers; organizational boundaries are quite porous, with connections at all levels and in all areas. Telecorp's work was indeed "increasingly distributed," impossible to categorize cleanly within the boundaries of companies, disciplines, or activities. The triangle diagrams with which activity theorists have been so enamored cannot contain this work.

To cope, these activity theorists have turned to developments such as netWORKing (Nardi et al., 2002) and knotworking (Engeström et al., 1999) to better describe this increasingly distributed work. Both developments are to some extent reactions to actor–network theory, which they criticize as inadequate to the task of describing this new structure of work. But I suggest that both underestimate the contribution of actor–network theory, which has a fundamentally different focus from activity theory. Whereas activity theorists are looking for cultural–historical, developmental explanations for human activity, actor–network theory is interested in political and rhetorical explanations for power and its exercise. Activity theory is interested in how *people* work; actor–network theory is interested in how *power* works. Partially because of this different focus, the two sides tend to talk past each other (see, e.g., Engeström, 1996b; Latour, 1996b, 1996c). In this chapter, I attempt a constructive dialogue between them – a *dialogue*, I emphasize, not a *dialectic*. The differences between the positions won't get resolved here, but we will draw comparisons, find common ground, and begin to see where the two perspectives diverge. They may not agree, but at least we'll reach some degree of stasis.

To start this conversation, we'll take an incident that happened at Telecorp during my study: the death of a customer's dog. I have discussed this incident at some length elsewhere, concentrating on its implications for responsibility and blame (Spinuzzi, 2007b). Here, I'll use it as a starting point for illustrating the differences and similarities in how activity theory and actor–network theory understand networks. It will also serve as our introduction to Telecorp and the telecommunications industry.

The chapter is arranged in this way: one dog's death; two ways to build networks; three aspects of Telecorp's work; four characteristics of networks; five events that led to the tragedy.

ONE DOG'S DEATH

On a hot August day in 2000, a customer called Telecorp to report interrupted local telephone service. A few days later, a telephone service technician opened the backyard gate to investigate the problem. Unknown to him, in the backyard lived a dog. Startled by the intruder, this dog fled the yard and ran into the street. He was promptly struck by a car. Let's call this dog "Rex."

Rex's lifeless body landed in the neighbor's flower garden – and at the periphery of Telecorp's complex sociotechnical network. When I say

"Telecorp's network" I do refer to the familiar *technological* aspect, the telecommunications equipment that has been strung together to transform voices into electronic impulses and back. But I also mean the *political–rhetorical* aspect: Telecorp can be seen as an *actor–network* composed of a spliced assemblage of sociopolitically aligned humans and nonhumans. And I additionally mean the *developmental* aspect: Telecorp can be seen as an *activity network* composed of interwoven, constantly developing, often contradictory cultural–historical activities. Textual knowledge constantly circulates through and is transformed within this multifaceted network, but not reliably: somewhere in the set of transformations, the vital message "dog in backyard" was lost.

Elsewhere, I address just where the message was lost (Spinuzzi, 2007b). Here, I'm more interested in how it circulated or failed to circulate and what that meant for Telecorp's network. First, I use the investigation to explicate two very different understandings of sociotechnical networks: the *woven*, cultural–historical and developmental understanding afforded by activity theory and the *spliced*, political–rhetorical, negotiated understanding afforded by actor–network theory. By holding these two understandings in dialogic tension, I explore three aspects of Telecorp's network and use them to explicate four characteristics of sociotechnical networks. Finally, I draw together an understanding of the dialogic tension between activity theory and actor–network theory, discussing how we might proceed with this dialogue. Think of this work as tracing through schematics to find design flaws or tracing through a circuit to find loose wires or damaged connections, but in this case we're looking at heterogeneous elements such as people, practices, and texts.

Let's start by contemplating how sociotechnical networks are built, using Telecorp as an example.

TWO WAYS TO BUILD A NETWORK

We can think of at least two ways to build sociotechnical networks: *weaving* and *splicing*. Let's separate these – artificially, of course, since any network involves both ways of building – and examine them closely here; we'll complicate the distinction in Chapter 3.

Woven networks are exemplified by the artisan who weaves nets for fishermen. In *Activity, Consciousness, and Personality* (1978, p. 63), A. N.

---

[1] Johndan Johnson-Eilola (1998) draws a similar distinction between "depth" (time) and "surface" (space).

Leont'ev points out that labor is divided in collectives: (some weave nets, some fish, some build boats, but all in the community can benefit from the catch) Perhaps at some point each member of the community had to do all the jobs, but it became more profitable to specialize. As one activity's labor is divided, it grows into several interwoven activities, and perhaps the interstices among the activities become wider: today I can walk into a sporting goods store and buy a fishing net from someone who knows nothing about fishing, manufactured by yet another company whose workers likewise know nothing about fishing. But genetically and historically, the activities interrelate. The net I buy from the sporting goods store is not so different from the one sedulously woven by the artisan. His net work involved weaving, developing, widening the net in ways that are based on a craft tradition – ways that involve reproducing the basic pattern even though elaborations and innovations eventually change it in a gradual progression that shows its history. Though the fishing nets may evolve, they recall their origins. The diverse types of nets we see in everyday life are constructed using tools and techniques originally employed by weavers of fishing nets. They started at a common point and *diverged*.

This sort of work organization is what Karl Marx called "organic," in which the same material is progressively transformed, allowing the different stages to be isolated and to yield a chained division of labor (1990, p. 463) in which work that had been accomplished in one place, by one person, is distributed in space and time (p. 464). In being distributed, the work diverges from its origins. Those divergences often involve attenuations, leading to weaknesses. For instance, the man who weaves nets for his fishing community has an intimate understanding of the work of the fishers. The man who toils in a factory making commercial fishing nets may have no experience at all with fishing. This separation of labor from craft skills introduces weaknesses into the network; the longer the network becomes, the more likely it is that disjunctions or contradictions will form among activities and consequently *the more attenuated and weaker the network becomes*.

In contrast, *spliced* networks are exemplified by the technician who splices together disparate electrical devices and existing networks to respond to unforeseen alliances and uses. When Bell Telephone's engineers built its massive network across the United States in the early 1900s, they did not envision connecting that network with microwave towers, satellites, the Internet backbone, cable television networks, or wireless telephony. All of these emerging technologies, heterogeneous as they are, had to be spliced in: wires had to be physically connected; equipment had to be invented, designed, and built; protocols had to be designed; legislation and regulations had to be produced; customers had to be made aware. My telephone is far more networked than the previous models, and its everyday operation requires people from widely disparate and historically unrelated activities to splice their technologies and their work together. These historically separate technologies – voice mail, Web browsing, e-mail, text messaging, games, photography – are brought together and hybridized in one device attached to one network. The technician's net work involved and still involves splicing, looking at existing networks, figuring out how to connect them productively (however that's defined), attempting to meet the needs of all these technologies, their users, and those who develop and maintain them. Whereas woven networks grow through development, spliced networks grow through opportunistic alliances, through unpredictable jumps and sideways connections. They do have a history, a history of *translations*, but that history is one of contacts and negotiations and compromises (see Spinuzzi, 2005). These sorts of networks – not just telecommunications but road networks (Spinuzzi, 2003b; Thévenot, 2002), petroleum networks (Bowker, 1987, 1994), railroad networks (Yates, 1989), electrical networks (Bazerman, 1999; Hughes, 1993), and sewage networks – are composed of different preexisting elements that have *converged*.[2]

These convergences lead to juxtapositions and connections among previously unconnected activities, strengthening the network as more actants are brought in to make the network solid and durable. For instance, as we'll see in Chapter 4, the Bell network has allowed other telecommunications companies to connect to it; the different companies use the same number assignation system, the same types of telephones, the same types of wires. This articulation strengthened the emerging network as a whole by aligning the interests and the methods of the disparate companies. This articulation work is still going on. Wireless local number portability, for instance, was mandated in 2003, making it possible for people to keep their telephone numbers as they switch from cellular to personal communication service (PCS) networks and from one provider to another. Commitments multiply and are built on previous commitments. *The longer the network becomes, the stronger it becomes.*

---

[2] I'm using the pair *converge/diverge* differently from the way it has been used by theorists such as John Law (2004b). In Law's taxonomy, convergence refers to the orienting of representations toward a single truth; here, I use convergence more along Geoffrey Bowker's lines (1994, p. 46): as the intersection of different, unrelated, spliced activities.

The woven understanding is usually taken up by activity theory, with its interest in developmental activity (though activity theory has developed a splicing account, as we'll see in detail in Chapter 3). The spliced understanding is usually taken up by actor–network theory, with its interest in shifting political–rhetorical alliances and negotiations. Of course, these two types of networks are vantage points on sociotechnical activities, not mutually exclusive types. You'll find that the artisan sometimes splices his nets just as the technician sometimes weaves hers. Or to put it another way, we can see networked activities as cultural–developmental (as activity theory does) and as political–rhetorical (as actor–network theory does). We can see strengths in both convergences and divergences. And in fact these two understandings have been brought into limited dialogue before. Engeström et al. (1999), for instance, have attempted to bring an account of splicing into activity theory, using the notion of *knotworking* to describe impromptu, temporary, collaboratively performed connections among actors and activity systems. Meanwhile, Latour (1995) has attempted to lend developmental stability to actor–network theory through various means. Nevertheless, the dialogue is still new and remains to be developed – especially because the dialogue's participants tend to talk past each other, as we'll see in Chapter 3.

THREE ASPECTS OF TELECORP'S NETWORK

Rex, as I said, landed at the periphery of the Telecorp network. As we explore aspects of that network, we will gain very different insights into the events leading up to Rex's death, and it's difficult to sort out how they interrelate. So in this section I separate these aspects, identifying and discussing each one. We'll start with the *technological network,* the bits of wire, wood, plastic, and glass that have been strung together to carry voices and data.

Telecorp's Technological Network

Network: 1. An interconnection of three or more communicating entities. 2. An interconnection of usually passive electronic components that performs a specific function (which is usually limited in scope), for example, to simulate a transmission line or to perform a mathematical function such as integration or differentiation. Note: A network may be part of a larger circuit. (ATIS, 2004)

For the purposes of this work, the process of networking will be the process of facilitating the exchange of information (oil, material, personnel) between high-energy centres along thin filaments (pipelines, rail routes, roads) that barely contact the traditional State. . . . the network's trend [is] to bypass the original state: to dig beneath it, build around it, then ship out of it. (Bowker, 1987, p. 629)

Telecommunications companies have *service areas*, usually designated by city ("Midsize City, TX") or on a map (in which an entire service area is solidly colored). Rex lived in one of these service areas. But examine the actual telecommunications network and you'll find that it occupies hardly any space: copper lines, fiber, switches, repeaters, phone jacks, resistors, inductances, capacitors, transistors, and power sources barely touch, let alone "cover" the area they claim. The telephone line that services your house, for instance, leads up to telephone poles or down into the ground and from there threads its way to more centralized nodes. As Geoff Bowker points out in his study of Schlumberger (1987), networks claim large areas but in practice are vanishingly small; their claim to power is that they transform the world so that things outside the network don't matter (see also Latour, 1993b, pp. 117–118). When we think of Telecorp as covering all of Midsize City, we forget that the network is inaccessible unless we happen to be precisely at the end of a wire with precisely the right equipment.[3] *In theory*, it would seem quite difficult to find the end of a pencil-thin wire. But fortunately, the wires go to predictable places: office buildings, pay phones, houses. So *in practice* it's dead easy to get on the right end of the right wire. We do it all the time, so we tend to forget the vast interstices in the network and think of the entire city as "covered."

A remarkable amount of work goes into maintaining this illusion of omnipresent service, but that work tends to be done quite well. Through diligent work, telecommunications companies have turned a thin, fragile, tentative tangle of filaments into a ubiquitous, reliable network. Interrupted service seems extraordinary. Yet these telecommunications networks are continuously being disrupted by felled branches that snap those thin telephone lines, by careless backhoes that dig up underground fiber, by power fluctuations that disrupt servers, by improperly entered instructions to switches, by miscommunications[4] with other telecommunications

---

[3] We'll leave aside the question of cordless phones and mobile phones. On first glance, these *appear* to be a different case, but the difference is in scale rather than kind.

[4] Not only miscommunications but also – it has been alleged in court – deliberate counter-activity, especially when customers switch from BigTel to Telecorp service. Telecorp has accused BigTel of systematically being hours late to vendor meets (appointments when Telecorp and BigTel techs meet with the customer to switch phone service) and of deliberately cutting off service to switching customers before Telecorp is able to set up their own service.

providers, and by hundreds of other events. Workers are constantly dispatched to repair this fragile, decaying network, constantly extending the network to include new buildings or to provide additional lines. Repairs and extensions both involve ruptures that expose the network's shakiness and limitations, but their impact on *individual* customers is so rare that the network as a whole seems solid as a rock (cf. Bazerman, 1999, p. 228). When individual customers do encounter a rare (to them) rupture in telephone service, they are often shocked and outraged.

Somehow this constantly decaying, recuperating, extending network appears solid and stable. Customers are constantly, unavoidably being inconvenienced; the trick is to make sure it's not the same customers each time and to minimize the duration of the inconvenience. So when two cables in Telecorp's interstate fiber network were severed by a contractor digging up a water main, Network Operations Center (NOC) workers rerouted calls over another company's network until they could repair the fiber. When a customer encountered crosstalk, an outside tech traced it to a poor cable splice. When the city's power failed, an inside tech immediately switched to backup power and rebooted a switch that had gone down. These were everyday events. Telecorp's telecommunications network was made of exceedingly thin bits of metal, glass, and plastic that were wired together by a variety of providers, yet Telecorp maintained the illusions of ubiquity and near-absolute reliability because those fragile parts were *multiply* linked; if one strand in the net snapped, the others could take up the load. This complex multiple linking was hidden from the consumers.

Like Telecorp's telecommunications network, Telecorp's service provided an illusion of unity that hid heterogeneity. For example, Rex's owner considered his local telephone company to be Telecorp. But his phone service was a "resale": he called Telecorp with problems, addressed his payments to Telecorp, praised Telecorp when problems were fixed quickly, and cursed Telecorp when his dog was struck by a car, but his actual service provider was BigTel. Telecorp bought BigTel's service at a legally mandated discount and sold it at competitive market rates. As one Telecorp employee put it, customers paid Telecorp to deal with BigTel so they didn't have to.

Even when customers were serviced by Telecorp's own fledgling network rather than BigTel's, their phone service was typically a collaboration among providers. Local providers have to hook up to each other's equipment and networks; long distance providers continually lease space to each other and bargain for the best prices on leased space. So even Telecorp's physical network consisted of many copresent, overlapping, spliced networks controlled by various companies. The technical, organizational, disciplinary, political,

and economic complexity of the system was *black-boxed* or hidden behind
a simple interface (Latour, 1987); customers just saw the "phone company."
The black box was maintained through thousands of daily, localized, often
ad hoc connections, including genres such as checklists, electronic notes,
and immense stacks of marked and highlighted printouts.

Telecorp's (Spliced) Actor–Network

[Actor–networks] bear only a distant resemblance to the technical networks (such as telecommunications systems, railways, or sewers) studied by economists. These can, in essence, be reduced to long associations of nonhumans that, here and there, join a few humans together.
Nor are they reducible to the networks of actors described by sociol-
ogists, which privilege interactions between humans in the absence of
any material support. Techno-economic networks [i.e., actor–networks]
are composite. They mix humans and nonhumans, inscriptions of all
sorts, and money in all its forms. Their dynamics can only be understood
if we study the translation operations that inscribe the mutual definition of the actors in the intermediaries put into circulation and "read"
the relevant inscriptions. Further, the translation operation is itself regulated by more or less local and revisable conventions. (Callon, 1991,
p. 153)

The word network indicates that resources are concentrated in a few
places – the knots and the nodes – which are connected to each other – the
links and the mesh: these connections transform the scattered resources
into a net that may seem to extend everywhere. Telephone lines, for
instance, are minute and fragile, so minute that they are invisible on a
map and so fragile that each may be easily cut; nevertheless, the telephone
network "covers" the whole world. (Latour, 1987, p. 180)

And that brings us to the actor–network. An actor–network is composed
of many entities or *actants* that enter into an alliance to satisfy their diverse
aims. Each actant *enrolls* the others, that is, finds ways to convince the others
to support its own aims. The longer these networks are, the more entities
that are enrolled in them, the stronger and more durable they become. An
actor–network, of course, is *spliced;* the actants intersect.
In the actor–network at hand, Telecorp, BigTel, and other service
providers had forged relatively stable alliances that allowed them to maintain the illusion of unified, ubiquitous, and reliable service. But examining
actants such as corporations and people gives us only part of the story.
Actor–network theory encourages us to see the political–rhetorical work as

occurring not just among corporations or people but also among non-humans and to use the same concepts for all of these entities. Just as Telecorp's workers enrolled BigTel's workers, they also enrolled fiber, switches, and pets like Rex, all of which are considered actants – all of which in turn enrolled the workers in their *own* aims, and all of which could betray each other at any moment. Cables could be cut, switches could fail, dogs could fight or bolt right out of their yards. Only by lengthening the actor–network, enrolling even more actants, splicing itself to other networks, could the actor–network remain durable. Is fiber so fragile that it is threatened by any contractor foolish enough to dig in its vicinity? Then its allies must erect warning signs, put some force in those signs through regulations and stiff fees, and retain other contractors to hastily and reliably repair them. Do switches depend on uninterrupted power? Then they shall have it: they shall be supplied with backup power generators and alert technicians who know how to coax them back online. Are dogs like Rex liable to fight or flee when a tech enters their backyard? Then the tech must be warned. When these actants betrayed Telecorp by being cut, by going down in a power failure, or by escaping from the backyard, Telecorp had to attend to these ruptures as quickly as possible and to reenroll the actants. Telecorp's actor–network was thick with actants, but particularly texts, which strengthened and lengthened the network, kept actants in line and reenrolled traitors so Telecorp could provide coherent, unitary service. These texts were the lightest and least substantial of allies – slips of paper, streams of characters on a screen, manila folders. But they spliced together this network. Such actants, Michel Callon says, define themselves by the intermediaries they put into circulation. Texts such as e-mails, technologies such as switches, humans such as technicians, and money in all its forms put each other into motion, mediate each other, and transform each other (Callon, 1991). They *persuade* each other. As Latour argues (1991, p. 115), rhetoric builds networks. These networks are nets that incorporate what they catch (just as early Christians were told to be "fishers of men," men who in turn became fishers of other men). Or as Latour puts it elsewhere, it can be said that a collective of humans and nonhumans is *articulated*

> in every sense of the word: that it "speaks" more, that it is subtler and more astute, that it includes more articles, discrete units, or concerned parties, that it mixes them together with greater degrees of freedom, that it deploys longer lists of actions. (2004, p. 86)

This principle of symmetry seems odd at first, and readers sometimes "get the disquieting impression that they are being pulled into a fable where animals, viruses, stars, and magic wands are going to start chattering away like magpies or princesses," as Latour (2004, p. 67) acknowledges. (That's partially his own fault: the protagonist in Latour's experimental novel *Aramis* [1996a] attempts to converse with doors, keys, and other nonhumans.) But as Susan Leigh Star argues (1995, pp. 21–22), symmetry is not pantheism. It's an attempt to avoid Cartesian dichotomies by applying the same concepts and vocabularies across the entire actor–network.[5] And once that has been done, we begin to see *the same sorts of actions* taking place whether the actants are human or not.[6] In Saint Brieuc Bay, scallops "vote" (Callon, 1986b); in Paris, mass transit systems "yearn to be born" (Latour, 1996a); in the French Pyrénées, roads "argue" (Thévenot, 2002). The actor–network continually finds ways to strengthen existing alliances and make new ones. Actants continually convince their allies to support them in their aims and form enough alliances that they can work around traitors. The actor–network, that is, constantly engages in a project that is essentially *political* and *rhetorical* and that involves both *consolidation* and *expansion*. Actor–networks expand through intersecting, enrolling, and translating other actants. They consolidate through the ties that bind – the ever-tightening mutual enrollment of intersected actants.

Actor–network theory, of course, is preoccupied with how power works (Latour, 1986). Latour (1992a) even claims boldly that the more actants are in a network, the more powerful it is, no matter the qualities of its individual actants! But in focusing on the political–rhetorical movements of complex heterogeneous networks, actor–network theory misses some important aspects of the Telecorp story. In particular, as Reijo Miettinen points out, actor–network theory's principle of symmetry leads it away from the study of cognition, human competence (other than the ability to form strategies and alliances), intentionality, "learning, development of expertise, complementarity of resources, and know-how in knowledge construction" (1999, p. 182). That is, as Andrew Pickering (1995) charges, actor–network theory does not provide a strong account for temporal change; it does not have a

---

[5] Many people think that it's outrageous to apply human terms (primarily drawn from politics and rhetoric) to nonhumans. Yet Edwin Hutchins (1995) and other distributed cognitionists apply nonhuman terms (primarily drawn from computer science) to humans, and for essentially the same reason – to provide a unified vocabulary that allows them to examine forms of agency across a given system. Kaptelinin and Nardi provide a sharp critique of how these frameworks handle agency, suggesting that a unified vocabulary leads to confusion between different types of agency (2006, Chapter 10).

[6] In the telecommunications literature, we find similar language: distributed digital processors "decide" and exhibit "intelligence," and "networks themselves have information, or content, built into them" (Aufderheide, 1999, pp. 10–11).

way to address cultural–historical development, something that impairs its discussion of agency. To recover these parts of the Telecorp story, I turn to activity networks.

Telecorp's (Woven) Activity Network

> An activity system does not exist in a vacuum. It is but a node in a multidimensional network of activity systems. Its relevant "neighbor activities" include *firstly* the activities where the objects and outcomes of the central activity are embedded (let's call them object–activities). *Secondly*, they include the activities that produce the key instruments for the central activity (let's call them object–activities). *Thirdly*, they include activities like education and schooling of the subjects of the central activity (subject-producing activities). *Fourthly*, they include activities like administration and legislation (rule-producing activities). *Fifthly*, they include activity systems essentially similar to the central activity. Some of those are regarded as in some respects more advanced than the central activity. These and other activities which are in some way, for a longer or shorter period, connected to the given central activity, potentially destabilize each other through their exchanges and interpenetrations. (Engeström, 1992, p. 13)

> Most often the outcome of an activity is not intended for the same collective which produces it, but to be "consumed" by some other collective in some other activity. Construction workers do not build houses for themselves only; researchers write publications for the scientific community to make use of. The activity network . . . describes the producing activities for each element of an activity. . . . (Korpela, Mursu, & Soriyan, 2002, p. 114)

If actor–network theory is preoccupied with how *power* works, activity theory is preoccupied with how *people* work: how individuals work in collectives to develop tools, practices, communities, rules, and divisions of labor as they cyclically transform the objects of their labor. Activity is typically studied in *activity systems*. Workers in the Network Operations Center, for instance, worked cyclically to transform Telecorp's equipment; their work involved maintaining, repairing, and extending it. (For introductory texts on activity theory, see Kaptelinin & Nardi, 2006; Nardi, 1996a; Spinuzzi, 2003b.)

Yet for all its advantages, the activity system doesn't scale up well to study broader social phenomena. Activity theory's roots are in the Soviet Union, where "the opportunity to study social phenomena was limited for political reasons," as Victor Kaptelinin (1996, p. 63) mildly observes. It's hard to freely explore questions of society and culture when injudicious questions can lead to a gulag. Consequently, some argue, activity theory's sociopolitical limitations led it to represent people as "simple executors," the ideal citizens in a system dominated by command socialism (see Lektorsky, 1999), and to ignore the issues of power and dominance (Häyrynen, 1999) that so fascinate actor–network theorists. It provided a weak account of political stakeholders and their negotiations. But later activity theorists, particularly in Western Europe and North America, have belatedly begun to develop activity theory in ways that account for these stakeholders, how discrete activity systems interact, interweave, and coevolve. They have often called these complexes *activity networks*.

As discussed in Chapter 1, activity networks are composed of activity systems that have become interlinked or interpenetrated. This interlinking is often – too often – described in terms of inputs and outputs (as in the Korpela et al. quote above). But activity networks can also be linked through shared tools, resources, or communities (see Gay & Hembrooke, 2004; Helle, 2000; Russell, 1997a; Spasser, 2000, 2002; Spinuzzi, 2003b). We'll see some of these distinctions in Chapter 3.

The term *activity network* is consciously modeled after that of *actor–network*; most of the work using this term cites actor–network theory and provides explicit comparisons with it (Engeström, 1996b; Engeström & Escalante, 1996; Miettinen, 1999; Miettinen & Hasu, 2002). Indeed, this development has largely served as a reaction or response to actor–network theory's insights (and its shortcomings reflect the fact that it has not yet matured from a reaction to its own independent account). These two frameworks have much in common, as Miettinen points out: they are materially oriented and monist; they study "the concrete networks of actors instead of interrelations between macro- and microscale phenomena"; they draw on distributed resources for doing and acting; and they allow for the independent activity of objects (1999, p. 171). They both have a strong interest in mediation (though they understand it quite differently; see Chapter 3). But despite their similarities, the two frameworks are quite different. Unlike actor–networks, activity networks *assume asymmetry*, casting nonhumans as mediators or objects of labor rather than as actants. They *emphasize development*, foregrounding human ingenuity, learning, and individual and social changes. And they *exhibit structure* in the composition of the activity networks and the activity systems that compose them.

Asymmetry

Since actor–networks assume symmetry between humans and nonhumans, they deemphasize human cognition, volition, and ingenuity (Latour, 1996b). These, like political power, are seen as qualities of an entire network rather than attributable to individuals. In contrast, activity theorists emphasize exactly these traits (see especially Kaptelinin & Nardi, 2006, Chapter 10) – which makes sense when you remember that activity theory is based on Marxism, which valorizes workers as agents. Activity theory's account is *asymmetrical.* Cables don't have interests – they are tools meant to mediate human communication or objects to be transformed through sedulous human labor. Switches don't yearn to continue running – they are materials designed and maintained by collectives of workers. Dogs are unpredictable organisms that may become the object of activity if they flee or bite. In sum, activity theorists tend to see humans as actors and nonhuman artifacts as crystallizations of human activity (cf. Latour, 1996c); only human beings can take initiative in constructing assemblages (Kaptelinin & Nardi, 2006, p. 200). An activity theorist would never have a conversation with a door, like the protagonist does in Latour's novel *Aramis,* but s/he *would* imagine the "embedded" or "crystallized" activity, the "dead labor" of the workers who designed and manufactured it (Bødker, 1991). (Each account sounds outlandish to the other's advocates.) In an activity network, human activity and ingenuity play the foregrounded role, even when implemented in a mediational genre such as a checklist.

Part of that role involves *development.* Although an actor–network theorist might provide a historical account of how actor–networks build associations, she would avoid explicit accounts of human competence;[7] activity theorists, in contrast, take human competence, development, and learning to be vital points of analysis. Cultural–historical development is everywhere you turn in an activity network. Individual workers enter the network through formal training, informal apprenticeship, trial and error, and socializing. The objects of the component activity systems change: as Telecorp began to provide local service, for example, it had to adjust to different practices, technologies, rules, and time scales. Divisions of labor are continually altered as Telecorp adds new products and services. And, of course, mediatory texts – computer programs, documentation, scripts, technologies,

---

[7] Miettinen (1999) argues that the Machiavellian Prince provides an implicit model of human competence in actor–network theory, but little is said about how that competence develops. At any rate, the Machiavellian Prince fades away in later ANT work.

ad hoc innovations, and thousands of others – are learned, adopted, adapted, and discarded by individuals and groups.

It is activity theory's interest in development that causes it to see activity networks the way it often does, as connected by inputs and outputs. The question is always: Where did this rule, artifact, subject, etc., come from? These connections are lines of development – of sorts. Often they are grounded in Marx's explanation of modular work, conceived as economic supply lines in which the goods, the material outcome of an activity, become the mediational means (in the case of manufacturing), the subject/actor (in the case of education), the rules or division of labor (in the case of legislation, regulation, and less formal organizational activities), or the community (in the case of disciplines and fields). (More on this in Chapter 5.) This understanding provides more structure than actor–network theory: it explains how these networks are woven over time, how they develop and become durable. But it traditionally keeps them separated as well. It encourages us to examine most connections as sequential rather than simultaneous, co-existing, and entangled. As we'll see in Chapter 3, "third-generation" activity theory has begun to address this problem by introducing its own account of splicing, meant to address the sort of knowledge work we see at Telecorp.

Structure

Finally, activity networks are much more *structured* than actor–networks. To recall a point made in Chapter 1: Engeström (1996b) complains that "Latour's actants seem to have no analyzable inner structure" and suggests using activity theory to "discover the intermediate institutional anatomy of each central actant[8] – that is, the historically accumulated durability, the interactive dynamics, and the inner contradictions of local activity systems" (p. 263; see Engeström & Escalante, 1996, for an extended example). Telecorp's activity network involved multiple activity systems, each developing in different directions under different influences. The activity network also involved other organizations besides Telecorp: BigTel, the Texas and U.S. legislatures, contractors, customers, etc. (We'll see more of these relationships in Chapter 4.) Activity systems both inside and outside Telecorp drew from their fields, trades, and disciplines. Network Operations Center workers typically learned their trade on the job, but they also learned tools, vocabularies, and practices through frequent collaboration with

---

[8] Engeström suggests examining these actants' inner structures "*instead of* jumping directly from actants to networks" (1996b, p. 263, my emphasis). Alert readers will note that Engeström misunderstands the nature of the actant here, since actants are also networks.

counterparts at BigTel and other telecommunications companies. That is, though these companies had been *spliced together* through relatively stable alliances, that splicing led to developmental *weaving* in which trades and industries codeveloped both individually and communally. Recent attempts at developing a fuller account of activity networks, such as netWORKing (Nardi et al., 2002) and knotworking (Engeström et al., 1999), are essentially attempts to explain splicing in terms of the woven structures of activity theory – ways to impart "institutional anatomy" to continually interconnecting actors. The latter article flirts with the sort of rhizomatic understanding that has been central to the actor–network theory approach: the activity has no center and changes constantly. But in the end, the authors return to the woven understanding of developmental work activity that is its root.

FOUR CHARACTERISTICS OF NETWORKS

Whatever their differences, actor–network theory and activity theory both suggest particular characteristics of networks. Here I'll aim for stasis rather than synthesis, building my own uneasy settlement by extracting similarities between the two understandings of networks. Sociotechnical networks can be seen as material assemblages that enact standing sets of transformations. These networks are *heterogeneous, multiply linked, transformative,* and *black-boxed.*

Heterogeneous

Sociotechnical networks are assemblages of humans and nonhumans: material assemblages that are constantly being enacted, that is, that interrelate in relatively stable ways. As we saw in Chapter 1, the heterogeneous assemblage at Telecorp included computer terminals, printed scripts, documentation, servers, telephones, wires, other telecommunications companies, provisioners, customer service representatives, salespeople, and hundreds or thousands of other humans and nonhumans. This assemblage in turn is made up of (or intersects with) other assemblages. For instance, salespeople, no matter what their product, tend to use day planners; Internet service personnel, no matter what their organization, tend to use scripts and databases of common problems; customer service personnel, no matter what company they serve, tend to keep records of their interactions with their customers. These assemblages are developed or woven over time; they are commonly called (that is to say, they comprise the everyday enactment of) trades or occupations or fields (In activity theory's terms, these assemblages comprise activities in which an object is transformed. Salespeople use day planners and the other tools and practices at their disposal to turn prospects into paying customers; Internet service personnel use their databases to make common problems tractable; and so forth. As each activity progresses, more elements are added to or changed in the assemblage to develop the activity: more humans (through changes in the community involved and in their division of labor), more nonhumans (through changes in the mediational means available), more practices (through changes in the rules that have been developed to keep the activity going). This proliferation, Latour tells us, is as certain as death and taxes. "Tomorrow, the collective will be more intricate than it was yesterday" (Latour, 2004, p. 192).

At Telecorp, most of these assemblages were progressively added in the few years before the study began, as the company began its rapid expansion into local phone service, Internet service, mobile phone service, and other features. That is, these woven networks have been progressively spliced together (which is, as we'll see in Chapter 5, a characteristic of knowledge work). Suddenly humans and nonhumans that had been developed in very different activities became networked together and were expected to interact to transform different things. Through this splicing or juxtaposition, the component activities became interpenetrated or interconnected with each other. The component assemblages began to interact and their parts became more mobile: humans, nonhumans, and their practices began to migrate across these component assemblages, interrupting the lines of development that these assemblages had followed. Of course, the new network began its own weaving as these spliced assemblages became incorporated into Telecorp.

Multiply Linked

That brings us to linkages. The telecommunications network is made up of innumerable parts, including lines, switches, utility poles, technicians, etc. Each part is terribly fragile. The phone line leading to my house is no wider than a pencil, for instance, and can be severed with wire cutters (as we see sometimes in horror movies) or falling branches (a more common occurrence in real life, fortunately). But the parts are so innumerable that individual parts can be routed around, spliced, and replaced easily. Networks are easy to disrupt, difficult to destroy because they have few if any centers, few if any vital parts.

These multiple links occur at all levels of scale. If you trace a line from the telecommunications network to a house, you'll find that it terminates at a box that is typically bolted to the side of the house (a "demarc," or demarcation point). Open that box and you'll see the network recapitulated, after a fashion: there's a smaller network of colored wires inside. Each node is itself a network. But we shouldn't be led to believe that networks are like Russian dolls, each containing the other. Each node connects to other overlapping networks. The wires in the demarc box, for instance, aren't black like the outside wires; they're colored in conventional ways that speak to electricians. Similarly, the Network Operations Center is a node, an activity, but it is saturated with overlapping connections to and dialogues with other nodes. Workers move from one functional area to another and they pick up values and social languages from those areas as well as from other activities in which they take part. We have to talk about *nets* as well as *knots*; agency, competence, expertise, and cognition are distributed across the entire network. As Donna Haraway (1996) puts it, "sticky threads" connect everything to everything else.

Such "threads" are often spun through texts. Technicians at Telecorp were guided by work orders; Customer Service workers typed instructions into switches and received feedback from them; servers sent signals to each other. Certainly more than just texts circulate in networks, but texts provide an inordinate number of the linkages. In this sense, texts aren't merely scripts, narratives, or documentary reality, although all of these functions were performed by various texts at Telecorp. As Callon argues (2002), texts weave relationships between individual actors (both human and nonhuman) and collectives. Texts translate the actors in such a way to define them and to facilitate smooth, predictable relations. Callon further alleges that writing helps manage complexity in increasingly complex markets through such definitions: the bewildering range of customers can be reduced to customer types that enjoy particular services; the bewildering array of detailed procedures can be reduced to principles. Narratives make actions and their unity compatible; they manage the multiplicity that comes from splicing together actors in an assemblage. This splicing work, Callon says, always involves negotiating and rearticulating – that is, *transforming* – texts.

Transformative

As I said in Chapter 1, sociotechnical networks represent *standing sets of transformations* (cf. Latour, 1999a). For a basic illustration, let's go back to the example of the fishing net. When you scoop a fish up in the net, the weight becomes *translated*: transformed, distributed, and redirected. Dozens of knots and strands take up the load; the fish's weight, which might have snapped a fishing line with its downward pull, becomes transformed into a sideways force that pulls on the entire net. Furthermore, if the tension in the net snaps a few strands or unravels a few knots, the net can still distribute that tension adequately.

Similarly, Telecorp was enacted through a standing set of transformations. For instance, when a customer called to complain about interrupted phone service, his complaint was written on a notepad, typed into a database, conveyed over the phone to other workers, and turned into a work order sent to a technician employed by another company. It moved from one place to another, from one part of the network (one position, social language, genre, activity) to another – and it moved by being rerepresented and *rearticulated* (again, in all senses of the word). In this case, the message "dog in backyard" would ideally be extracted from the customer during a phone conversation, transformed into F1 notes in a database, made a part of the vital information, and orally presented to the tech. The message, like the customer, was rearticulated at each node (as we saw in Chapter 1).

Transformations happen as movements to different physical and social locales – different media, different activities, different groups with different social languages. And that brings us to the *nodes* of the network, the local areas in which the message was rearticulated. These nodes are local activities in the sense used by activity theorists, but as Engeström et al. (1999) point out, these are often ad hoc activities, often deeply interpenetrated in each other. These activities are standing sets of transformations, but their complex interpenetrations mean that their transformations can be idiosyncratic and unpredictable. Each node has its own logic, its own connections, its own texts, and its own scales of space and time. At the Network Operations Center, for instance, workers coordinated the repair activities of the company, and the genres they used were oriented toward representing and facilitating this work. On one wall, a map of the entire country was projected on a large screen, showing only the characteristics of the country that are germane to the repair work, that is, the telecommunications network. Similarly, the trouble tickets authored by NOC workers reduced the life of the account's service to a set of problems and solutions that were described in particular ways with a particular vocabulary.

Black-Boxed

That brings us to one of Latour's favorite terms. We *black-box* the nodes to reduce and manage complexity; that's how they become nodes. At some point in the past, for instance, the functions of solving network problems and coordinating technicians had belonged to Customer Service; as the company grew, it became advantageous to divide that labor, to concentrate it within a functional unit, and to hide its complexity from the other units. The NOC became a black box, a simple interface for a complex set of workings, in the same way that the box bolted on the side of a customer's house hides the complex set of components within it. Black boxes tend to hide not just complexities but also local transformations. Send a signal into a black box and the output will be a transformation – you may not know *how* it was transformed, but you'll be able to predict the *results* of the transformation.

Telecorp itself was a black box. It strove to be seen as a single continuous company: customers called in, ordered service, received service, and got monthly bills, just like the many other utilities to which they subscribed. But inside that black box, Telecorp's service was a patchwork of services provided by different teams and companies. On the local side, Telecorp resold BigTel's service, serving as a buffer for those who didn't like and didn't want to deal with BigTel. Telecorp also provided its own dial tone – it had built its own fiber loop around certain cities and connected its own switches through its own physical network – but that fiber usually had to interface with BigTel's network, since that infrastructure already existed and was usually connected to the houses, apartments, and office buildings that housed Telecorp's customers. (That is, your house has only one set of phone jacks connected to just one telephone box on the outside of your house. You don't have a box and a set of jacks for every service provider, like spigots at a soda fountain.) On the long distance side, Telecorp had its own network, but that network consisted of pieces of cable and fiber that were connected to other networks owned by other regional providers, national providers, and consortiums; Telecorp rented paths through these other networks, and these paths were renegotiated by the month as prices fluctuated. Telecorp offered mobile service by rebranding the service of an existing national telecommunications company. So although we may think of Telecorp as "the phone company" that "provides phone service," much of Telecorp's work consisted of coordinating with many other companies and vendors at the local and national level. As Telecorp expanded into other markets – for instance, as deregulation allowed it to become a competitive local exchange carrier or CLEC (see Chapter 3) – it had to associate with more entities and develop more internal departments to interface with them. All of these allies had to be continuously coordinated and negotiated with, and each could turn on the others at the drop of a hat. Telecommunications partners are constantly litigating against each other, recording one another's mistakes, and documenting their own procedures in case those records are needed in a lawsuit – as Nathaniel matter-of-factly pointed out. Most of the time, those ruptures are kept invisible to the customers, who can black-box the whole mess and think of it as "the telephone company."

Now that we've covered the theoretical ground, let's get back to the question of Rex's death.

FIVE EVENTS

Now we can represent Telecorp's sociotechnical network as a sort of schematic through which we can trace to find ruptures and breaks – in this case, the rupture that led to Rex's death. But our task is somewhat more complicated and less sure than that. The network is more complex, its parts are more likely to converge and diverge (in the senses that I have set out here). A successful message would be easy to trace, since everyone who touches it leaves their time-stamped traces, and in retrospect a clear path is traversed, a clearly documented achievement with precisely recorded communications and handoffs. But an unsuccessful message, as my informants suggested, leaves no such traces: a blockage means no path, and the potential routes are many and unpredictable. Unlike a cut fiber, downed server, or poorly spliced cable, a dropped message is detectable only in that it has not been achieved. Yet we can examine how the message *should* have impacted the network, trace the possible routes, and search for junctures – obligatory passage points (Latour, 1987) – that it should have traversed. As we do so, we'll examine the network as a standing set of transformations that are heterogeneous, multiply linked, transformative, and black-boxed.

Before we get into the analysis, let's summarize what happened as best we can (see Spinuzzi, 2007b, for a fuller account), tracing the events forward through the network. In Figure 2.1, I represent Telecorp as a black box, a sort of machine with inputs (the call reporting service outage) and outputs (repaired service). This is the customer's view. But inside that black box, things become murky and confused. And that confusion spills over in the case of Rex's death, cracking open the black box and exposing some of the complexity within (if *within* is indeed an appropriate term).

In sum, here are the events that led to Rex's death:

1. Rex's owner noticed interrupted phone service.
2. He called Telecorp to complain about his phone service, speaking to Customer Service (most likely), Sales (less likely), the Network Operations Center (even less likely), or some other department (remotely possible). He did not mention that Rex is in his backyard.

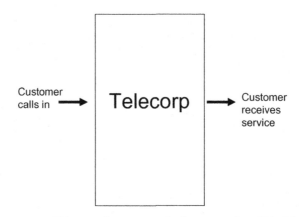

FIGURE 2.1. Telecorp, the customer's view – as a closed black box.

3. At this point it's unclear who took the call, but we can speculate what certain parties might have done with it. A customer service rep would relay the message to the NOC; a sales rep might call the NOC, Customer Service, or even another department. The message would eventually find its way to the NOC.

4. An NOC worker then called a counterpart at BigTel and set up a time for a technician to visit the customer's residence.

5. BigTel's technician visited the customer's residence, letting Rex escape and sending him to his final reward.

Figures 2.1 and 2.2 represent these five events.

Here, our attempt to trace through the network is quickly stymied because, although things appear fairly simple to those outside the company (Figure 2.1), the connections multiply and snarl once we follow the message into Telecorp (which is to say, once we leave the customer's black-box representation of the problem; see Figure 2.2). We might begin to follow the actual route of this particular call by painstakingly examining the records (e.g., the F1 notes), but we can't deduce it simply by examining the organizational and technical structure because the structure provided multiple, multiplying, unpredictable pathways for handling such calls. We can't determine the personnel who handled the call, the teams that moved it forward, and the routine, predictable phone lines along which customers' calls were routed. And even if we were able to painstakingly examine the records and reconstruct the answer *for this particular case*, the problem in the network remains. *Telecorp was run on the assumption that the black box*

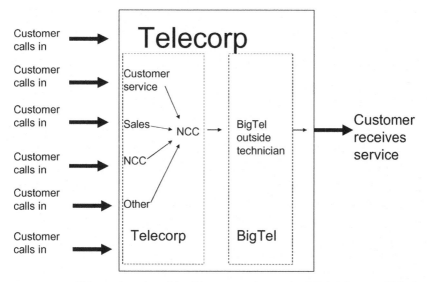

FIGURE 2.2. Telecorp, as viewed by Telecorp workers – the (slightly) opened black box.

was sustainable, though it was not, even in routine interactions. Whenever a problem cropped up – a problem being defined as a disruption in the ideal transaction, from a minor breakdown to an extended interruption of service – the black box was cracked open a bit more.

To oversimplify: Telecorp had been ideally set up as a standing set of transformations in which inputs enter the black box, are successively transformed, and result in a desirable outcome (Figure 2.2). These successive layers of transformations were handled by heterogeneous activity systems, each with their own fields, tools, and ways of doing things. But the activity systems were almost all massed on Telecorp's border, at the very permeable edge of the black box, and any one of them could take initial input such as a call about interrupted service. *Telecorp was almost all border.* Its people were perpetually massed at the border of the organization because the border was everywhere: nearly every worker at Telecorp could be contacted at any time by a customer, a vendor, a collaborator, or a competitor, and thus nearly every worker could be pulled into different activities and asked to function in novel ways. This is typical in knowledge work, in which business-to-customer and business-to-business contacts proliferate (Zuboff & Maxmin, 2004). Since these activities represented different points or functions in the call's transformation, functional groups did not receive that initial call in the same way; members of different groups asked different things, recorded different things, and routed the information in somewhat different ways. This posed a real problem in terms of tracking, routing, and maintaining quality. Telecorp was in a bind here, since the two most obvious solutions were quite unworkable.

Solution 1: The *Cordon Sanitaire*

One solution was to restrict contact with customers so that only one group could receive calls: that is to say, guard the borders, removing the multiple linkages between customers and workers. Doing so would involve returning to a modular work organization in which workers interacted only with others in their subset of the organization (see Chapter 5). Yet the borders between Telecorp and its customers were unsustainable, the connections between the groups too dense. Nobody was guarding the border between company and customer; indeed, the majority of Telecorp's workers were *on* the border, able to contact and be contacted by the customers. And they *had* to be: sales reps *had* to be able to take calls from their customers and maintain relationships; Customer Service *had* to be able to take calls from residential customers with problems; and so forth. Each group had access to customers for a reason, since each group could be the starting point for a different sort of transformation. Like the hygienists in Latour's *The Pasteurization of France* (1988a), who sought to rebuild entire cities hygienically because they could not pinpoint the cause of disease, Telecorp faced an impossible task if it tried to erect a *cordon sanitaire* across all capillaries of its network. This solution was a nonstarter.

Solution 2: The Uniform Regimen

The other solution was to inculcate the same procedural knowledge in all workers, turning them into uniformly trained soldiers who could patrol the border the same way, like Spartans. But that solution didn't work either because it attempted to erase the very heterogeneity that made the transformations work in the first place. Workers at Telecorp labored in a far-flung activity network with very different activity systems that handled very different types of problems and knowledge. Uniform training and a uniform understanding of work would not only be very difficult to achieve under these extremely heterogeneous conditions, it would actually be counterproductive since it would squeeze out the very differences in activity that allow Telecorp to make productive transformations. Nevertheless, this second solution was quite attractive to one Customer Service worker, who suggested this very solution in an internal survey dated March 2000:

> All products can start or finish in customer service. Every Telecorp employee should know what Telecorp sells and services and what has to be done to service a customer. I think it would help with communication with the company itself to know what is actually expected out of their Customer Service Reps. All employees should sit in a CS rep seat for a day and actually be expected to take care of whatever daily task that day.

This solution is nostalgic, hearkening back to the simpler years when Telecorp was more homogeneous. In these early years, one 18-year veteran told me, everyone began in Customer Service and "knew everything from the ground up" so

> you're not just doing it blind.... I like to know enough about it that I feel like I know when I look into an account what I'm looking at. That's something we don't do anymore. But we've gotten so large it's hard to say, okay, why don't you set up this account now. Setting up an account is not like it used to be, it's a lot harder.

Indeed it is. Telecorp began by reselling long distance service, but now it offers an ever-expanding number of services: calling cards, long distance pagers, DSL, Internet dial-up, mobile service, conference calling. Who could learn all aspects of this business, which is at the same time rapidly diverging (as old fields engender new occupations and traditions) and converging (as fields are brought into contact and combined)? Especially with a labor shortage making it easy for workers to job-hop and a booming telecommunications business making it imperative to hire more people – two factors that pushed turnover higher and higher across the company and the industry in 2000–2001. Telecorp was constantly changing and developing; it was a moving target. And as its often short-term employees came from other, very different workplaces (telecommunications companies, the local university, telemarketing, Internet service providers, etc.), they spliced that knowledge into Telecorp too (just as call center workers did in Wenger's [1998] study of an insurance company). Consequently, waves of localized transformations and innovations changed local practice and made universal regimens nearly impossible.

Nevertheless this second solution, the universal regimen, was at the core of the strategy Telecorp had begun to implement in 2000–2001. It initiated a new cross-training program that involved having workers spend time in various sections, learning "how the company works" – an attempt to cultivate a stable, essential core of knowledge that could function as a universal regime for the company. Simultaneously, and with the same intent, it encouraged workers in each department to apply for jobs in other departments so that each department could share knowledge about the others. For instance, one sales assistant ("Sheila") was recruited from Customer Service to help bridge the contradictions between the two departments. Sheila laughingly recalled that a co-worker in Customer Service threatened to come "kick my ass" if she developed an attitude like others in Sales.

How would this solution work out? Not very well, as I discuss in Chapter 6. Cross-training might indeed help spread understanding about how Telecorp's heterogeneous parts work, but Telecorp is becoming more complicated by the day, and local knowledge has a short shelf life. In the few short months since Sheila had left Customer Service, the department had already spun the task of data entry off to a specialized subgroup – a fundamental change in this department's division of labor. How much of Sheila's knowledge would be relevant six months later? Could she continue to bridge the widening gap between Sales and Customer Service, or would her former co-worker eventually perceive her as a traitor and feel compelled to kick her ass? Similarly, one worker who moved from Customer Service to Network Coordination ("Marisela") told me that her former colleagues were still calling her with Customer Service questions *eight months later*. How can Customer Service continue to function when the people who have accumulated the most information about their activity are moved away and lose touch?

Let's develop this point a bit further. When Rex's owner called Telecorp to complain about his phone service, he was able to treat the telephone company as a black box,[9] a simple interface for a complex and messy sociotechnical system. See Figure 2.1 again. Isn't it simple? The black box marked "Telecorp" really does not do justice to the enormous complexity of the telecommunications industry that the customer's request had to traverse, but he neither knew about nor cared for that complexity. *His task was simple for him because Telecorp was simple for him.* He picked up a phone, called a number, and talked to someone on the other end who promised to take care

---

[9] This black-boxing is abetted by legislation and the actions of independent telecommunications providers. You don't have to switch to a different dialing scheme or learn a new set of area codes when you switch phone providers, for instance, because legislation dictates that they all use the same scheme. Similarly, if you choose Company A to provide your service, Company B can't block your calls to customers using their service. In this context, only one company profits when the black box of local telephone service is opened: BigTel, which is the largest and most established of the regional companies, sets the standard for telecommunications service.

of the problem. Ideally, a few days later, the phone line would start working again. If this outcome actually happened – as it almost always did, because Telecorp provided good reliable service in the overwhelming majority of instances – the black box remained closed.

Inside that black box, things were quite different. As we've seen, Telecorp's management took the opposite strategy in its attempt to develop a universal regime. Rather than building black boxes for its workers, Telecorp's management worked hard to open all of those black boxes at once, turning them into Pandora's boxes (Latour, 1999b), multiplying complexity rather than reducing it. *The workers' jobs were complex because their relations to other departments, other activity systems, were complex and getting more complex all the time.* Few departments had simple interfaces to other departments; although predictable paths existed for transforming information, they always involved side paths and exceptions, multiple links described only through lore. And that lore had few chances to develop into more enduring texts. Too many changes were occurring within Telecorp and in the broader telecommunications market (and, we might add, in knowledge work in general; see Chapter 5). Splicing events such as turnover, acquisitions, cross-training, and regulative changes meant that workers could not close the black boxes themselves by *operationalizing* (to use activity theory's term) their routine actions. The weaving activity that would allow for communal operationalizing – the formation of shared tricks, habits, and genres, the sorts of things that make black boxes possible – was difficult to sustain because the activities of the different activity systems were weaving too rapidly, diverging too quickly, converging too chaotically, splicing across heterogeneous fields too frequently, and losing too many individuals too quickly. Workers sometimes suggested that "this is a different kind of industry" and that some parts of the job were simply unteachable, and they were right: these jobs *were* unteachable as long as networks were woven and spliced without affording a chance for workers to manage the attendant complexity and change. *Without relative stability on which sustainable practices could be founded and formalized, workers could only learn by encountering contingencies and tailoring responses to each one of them* (see Chapter 6). Stable mediational relationships (with people and with artifacts) could not reliably develop and spread across the company because the work was too ad hoc and mercurial, not black-boxed enough, to make them possible on a broad enough scale. NOC workers blamed other departments for Rex's death, but there was no way to guide interactions, enforce compliance, or hold anyone accountable. There was no stable settlement on which to base responsibility.

A black box is a settlement among different interests, a settlement that has hardened over time and that can serve as a building block for more complex sociotechnical structures. It provides a way to bracket off complexity, a way that can be communally agreed upon so interested parties can conceptualize scale and activity. Opening the black box means renegotiating everything: the parties involved, the way they divide the labor, the tools they use, the objectives they profess, the multiple linkages they make with heterogeneous others. Activity systems are themselves an attempt to black-box work, but in Telecorp's case those black boxes didn't hold together: in this increasingly spliced environment, work is no longer separable into woven fields and disciplines (if it ever had been); those activity systems are always spliced, always deeply interpenetrated. NetWORKing (Nardi et al., 2002) and knotworking (Engeström et al., 1999), in my reading, are attempts to reimpose developmental understanding. We can see their value but also the need for caution: black boxes should be closed, eventually, but not too hastily.

Garrisoning the Passes and Interrogating the Locals

So have we found the rupture, the point at which the mistake was made that would eventually kill Rex? No. We've found a severe problem with the network, one that we'll revisit in later chapters. But this complex interconnection among departments, this tangled knot, raises the question of whether we can indeed hold one part of the network accountable. If only this "schematic" through which we're tracing were as static and bounded as it appears in Figure 2.2! We would have a tangle, but at least it would present a fairly limited number of possibilities to examine. But unlike a conventional schematic, this one constantly redraws itself; its lines can potentially connect anything to anything else. Customers and departments could contact each other at various points in the work, route around each other, loop through or bypass transformations. If someone later in the set of transformations noticed that a piece of information is unspecified (e.g., whether a customer has a dog in his yard), she could call or e-mail others to get that information, including the customer himself. In his discussion of war in the *Discourses*, Machiavelli describes an analogous situation with regard to mountain passes:

[V]ery few generals of any virtuosity have attempted to hold such passes ... because it is impossible to close them all, for in mountains, as in open country, there are not only the commonly frequented routes, but many others which, if not known to foreigners, are known to peasants, whose help you can always enlist in any place to the discomfiture of your opponent. (Machiavelli, 2003a, p. 172)

With the right guides and the right local knowledge, the well-worn paths can be bypassed. Someone who takes Sun Tzu's advice on the same subject ("On enclosed ground, if we occupy it first, we must block it and wait for the enemy" [2002, p. 62]) might be in for a surprise. And if we apply the arborescent logic of discrete, linearized relationships among activities to this rhizomatic organization – the logic that is implied in the inputs and outputs of the activity network depicted in Figure 3.2 – we will be similarly surprised: although they were woven, these activities were also spliced together, and those splicings were often both dense and unmapped. Inside Telecorp, every point was potentially connected to every other point and could mediate the others, not metaphorically but quite literally. Texts such as comprehensive phone lists, F1 notes, and e-mails were available to all workers, allowing spontaneous contact among any workers at any time. The phone system, the internal mail system, and databases facilitated those contacts in various modes; every worker had access to these technologies, though some restrictions in database permissions existed. Workers circulated among jobs, regularly interfaced with others in different departments, and were encouraged to make social connections across the company during gatherings and lunch hours. Even if the connections didn't show up on an organization chart, these hidden passes were there.

A few customers could and did route around the garrisoned passes by exploiting local knowledge, contacting workers deep in the company's interior, workers who weren't officially supposed to talk to the public. For instance, one customer obtained the direct number for a provisioner and called him directly about an order; the provisioner expedited the order, then reprimanded the worker who had given his number to the customer. In another instance, a new hire working with a data entry group received an angry call from a customer who had obtained her name from another worker, then had her paged; she answered the page because she assumed it was a personal call and reported feeling intimidated and vulnerable afterwards. To extend the martial metaphor, the more obvious passes have been garrisoned through procedures and training, but the hidden passes cannot all be garrisoned. On the other hand, the same hidden passes were often a source of strength. If a worker found that one pass was blocked (e.g., information was missing from an F1 note), she could route around that mediatory relationship by drawing on another one (e.g., by calling

another worker or consulting a different part of the database). The dense set
of mediatory interconnections provided a robust environment for information gathering – a characteristic of networks – but this terrain was largely
unmapped, workers were not trained in traversing the passes, and no way
existed to close them to motivated customers.

With that realization, we can recognize that the question has been framed
too hastily. Rather than looking at the beginning of the process, at the
permeable border between customers and Telecorp (who failed to take the
information?), we should look at the end of the process (who was the last
person who could have obtained the information?). The question isn't where
the information *enters* Telecorp, it's the relatively narrow point where the
information *leaves* Telecorp. The only mountain pass that cannot be routed
around, the narrowest point in the network, is the last one: the strictly
regulated interface between the NOC and BigTel's technician. This interface
is wholly different from Telecorp's internal connections. Only one group –
a handful of people – had contact with BigTel's technicians; only they
had the relevant contact information; only they had cultivated an ongoing
relationship with BigTel. Here it is practical to set up a garrison, and in Rex's
case, the garrison has let Telecorp down. The NOC worker who last touched
the order – and who should have checked with the customer – is the only
one who can be held responsible.

CONCLUSION: WHAT IS A NETWORK?

What is a network? In this chapter, I have attempted a tentative answer
to that question based on a dialogue between activity theory and actor–
network theory. But a dialogue, unlike a dialectic, does not imply a process
that will lead to agreement or a single answer. At this point, at least, that
seems productive. We can see a network as woven and spliced, divergent and
convergent, culturally–historically developed and anachronistically associated, material and performed. We can see its length and interconnections as
directly proportional to the number of embedded contradictions that desta-
bilize it, and we can also see its length and interconnections as a source of
stability and strength. I won't try to reconcile these differing views here. This
dialogue, I think, is valuable as we go on to examine Telecorp and its industry in various ways. At the same time, we can reach some degree of stasis
in this discussion. Activity theory and actor–network theory disagree about
many things, but they agree that networks are (in the terms I've defined
here) heterogeneous, multiply linked, transformative, and black-boxed.

These are common characteristics that we can apply to Telecorp's network throughout the rest of this book.

This ongoing dialogue, then, has leveraged the differences between the two approaches without trying to resolve them. As Engeström points out, contradictions drive change and development (1990, p. 84); and as Latour has noted, contradictions are often dealt with by rerouting around them rather than meeting them head-on (1999a, p. 16). That's what I've attempted to do in this chapter: establish stasis and use it as a base for pulling insights from these divergent approaches.

Now that we have established this dialogue, let's take a step back from Telecorp and engage the dialogue more fully. For activity theorists and actor–network theorists have for too long talked past each other. In the next chapter I'll examine their ongoing dispute in more detail to answer the question: how are networks theorized? This theoretical work will provide the basis for the empirical work in the rest of the book.

3

How Are Networks Theorized?

As we saw in the previous chapters, different parts of Telecorp relate in different and complex ways. I've introduced activity networks and actor–networks in thumbnail fashion as two different ways of getting at how these parts relate. Now it's time to roll up our sleeves and see what's actually involved in analyzing such networks. As we've seen, activity theory and actor–network theory have common ground but also disagreements stemming from their very different projects. As I said in Chapter 2, I'm not going to provide a middle way or "just right" solution (that's a tired trope, and nobody really believes it anyway). I'll settle for a dialogue – one that honestly examines the dispute, not the sniping that has until now taken place between the two camps. Let's have a real argument!

And it's high time that this argument take place. Activity theory and actor–network theory have traditionally worked in separate areas. Activity theory is primarily a theory of distributed cognition and focuses on issues of labor, learning, and concept formation; it's used in fields such as educational, cognitive, and cultural psychology, although it's also making inroads in human–computer interaction, computer-supported cooperative work, communication, and anthropology. In contrast, actor–network theory is primarily an ontology – an account of existence – and focuses on issues of power in science and politics: rhetoric, production of facts, agreements, and knowledge. It's used in science and technology studies, philosophy, and sociology. But recently the edges of these projects have begun to meet and contend with each other. Activity theory, in its "third generation" (discussed below), is attempting to move from the study of individuals and focused activities to the study of interrelated sets of activities, and thus into work organization, and it's also beginning to investigate issues of power and mastery (e.g., Blackler & McDonald, 2000; Nardi, 2005). Simultaneously, actor–network theory is expanding from studies of scientific knowledge into popular science and technology and from there into work organization as well (e.g., Berg, 1997; Latour, 2006). So it's not surprising that advocates of the two approaches are beginning to grapple with each other's approaches. And their apparently deep differences mean that they have begun to have sharp confrontations. But confrontations are not necessarily dialogue.

So, on the one hand, actor–network theorists such as Latour have made vague, undersourced attacks on dialectics and contradictions, which are key elements of activity theory analyses. We're told that dialectical arguments are an attempt to rescue the subject–object divide, "to save the dualist paradigm under the pretense of subsuming it" (Latour, 1993a, p. 388; cf. Latour, 1993b, p. 57; 2006, pp. 169–170). And that "dialectics recites a logic so impoverished that anything and everything can be drawn from it" (Serres & Latour, 1995, p. 155). These attacks on dialectic don't take into account the differences between Hegelian and Marxist dialectics (Miettinen, 1999), a distinction that is brushed aside rather than addressed (Latour, 1996c).

On the other hand, activity theorists have been more aggressive and specific with their brief against actor–network theory. Actor–network theory is said to be practicing a poor-cousin version of dialectics (Engeström, 1996b; Miettinen, 1999). It is said to embody a contradiction between the principle of symmetry and an extreme version of asymmetry (Engeström & Escalante, 1996; Miettinen, 1998, 1999; Nardi, Whittaker, & Schwarz, 2002). It is said to strive for irreversibility (Engeström & Escalante, 1996) and assume durability and inertia (Miettinen, 1999). These criticisms are based on some basic misunderstandings of actor–network theory. Engeström even criticizes actor–network theory as a poor theory of learning (2001), which is like criticizing a hammer for making a poor spatula.

So there's plenty of mischaracterization on both sides of the dispute, resulting from the failure to enter into a genuine dialogue and examine the differences of the programs on their own terms. And that's too bad, since the projects also have much in common, as we saw in Chapter 2. So let's raise the white flag and parley a bit.

We'll get back to Telecorp's strategic posture in the next chapter with a historical examination of the landscape in which it operates. But first, in this chapter, let's frame where activity theory and actor–network theory get their notions of networks. As I said in Chapter 2, there has been a running battle between these approaches – mostly waged by activity theorists, who came to the notion of network later and who see the opportunity to leverage the concept in their own work. Here I'll discuss some of the key concepts, outline objections, and discuss points of misunderstanding in their dialogue.

I'll start with their historical roots and move quickly through the highlights, and I apologize in advance for compressing such large bodies of thought into a single chapter. Much is lost here, and I hope I can recover some of it adequately in later chapters.

To get at this difference, let's draw on the discussion of weaving and splicing from the last chapter – a distinction that may be a bit facile but that puts a name to the differing orientations of the two approaches and (as we'll see below) explains quite a bit about why they diverge in the ways they do. I characterized activity theory as weaving and actor–network theory as splicing, but I acknowledged that neither was necessarily "pure": each necessarily deals with both splicing and weaving. And technologies are "full partners" in cognition in both approaches. So exactly what is the key difference? To understand that, we must get under the hood of these two different approaches.

Let's begin with an illustration.

THE FIRST STROKE

We'll revisit Telecorp later in the chapter, but first let's talk about steam engines and water pumps.

According to Frederich Engels, Sadi Carnot's theorization of the steam engine "provided the most striking proof that one can impart heat and obtain mechanical motion. 100,000 steam engines did not prove this any more than the one" (1954, p. 303). By doing away with the "subsidiary processes," Carnot found the underlying principle of the steam engine (p. 303), which "presents the process in a pure, independent, and unadulterated form" (p. 304). That is, Carnot worked inductively from many examples of the steam engine to determine the essential principle underlying it; once that principle was identified, other and better steam engines could be built on it. The principle Carnot extracted became the second law of thermodynamics.

Invoking Engels's illustration, Yrjö Engeström describes Carnot's "ideal" steam engine as "the germ-cell, the initial inner relations behind any particular form of steam-engine. This kind of an abstraction does not seek and classify the common external features of all the particular cases. Rather, it seeks the *genetic origin* of a totality" (1990, p. 52, my emphasis; cf. Ilyenkov, 1982, pp. 170–171). The steam engine is an example of a materialist, non-idealist emergence of a concept in which someone thoroughly analyzes a particular instance of a phenomenon, reduces it to a single abstract concept or principle (the "germ-cell"), then uses the concept or principle to develop further variations. Elsewhere activity theorists call this "ascending from the abstract to the concrete," that is, inductively establishing the basic principle that can then serve as the basis for further development (e.g., Engeström, 1990). As the "germ-cell" metaphor implies, this is a developmental account. When constructing the fabric of the network, *the first stroke is a weave.*

From this perspective, *of course* 10,000 steam engines did not prove the principle more than the one. Carnot induced from the workings of a steam engine the principle that steam engines have in common – the second law of thermodynamics – which in turn came to underpin the design and production of 10,000 more. This principle, this germ-cell, was true no matter how many steam engines had been derived from it, even if there had been none. Weaving is *arborescent* or treelike (Deleuze & Guattari, 1987; Law, 2002a). It emphasizes the evolution and development over time from a root (the germ-cell, the "abstract") to branches (the various implementations, the "concrete"). The weaving perspective assumes such genetic, historical–developmental relations; although those relations might involve splicing with other woven relations (Deleuze & Guattari, 1987, p. 20), the origin point is a weave.

Compare this account with Marianne de Laet and Annemarie Mol's (2000) discussion of the Zimbabwe Bush Pump, a water pump that the Zimbabwean government distributes to villages to supply safe drinking water. "A national standard, the Zimbabwe Bush Pump is a nation-builder that gains strength with each new installation" (p. 236). *The more pumps, the more real the pump becomes*; the more it is installed, the more it must adapt itself to new conditions in order to spread. Whereas Engels thought the steam engine could be reduced to a germ-cell, de Laet and Mol insist that the Zimbabwe Bush Pump has indistinct boundaries and cannot be reduced to a single germinating principle:

> Even if nothing can be taken from it, it is not clear where this pump ends. For what is the Zimbabwe Bush Pump? A water-producing device, defined by the mechanics that make it work as a pump. Or a type of hydraulics that produces water in specific quantities and from particular sources. But then again, maybe it is a sanitation device – in which case the concrete slab, mould, casing and gravel are also essential parts. And while it may provide water and health, the Pump can do so only with the Vonder Rig – or some other boring device – and accompanied by manuals, measurements, and texts. Without these it is nothing, so maybe they belong to it too. And what about the village community? Is it to be included in the Pump – because a pump has to be set up by the community and cannot be maintained without one? But then again, perhaps the boundaries of the Bush Pump coincide with those of the Zimbabwean nation. For in its modest way this national Bush Pump helps to make Zimbabwe as much as Zimbabwe makes it. (p. 237)

Where an activity theorist would look for a germ-cell or abstract principle from which the many instances of the pump develops, de Laet and Mol describe a multiplicity of pumps; each instance or aspect provides yet another relational link that lengthens the network, that makes the whole enterprise cohere more tightly and makes the pump more real. This account is one of associations and alliances.[1] In an actor–network, *the first stroke is a splice.*

From this perspective, *of course* 100,000 steam engines prove the principle more than the one. It is only because Carnot artificially erased the network of relations that sustain and make possible the steam engine that he could come up with what we call a "concept," an abstract principle that we take to be common to and fundamental to all subsequent iterations (cf. Latour, 1999b, Chapter 3). But Carnot's concept in itself does nothing; it is only when we reproduce and continue to fiddle with the entire network of relations that the steam engine can actually do anything. The stronger and denser the network of relations, the more real the steam engine is – the more manufacturers of spare parts within tolerances, the more mechanics on call, the more documentation for repairing such machines, the more uses developed for them. One steam engine is hardly real at all, which is why experiments are basically detailed instructions that are repeatedly carried out by different individuals in different places: they are programs meant to reproduce phenomena in order to make them more real in different areas, to be transportable without transformation (cf. Bazerman, 1988; Latour, 1987; Shapin & Schaffer, 1985). Splicing is *rhizomatic* (Deleuze & Guattari, 1987; Law, 2002a). In this perspective, existence is achieved through accretion rather than development, associations rather than evolution. Splicing does not assume a unitary existence for humans and nonhumans but a purely associational one, and thus historical–developmental accounts (which assume a sort of unitary existence) are questionable. Weaving is filiation, but splicing is alliance, uniquely alliance (Deleuze & Guattari, 1987, p. 25).

Why the difference between these two accounts? Engels was searching for a materialist theory of knowledge, an account of development in all its forms (cf. Ilyenkov, 1977). de Laet and Mol, and others working with actor–network theory and its postvariants, are looking for a way to define technologies relationally and nonessentially. Their different projects demand different tacks. Engels and his activity theory descendants are interested in learning and development, so they are concerned with how to describe concept formation; they study how psychological and physical tools are

---

[1] Vygotsky (1962) understood association as an immature stage of concept development. I discuss this point further in Chapter 6.

developed over time and made into mediators that guide further activity. Actor–network theorists are much more concerned with ontology and find abstractions such as concepts to be quite untenable as ways to address that problem; they are more concerned with the associations that constitute each phenomenon.

With this in mind, we can begin to discern where the central dispute between activity theory and actor–network theory lies, and we can turn a more discerning eye on their complaints. For instance, Reijo Miettinen critiques actor–network theory from an activity-theoretical standpoint, arguing that it makes no sense to discuss political–rhetorical interests without an understanding of how those interests developed and how they persist. "An explanation of the motives for participating in a network *presupposes* an analysis of the history and dilemmas associated with the participating activity systems," he argues (1998, p. 446, my emphasis). So "an analysis of network formation in terms of interests, goals, persuasion, and enrollment is not enough. I propose that, if we are to understand the content of collaboration and the motives of participants, we need an analysis of the historically formed objects of participating activity systems, and also of the objects constructed together by them" (p. 426). Indeed, activity itself is defined "in terms of a subject's relation to a world" (Kaptelinin & Nardi, 2006, p. 247). For activity theorists, any account of splicing has to be predicated on a woven understanding; *development precedes and underpins political–rhetorical interests.* The first stroke is a weave. On the other hand, Latour critiques classical sociology for its *a priori* assumption of preexisting social structures and subject–object relations, as well as for providing itself with a metalanguage that allows its practitioners to discern rules, laws, and goals that are not accessible to those who live in that society. Instead, he says, the actors should be allowed to define each other through their relations (1996a, pp. 199–200; cf. Callon, 1991, p. 140). These relations are reversible and renegotiable at any time, though the thicker the relations, the less likely they are to be reversed (Callon, 1991). For actor–network theorists, any account of weaving has to be predicated on a spliced understanding; *political–rhetorical interests precede and underpin development.* The first stroke is a splice.

So each side accuses the other of putting the cart before the horse. Let's look at each account in turn, starting with activity theory, and use them to revisit the case from Chapter 2.

WEAVING A NETWORK: ACTIVITY THEORY'S ACCOUNT

From activity theory's perspective, activity networks consist of a developing set of activities anchored by a common object toward which people strive. The root of this developmental view is *dialectics*, the interactionist understanding of change that permeates Marxist accounts of activity.

An Engelsian View: The Science of Interconnections

Dialectics is associated with Marx, who used a non-Hegelian materialist dialectics in his work. But dialectical materialism was popularized – and universalized – by Marx's collaborator and posthumous editor, Frederich Engels (Wilde, 1991). Seminal works in the development of activity theory (Leont'ev, 1978; Vygotsky, 1962, 1978) are based on an Engelsian understanding of dialectics. Later work such as Engeström's has drawn more heavily on Marx and Soviet theoreticians such as Evald Ilyenkov but still borrows from Engels.

Engels argued that dialectics, once made materialist rather than idealist, constitutes a general law of nature. For him, dialectics was the "science of interconnections" (1954, p. 83), a science that explains the natural world as well as the social one: "The dialectical laws are really laws of development of nature, and therefore are valid also for theoretical natural science" (p. 84). Not only does dialectic constitute a "universally valid... general law of development of nature, society, or thought," it also constitutes a universally valid law of development for the natural world (p. 91). Indeed, "Nature is the proof of dialectics, and it must be said for modern science that it has furnished this proof with very rich materials increasingly daily, and thus has shown that, in the last resort, Nature works dialectically and not metaphysically; that she does not move in the eternal oneness of a perpetually recurring circle, but goes through a real historical evolution" (1975, p. 48). The term *evolution* is key here, since Engels aggressively sought to tie dialectics to Darwin's work. He saw dialectics as an interactionism that sticks, an irreversible process of developmental changes. Just as you can't ungrind the hamburger or put the toothpaste back in the tube, you can't undo dialectic interactions. (We can see clearly why Deleuze and Guattari label dialectics as arborescent [1987, p. 5].)

And where does dialectics lead? "Objective" dialectics, which "prevails throughout nature . . . [is] the motion of opposites which asserts itself everywhere in nature, and which by the continual conflict of opposites and their final passage into one another, or into higher forms, determines the life of nature" (Engels, 1954, p. 280). This science of interconnections provided a unified theory that would explain the workings of people, economies, societies, biology, physics, and chemistry with equal insight, predicated on the continuously developing interactions among parties rather than on rigid cause–effect relations or essentialist understandings of things-in-themselves (Engels, 1975, pp. 47–48). This understanding of dialectics underpins the work of Lev Vygotsky, which in turn underpins activity theory. Although activity theorists have ratcheted back Engels's claims of universality, they continue to take development-through-interaction as the central principle by which activity must be analyzed; they continue to see the first stroke as a weave.

So let's talk about the development of activity theory itself. Yrjö Engeström (1996a) outlines three "generations" of activity theory in which its tenets were established. In the first generation, Lev Vygotsky and his collaborators built directly on Engels's ideas to develop the concept of mediated human activity in the individual, laying the foundations of activity theory. In the second generation, A. N. Leont'ev applied the concept of mediation to larger social groups, yielding the unit of the activity system; this innovation is widely considered to be the beginning of activity theory. And in the third and current generation, Engeström and his collaborators drew on the works of Evald Ilyenkov (1977, 1982) to apply contradictions to activity systems and to conceptualize activity networks. Also in this third generation, activity theory began to come to grips with two aspects of splicing: polycontextuality and boundary crossing.

Mediation

Vygotsky argues that human activity is marked by a reliance on cultural artifacts: external stimuli that allow humans "*to control their behavior from the outside,*" that is to say, indirectly (1978, p. 40, his emphasis). These external artifacts, Vygotsky emphasizes, do not simply help humans do things they would do anyway; the artifacts qualitatively transform the activity, often in ways that exceed the unmediated capacity of the human being. (One of Vygotsky's favorite examples is tying a knot in a handkerchief, a Russian aide-mémoire similar to tying a string around one's finger [1978, p. 50].) In using mediational artifacts, Michael Cole argues, people themselves are psychologically transformed: they begin to think, act, and value differently (1996, p. 108).

The notion of mediation is terribly important here, and Vygotsky illustrates it well with accounts of his many studies. He argues that we rarely do what animals do – act directly on the environment – but instead work through mediators. For example, an infant might reach vainly for an object that is then handed to her by a parent. Eventually the grasping (an attempt to control the environment directly) becomes pointing (a sign that helps to "control" the parent). The mediator not only helps to carry out an activity that would be difficult otherwise, it changes the character of the activity; it qualitatively transforms it. And in learning and taking up a culture's mediators, we become acculturated (Luria, 1976).

The person-mediated-by-tools functions differently from the person alone. For instance, in one of his remarkably economical experiments, Vygotsky (1978, pp. 40–45) studied how well children performed on a memory game. The researcher would ask each child the color of a series of items, and the child would answer using each color no more than once and avoiding two "forbidden" colors. In one iteration, the child would rely on only her own memory; in the other, she was given a set of colored cards and no instructions on how to use them. For children ages five and six, the colored cards made no difference. But for older children, who began to use the cards to keep track of allowable colors, the card-mediated task was far more successful than the unmediated one. Once an individual learns how to mediate her task with physical tools (such as cards) or psychological tools (such as structured memory techniques – think of singing the alphabet), the quality of her activity changes. The individual exceeds her unmediated limits. For Vygotsky, then, the basic unit of psychological analysis is not the individual but the mediated action in which she takes part (1978, p. 40).

As the example above suggests, activity theory does not assume a divide between the cognitive and the social (see Hakkarainen, 2003, p. 680) or between the individual and her tools. Vygotsky insisted that human activity must be understood as mediated by physical and psychological tools, a stance that can be understood as distributed cognition (Cole & Engeström, 1993; but see Nardi, 1996b). Human activity at the individual level is a dialectic among humans and their mediators.

Structure of Activity

This essential unit of mediated action was sufficient for studying individuals psychologically. But in his later work, Vygotsky attempted to extend the concept of mediation to groups, laying the foundations for what we now call "activity theory." The development of activity theory itself was achieved by Vygotsky's collaborator A.N. Leont'ev, who extended Vygotsky's insights on the basis of Marx's and Engels's work. Leont'ev proposed that the essential unit of analysis should be the *activity system*, a unit that included Vygotsky's triangle of individual mediated action but also the individual's community, the rules that mediated the individual's relation to that community, and the division of labor that mediated between the community and the object of

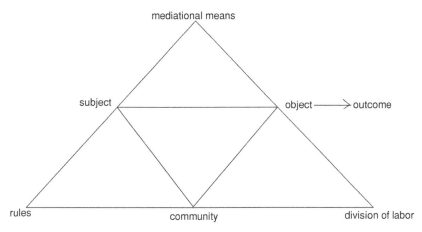

FIGURE 3.1. An activity system.

the activity. Leont'ev did not diagram the activity system, but Engeström later popularized it through diagrams such as the one in Figure 3.1.

As Stephen Witte (2005) argues, the activity system is an expanded version of Vygotsky's triangle of mediated activity: The points of the triangle are three different types of mediators (tools, rules, and division of labor). In an activity system(individual collaborators use *mediational means* (physical and psychological tools) to cyclically transform a particular *object* with a particular outcome in mind.)Repeatedly, the farmer transforms a field into a harvest; the traffic safety worker transforms raw traffic accident data into recommendations; the Telecorp provisioner transforms service requests into phone service. These transformations are meant to produce certain *outcomes*: subsistence or profit, safer roadways, a reliable telecommunications system. These mediated activities are rooted in and given meaning through their relationship with the *community* in which they are enacted. The community relates to collaborators through communal *rules* that establish the nature of the relationship between collaborator and community. It also relates to the object through a *division of labor* that implicitly or explicitly spells out the roles each collaborator undertakes in transforming the object.

Understanding the object is vital here, especially since *object* is used in a very specific way that is often not intuitive to English speakers. Rather than *artifact* or *thing*, it means the *transformational focus*[2] of an ongoing activity (as in "the object of the game" or "the object of this exercise"; see Nardi,

---

[2] David R. Russell has attempted to convey this specific meaning in English by using the term *object(ive)* (1995).

2005, p. 40). The object of an activity "is both the projection of a human mind onto the objective world and a projection of the world onto human mind" (Kaptelinin, 2005, p. 5) in that it dialectically transforms both (p. 20; cf. Hyysalo, 2005). In doing so, it makes sense of human activity: it "gives meaning to and determines values of various entities and phenomena" (Kaptelinin, 2005, p. 5).

The object is shared by all in the activity system, though it may be poly-motivated; that is, different individuals may have different motivations as they collectively work to transform it (Kaptelinin, 2005; Miettinen, 2005; Nardi, 2005). And the object is typically not a single entity: it is "an assembly of material entities embedded in economic and social relationships" (Miettinen, 2005, p. 58). When the farmer transforms a field, the traffic safety worker transforms a roadway system, or the provisioner transforms a service request, they work on coherent assemblages treated as a single developing object. Such assemblages – and their components – are also members of other activity systems, where they fulfill different roles. For instance, the phone line that functions as an object for the telecommunications worker also functions as a mediational means for her customer.

It is this understanding of the object as the transformational focus of collective dialectical development that leads us to activity theory's account of developmental change: contradictions.

Contradictions

Contradiction is absolutely central to the dialectical account of developmental change that activity theory proffers. "Contradictions are historically accumulating structural tensions within or between activity systems" (Engeström, 2001, p. 137). Such tensions, Engeström argues, take four forms:

> The primary contradiction of activities in capitalist socio-economic formations lives as the inner conflict between exchange value and use value within each corner of the triangle of activity.
>
> The secondary contradictions are those appearing between the corners. The stiff hierarchical division of labor lagging behind and preventing the possibilities opened by advanced instruments is a typical example.
>
> The tertiary contradiction appears when representatives of culture (e.g., teachers) introduce the object and motive of a culturally more advanced form of the central activity into the dominant form of the central activity. For example, the primary school pupil goes to school in order to play with his mates (the dominant motive), but the parents and the teacher

try to make him study seriously (the culturally more advanced motive). The culturally more advanced object and motive may also be actively sought by the subjects of the central activity themselves.

The quaternary contradictions require that we take into considera- tion the essential "neighbour activities" linked with the central activity which is the original object of our study. (Engeström, 1987, Chapter 2; cf. 1992, p. 21)

Contradiction is firmly embedded in dialectical materialism, a mainstay of the Marxist ideology that dominated the Soviet Union during activity theory's initial development (e.g., Hyysalo, 2005; Kaptelinin, 2005). So it may be surprising to note that contradiction did not become an important part of activity theory analyses until late in its development. Yes, contradiction was freely discussed in the abstract and applied vigorously to critiques of the West, but applying it to internal Soviet matters – such as schooling and work – was a dangerous exercise. Contradiction emphasizes change, and change was not always welcomed in the Soviet Union. In Engeström's words, "contradictions in activity remained an extremely touchy issue" (1996a, p. 132).

But in the 1970s, researchers in the West picked up the concept of *activity* and began applying it to different domains, such as work (p. 132). And in the West, the notion of contradictions was more palatable (or at least less dangerous). Engeström credits Ilyenkov (1977, 1982) with conceptualizing "the idea of internal contradictions as the driving force of change and development in activity systems" (p. 133) but modestly downplays his own considerable role in elaborating and popularizing the idea.

Contradictions are engines of change: they provide the impetus for the sorts of reorganizing, reconceiving, and reworking that characterizes a living activity system or network. They are "not just inevitable features of activ- ity but central features" (Helle, 2000, p. 88). Identifying a contradiction *in progress* can help researchers conceptualize the problem and develop appro- priate responses to it (the rationale behind Engeström's developmental work research [Engeström, 1996a; Gay & Hembrooke, 2004; Helle, 2000]). And identifying contradictions *in the past* provides a historical approach (as we'll see in Chapter 4) that can help researchers identify and examine particular crises that were key to the development of new innovations and solutions (Engeström, 1990; Miettinen, 1998; Spinuzzi, 2003b, Chapter 3). In either case, *contradiction* puts a name to the oppositional nature of dialectics as Engels describes it: "the continual conflict of opposites and their final passage into one another, or into higher forms" (1954, p. 280) is applied to different activities that must meet and be merged or changed through their interaction.

Activity Networks

Importantly, developing the notion of contradiction allowed activity theorists to study development at the level of activity, and that led to examining development *between and among* activities. This work led to what Yrjö Engeström calls the "third generation" of activity theory, which "needs to develop conceptual tools in order to understand dialogue, multiple perspectives, and networks of interacting activity systems" (1996a, p. 133). In a review of this work, Engeström discusses James Wertsch's (1991) and Ritva Engeström's (1995) separate work on dialogue; Holland & Reeves's (1996) work on perspective; and the question of activity networks, which has been developed by Saarelma (1993) as well as Engeström and his collaborators. A "discussion" between actor–network theory and activity theory "has been initiated" (though, as I said at the beginning of the chapter, it has not been extensively engaged) and Engeström points to boundary crossing as another "tool" (cf. Engeström, Engeström, & Kärkkäinen, 1995; Tuomi-Gröhn & Engeström, 2003). In this third generation of activity theory, "the basic model is expanded to include minimally two interacting activities" (Engeström, 1996a, p. 133).

The notion of activity networks, first forwarded by Engeström with explicit reference to Latour (1992, Chapter 1), is a way to deal with the insularity implied by Leont'ev's activity systems. Activities could be understood as related to one another rather than as independent. And those relations – those networks – take the form of standing sets of transformations, just as orders for Telecorp's phone service are regularly transformed into the service itself. There are two variations of activity networks, though this fact is almost never acknowledged in the activity theory literature,[3] and the lines between the two are fuzzy.

Variation 1: Chained Activity Systems
One variation understands activity networks as *chained activity systems*. An activity becomes more complex, divides, and the resulting activity systems develop in concert while simultaneously becoming more distinct and specialized. In this variation, activity systems are linked by their "corners"

---

[3] Bødker and Andersen (2005) do draw a similar distinction in their discussion of "chained" and "juxtaposed" mediators. Characteristically, their focus is on development.

(Helle, 2000, p. 89), and each corner is something that has been produced by one activity system to be consumed by another (Korpela, Mursu, & Soriyan, 2002; Miettinen, 1998). This production-and-consumption relationship characterizes the standing set of transformations performed by the activity network. The individual activities are typically taken to be split by "organizational boundaries" (Korpela et al., 2002, p. 114) or disciplines (Miettinen, 1998). This variation looks a lot like a supply chain, and I don't think that's coincidental:

> It is a simple every-day observation that organisational boundaries are an important fact that affects how seamlessly or otherwise the activity networks operate. From an Activity-Theoretical point of view, we can define an organisation or institution as a group of activities that are coordinated and controlled by a common management activity. In other words, the management activity of an organisation is the primary source for the rules applied within and between the other activities of the organisation. Conversely, we can identify an organisation – an informal community, a department, a company, a branch of administration, a state – by identifying a management activity which sets the rules (or some of the rules) for a number of other activities. Of course, any baseline activity can belong to many organisations at the same time. (Korpela, Soriyan, & Olifokunbi, 2000, p. 197)

That is to say, in this variation, an activity network describes a *mass production* or *modular* configuration of work (Victor & Boynton, 1998; Zuboff & Maxmin, 2004) with a strict division of labor, specialization, and central coordination. It black-boxes the organization chart (never mind that the boxes are represented as triangles!). Figure 3.2 shows a chained activity network based on the figures in Chapter 2.

Chained activity networks may be suitable for analyzing mass production work, but they are problematic for two reasons. First, as Ilyenkov suggests, we can't understand networks of activity by simply looking for ways in which discrete activity systems link up and form *external* contradictions, because external contradictions don't lead to significant development. Rather, we have to understand these linkages as interpenetrating activity systems that foster *internal* contradictions, contradictions that inescapably motivate development and change (Ilyenkov, 1982, pp. 238, 266). Second, work boundaries are not nearly as clear-cut as this portrayal makes them out to be. As Osmo Saarelma points out, "the meaning of the links may be multiple" (1993, p. 103). Saarelma brilliantly shows how workers in the Finnish health care system describe the same activity network in very

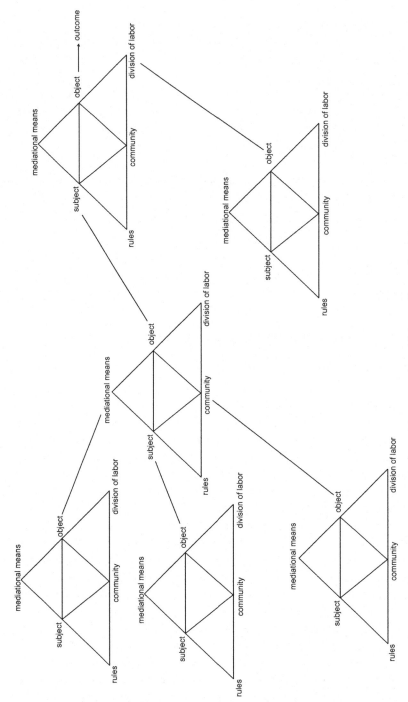

FIGURE 3.2. An activity network as a "chained" set of activity systems.

different ways, turning up unexpected links as well as multivalences of common links (pp. 107–108). This comparative work alerts us to the problem that activity systems' boundaries are often difficult to define (cf. Fitzpatrick, 2000; Witte, 2005); they are frequently less modular than organizational and disciplinary boundaries.

For instance, the activity network in Figure 3.2 draws artificially distinct boundaries between activities. But as we saw in Chapter 2, organizations can have "hidden passes" or informal linkages that potentially connect any part of the organization to any other. Such hidden passes and multivalent links multiply in knowledge work, where the static, modular organization of mass production gives way to more deeply interpenetrated and dynamic work organization (Victor & Boynton, 1998; Zuboff & Maxmin, 2004, see Chapter 5). Recent work by Yrjö Engeström, Bonnie Nardi, and their respective colleagues has begun to recharacterize activity networks in these terms: as dynamic, overlapping activity systems clustered around a common object. And that brings us to the second, more sophisticated variation of activity networks.

Variation 2: Overlapping Activity Systems
In this second variation, activity networks are seen as *overlapping activity systems*. Multiple activity systems converge on the same object, although that object is construed in different ways. Engeström, in fact, counsels us to "follow the objects" (2004, p. 7) to understand how activity networks develop. In this variation, activities with entirely different developmental paths can converge on the same object and, through their combined work, can become spliced together and influence each other. This engagement can be permanent or quite transitional. For instance, when examining an incident in which different activities meet temporarily to help apprehend a mentally ill person (Engeström, Engeström, & Vähääho, 1999), Engeström and his collaborators describe transient ("knotworking," or "work that requires active construction of constantly changing combinations of people and artifacts over lengthy trajectories of time and widely distributed in space") (p. 345). Such work has no center or stable configuration (p. 346). Nardi et al. (2002) describe ("netWORKing," a similar but distinct phenomenon in which "intensional networks" are constituted by long-term relationships among professionals that self-organize in "more flexible and less predictable configurations of workers.") "*Configuring labor is up to workers themselves*," they emphasize (p. 230).

Earlier, I suggested that the first variation of activity networks, as chained activity systems, was based on mass production work. This second variation, in contrast, is explicitly meant to describe "new economy" work organization (Nardi et al., 2002, p. 232) or "co-customization" (Engeström, 2004; Engeström, Puonti, & Seppänen, 2003; cf. Victor & Boynton, 1998). In this second variation, the standing set of transformations is not necessarily orderly, progressive, modular, or relatively static; it's more likely to be conflicting, overlapping, and dynamic. That is to say (activities that have developed independently are now being spliced together.) This understanding of activity networks is strongly associated with "new economy" or knowledge work organizations such as Telecorp (see Chapter 5).

The differentiation between these two types of activity networks is important because they lead in different directions. Variation 1's modular account emphasizes weaving, while Variation 2 – which I'll prefer throughout the rest of this book – emphasizes splicing. And Variation 2, in turn, opens activity theory's woven account to two particular issues associated with splicing: polycontextuality and boundary crossing. These issues are attempts to deal with splicing but from within a woven framework. The first stroke is a weave, but subsequent strokes can be splices (cf. Deleuze & Guattari, 1987, p. 20).

To see how this shakes out, let's turn to Engeström et al.'s (1995) discussion of expertise in work. They charge that expertise has been traditionally defined *vertically*, in terms of the stages a person passes as she becomes more expert in a specific domain: she starts out as a neophyte, then progressively gains more expertise until she is an expert. But the authors argue that there is also a *horizontal* dimension to expertise:

> In their work, experts operate in and move between multiple parallel activity contexts. These multiple contexts demand and afford different, complementary but also conflicting cognitive tools, rules, and patterns of social interaction. The criteria of expert knowledge and skill are different in the various contexts. Experts face the challenge of negotiating and combining ingredients from different contexts to achieve hybrid solutions. The vertical master-novice relationship, and with it, in some cases, the professional monopoly on expertise, is problematized as demands for dialogical problem solving increase. (Engeström et al., 1995, p. 319)

The expert is generally seen as a unitary subject who learns and develops as she traverses the parallel activity contexts (but see Nardi et al., 2002, p. 207). And these contexts' increasing interpenetration yields increasing potential for contradictions among the activities, and at the same time these activities are too massive, complex, abstract, unstable, and interpenetrated with other activities to simply be synthesized (Blackler & McDonald, 2000; Engeström, 1996a). Those separate "contexts" and separate "dialogues"

(Kaptelinin & Nardi, 2006, p. 23) aren't going to go away; linked activity systems will not shake off their separate developmental histories to simply merge together. So activity theorists such as Engeström et al. (1995) are positioning activity theory to address work multidimensionally. They address "two central features of this newly emerging landscape": polycontextuality and boundary crossing (pp. 319–320).

Polycontextuality
Polycontextuality (which, as I indicated in Chapter 1, is roughly equivalent to multiplicity; cf. Miettinen, 2005; see also Kaptelinin & Nardi, 2006, on polymotivation) involves working on tasks from different activities or frames of work simultaneously. And on the level of activity, polycontextuality "means that experts are engaged not only in multiple simultaneous tasks and task-specific participation frameworks within one and the same activity. They are also increasingly involved in multiple communities of practice" (Engeström et al., 1995, p. 320). These multiple communities of practice operate within "parallel activity contexts," that is, activity systems with their own internal rules and expectations as well as external relations with other activity systems (Tuomi-Gröhn, Engeström, & Young, 2003, p. 3). The developmental transfer between activity systems thus becomes a focus of the analysis (p. 4).

Elsewhere, polycontextuality is dealt with using somewhat different terms borrowed from different traditions: perspective (Blackler, Crump, & McDonald, 2003; Blackler & McDonald, 2000; Holland & Reeves, 1996) and dialogue[4] (Engeström, 1995; Russell, 1997a; Wertsch, 1991).

Boundary Crossing
Polycontextuality leads to boundary crossing. When two different activities are linked together – such as two organizations that must collaborate to provide a service or two workplaces that have emerged separately but have been acquired by the same company and must now work together – "the two contexts" in linked activities must be "iteratively connected." The tools, relationships, social languages, and so forth may be very different; the linked activities need "boundary crossers" who can mediate between them (Engeström et al., 1995, p. 321). As we've seen, boundary crossing work is more complicated in the second variation of activity networks, in which boundaries cannot be defined by hard organizational or disciplinary edges (Fitzpatrick, 2000).

---

[4] The reliance on dialogue is ironic since it draws primarily from Mikhail Bakhtin, who advanced dialogism as an *alternative* to dialectic (1984).

This boundary crossing work, again, is developmental in nature. This is particularly true in Engeström's developmental work research, which is "a distinctively educational approach" to boundary crossing at work (1996a, p. 134), but it's also true in other activity theory-based work. The notion of contradictions takes a major role here as the source of change and development; an activity system must continue to change so that it can loosen the double binds and reconcile the contradictions that dog it. A "third generation" analysis recognizes the contradictions set up across multiple activity systems, some of which become visible as the result of moving from school to work or from job to job (Engeström, 1996a).

Like Engeström, Terttu Tuomi-Gröhn focuses on the developmental aspects of splicing, arguing that "significant learning processes are achieved by collective activities" and "meaningful transfer takes place between collective activity systems" (2003, p. 200). In this view, novel solutions come from the expertise of the overlapping activities, in a multifaceted and multidirectional fashion. "In the case of developmental transfer," Tuomi-Gröhn adds, "the ZPD [Zone of Proximal Development] is expanded to encompass the collaboration of different activity systems" (p. 200). (Again, activity networks are developmental first and foremost.) This leads to a discussion of boundary crossers as "people who move from one activity system to another and work in two or more activity systems simultaneously, sharing the boundary object and the work based on it with some partners in the other activity system" (p. 203).

One example is that of sales engineers, who learn their work by gathering knowledge simultaneously from all the different activities whose borders they cross (Ludvigsen, Havnes, & Chr. Lahn, 2003, p. 292). This boundary crossing work involves negotiating the conflicting goals of different activity systems: "The sales engineers from Norex do not consider themselves as members of the project organization responsible for constructional design, but they try to make alliances with nodes in the network" (p. 307). Of course they do. But of these alliances, and the political–rhetorical actions that sustain them, activity theorists tend to say little.

Summing Up

Activity theory is a richly developed and frequently complicated approach to understanding human activity. Based on dialectics, it emphasizes the sorts of things that dialectics emphasizes: change, development, interaction, irreversible evolution, all performed through the cyclical resolution of dialectical contradictions. In this account, the human being mediates her own and others' work with physical and psychological tools, but ultimately human beings hold agency and nonhumans don't; it is a decidedly asymmetrical account. Activity theory provides a sophisticated set of theoretical and methodological tools in service of this account.

Despite its forays with splicing, activity theory's understanding of networks is founded on a *woven* understanding: an arborescent, evolutionary explanation of how activities link, combine, merge, interpenetrate, and divide over time through a process of developing and resolving contradictions. This account does a remarkably good job of explaining weaving, but it has only lately begun to grapple with splicing in earnest and is still working through the issues that have been raised by these later explorations. Its account of splicing is informed by the underlying assumption of weaving, development, education, founding, dialectics.

SPLICING A NETWORK: ACTOR–NETWORK THEORY'S ACCOUNT

In contrast, a spliced understanding of networks involves understanding them as (becoming interconnected in ways that are not necessarily organic, self-contained, or unified.) Like dialectics, a spliced or rhizomatic understanding rejects simple cause–effect relationships; unlike dialectics, it assumes multiplicity rather than immanent unity in everything and understands change as not necessarily developmental. (As Deleuze & Guattari [1987, p. 32] point out, multiplicity is meant to escape dialectics.) In a spliced understanding of activity, we can think of sociotechnical networks as conversations in which different actants interact, sometimes in more stable ways than others. Actants are multivalent and rearticulated; cross-developmental alliances are possible; actors are interested and persuaded.[5]

Actor–network theory's spliced understanding follows a pragmatic strand of thought that draws from Michel Serres (Serres, 1982, 1983, 1995; Serres & Latour, 1995) and to a lesser extent Gilles Deleuze and Felix Guattari (1987). That pragmatist strand can be traced back to Niccolò Machiavelli. Below, I discuss actor–network theory's roots in Machiavelli, then its major concepts.

A Machiavellian View; Or, Sympathy for the Devil

Machiavelli has been denounced periodically as a devil, an archetypically amoral figure interested primarily in power and manipulation. But these

---

[5] I don't want to equate rhizomatics with rhetoric here. But we can understand rhizomatics in rhetorical terms and make it a rhetorical project, as others have (Davis, 2000).

are crude representations of Machiavelli's thought. What attracted actor–network theorists to Machiavelli in 1986 – and, I would argue, what still animates Latour's work, despite his carefully worded protestations – is Machiavelli's pragmatism and antireductionism.

Machiavelli's *pragmatism* is on display in *The Prince* (2003b). Rather than rely on abstract social structures, ideals, or general laws to provide explanations, Machiavelli examines the relations forged among actors and allows those relations to be their own explanation (p. 50). This pragmatic approach had a profound effect on actor–network theory. For instance, in *Aramis* (1996a), Latour contrasts classical sociology with his (Machiavellian) relationist sociology. Classical sociology, he says, presumes an abstract social structure that functions as an explanatory device; it "can comment on what the patients say because it possesses metalanguage, while they have only language" (p. 199). But his relationist sociology doesn't use this explanatory device: it "has no fixed reference frames, and consequently no metalanguage. It expects the actors to understand what they are and what it is" (p. 200). Classical sociology has "dreamed up republics and principalities which have never in truth been known to exist," to recall Machiavelli's words (2003b, p. 50), while relational sociology has taken a more pragmatic, Machiavellian route.

Pragmatism amounts to – or is articulated here as – relational interactions that, unlike dialectical interactions, can always be reversed. Settlements can unravel, splices can be undone. No inertia exists that will carry these settlements forward, because at any moment these "allies" can betray each other. The focus is perpetually on alliance: "Interaction is all there is," John Law argues (1992, p. 380).

This pragmatism leads to the *antireductionism* that Callon, Law, and Rip describe:

> Is it not tempting to reduce the evolution of societies to the actions of a few princes who exert their power? Or, alternatively, to consider princes as puppets without substance, whose strings may be pulled by such powerful social actors as the people or the nobles? Machiavelli avoids both temptations. He shows us a prince who is skillful in the art of managing variable and unexpected social forces. The prince is not a lonely man, drawing force from his tactical genius alone, yet neither is he the simple plaything of forces that transcend and manipulate him. (1986, p. 7)

This antireductionism translates to the principle of symmetry that actor–network theory espouses. In this view, power is not a possession of a prince, it is a *consequence of the system*: orders are followed not because the person who issued them is powerful but because they are transformed into actions that serve the interests of those who execute them.)"If it were not the case, then the order would not have been 'obeyed' in the first place, and the person who gave the order would be said to be powerless!" (Latour, 1986, p. 268).

Such an understanding of power contradicts the popular conception of Machiavelli as a schemer bent on consolidating dictatorial power. But Machiavelli was an ardent republican who thought that in most respects the people were better decision-makers than a prince (2003a; see also 2001; and see Latour on this point, 1988c). Machiavelli's most famous work (2003b) is arguably based on his understanding of history, which was that republics tended to decline into aristocracies and then principalities before being reborn as republics again (2003a; cf. Aristotle, 1992). Even princes, though, had to understand that they must negotiate with their people, their generals, and their neighbors, as well as with the material conditions that surrounded their countries (2001, 2003b). This strand of symmetry-as-negotiation runs throughout the actor–network theory literature – not just in fits and starts as some have alleged (Kaptelinin & Nardi, 2006; Miettinen, 1999) but continuously.[6]

For instance, take Latour's analysis of the *Gorgias* in Chapters 5–6 of *Pandora's Hope* (1999b), focusing on the confrontation between Socrates and Callicles. Socrates represents Right: the lone man with knowledge and virtue on his side who invokes absolute truth and declares that he will be vindicated in the afterlife. Callicles represents Might: the strongman who commands the dumb masses through force of personality, ruthlessness, and deception. Callicles is the very image of the Prince, at least the Prince that we have come to expect from the many slanders leveled against Machiavelli. But Latour scorns both Socrates and Callicles. If they just looked out the window, he says, these two would-be rulers would see the *real* rulers of Athens: the citizens in the marketplace, bargaining, negotiating, persuading, and

---

[6] Latour conspicuously criticizes Machiavelli in his later work to distance himself from the charges of Machiavellianism, but he does not renounce the methodological insights that actor–network theory gleaned from Machiavelli early on. This is perhaps best seen in *Aramis*: Latour takes pains to distance himself from crude Machiavellianism, even denouncing intrigues as "Machiavellian" (1996a, pp. 166–173), but at the same time he retains the republican and strategic elements of Machiavelli. In fact, a few pages after denouncing these "Machiavellian" intrigues, he includes what appears to be an uncited reference to Machiavelli's *The Art of War* (Latour, 1996a, p. 177; cf. Machiavelli, 2001, p. 75)! Similarly, in *Pandora's Hope*, Latour criticizes Machiavelli – but in the context of discussing a straw Callicles and a straw Latour (1999b).

trading. Actor–network theorists take this stance even further, extending symmetry-as-negotiation to nonhumans as well. In other words, a negotiator can be human, nonhuman, or a combination: "It is never certain whether the Prince, like Proteus, is an individual, an assembly, a technostructure, a nation or a collective" (Latour, 1988c, p. 25). One actant's point of view, one prince's machinations, does not constitute the organizing principle for the entire network (Callon, 1992; cf. Serres, 1982). As an *analytical* stance (not an ethical one; see Law, 1992), symmetry provides an account of how artifacts participate in the negotiations, not least by resisting the interpretations that humans attempt to impose on them (see Latour, 1996a). Symmetry, then, is epistemological and ontological as well as political (Law, 2004a, p. 102).

Taken together, pragmatism and antireductionism lead to an understanding of activity that is quite different from activity theory's. Pragmatism leads away from abstract structures and causal explanations and toward relational sociology. Antireductionism leads to symmetry, multiplicity, and monoscale explanations. What concerns us here is how this sophisticated Machiavellianism is enacted in actor–network theory.

Actor–Networks

Whereas activity theory came to networks relatively late in the game, networks were a vital part of actor–network theory from the beginning (as the name implies).

So what is an actor–network? "All groups, actors, and intermediaries describe a network: they identify and define other groups, actors, and intermediaries, together with the relationships that bring these together" (Callon, 1991, p. 142). And "the network of intermediaries accepted by an actor after negotiation and transformation is in turn transformed *by* that actor. It is converted into a scenario, carrying the signature of its author, looking for actors ready to play its roles. For this reason I speak of *actor–networks*: for an actor is also a network" (p. 142). That is, "*it is the same task to define the artefact tying together the various groups or the groups tying together one artifact*" (Latour, 1993a, p. 381, his emphasis).

When Callon says that the actants in an actor–network *define* each other, he means more than that they interact and change each other. An actant in an actor–network is not a unitary subject passing through boundaries between multiple activity contexts like an astronaut passing through different worlds. An actant, rather, is an effect of the network (Law, 1992), something that gains its identity through the interactions of an ecology. An actant is less like an astronaut and more like Donna Haraway's (1991) cyborg: decentralized, interconnected, an assemblage with constructed, confused boundaries rather than an organic unity. (That is, an actant is *also* a network; see Law, 1992.) This account of actants rejects not only the subject–object distinction but also dialectics, which Haraway characterizes as a "totalizing and imperialist language" that provides "perfectly faithful naming of experience" (1991, p. 173). By turning to a relationist materialism rather than a dialectical materialism, actor–network theory makes an arborescent (weaving) account impossible: if actants emerge from the network of relations, if they don't maintain an organic unity across contexts, then there's nothing to develop.

It's really vital to get this point, which is more than just word games, more than changes in roles, and more than changing interpretations: it is not epistemological but ontological in nature, not a matter of how we interpret something but how that something is "enacted into being" (Law & Singleton, 2005, p. 334). Let's take Gregory Bateson's (1972) famous example of the blind man's cane. Bateson asks: is a blind man's cane part of him? When the blind man taps his stick along the sidewalk and feels a curb, where is the curb perceived? At the end of the stick, where the stick reaches the hand, or elsewhere? Bateson's answer is that the whole has to be understood as a system of blind man + stick + curb; it's a molar unit, an assemblage or rhizome (Deleuze & Guattari, 1987; cf. Serres, 1982). The assemblage is not just a collection of atomic elements ("man," "stick," "curb"): each of these can be sliced or interconnected infinitely, each has fractional rather than absolute coherence (Law, 2002a, p. 2). Assemblages make sense of a heterogeneous jumble of infinitely recombinable parts, not just semiotically but functionally (Deleuze & Guattari, 1987, p. 71). And changes in the relations of the assemblage result in new actants, identities, and groups (Akrich, 1992, 1993). New telecommunications technologies, for instance, cause new groups and identities to emerge, such as "teenagers-with-mobile-phones" and organizations opposing relay towers; epidemiological studies turn up previously unknown viruses, microbes, and toxic molecules and thus define the groups that suffer from them (Callon, 2004; cf. Sheller, 2004). And lest these differences seem to be merely interpreted, merely epistemological, note that this process doesn't have to include human interaction at all: a drop in the climate's temperature effects a separation between warm- and cold-blooded animals; a new organism in an ecology effects a separation between resistant and nonresistant organisms.

Bateson defined information as "differences that make a difference" (1979, p. 99), and that's as good a description as any of how actors emerge in an actor–network.

At first glance, these interrelationships look a lot like dialectic, and critics of dialectic are often baffled by actor–network theorists' tendency to rail against dialectic while apparently performing it (Engeström, 1996b; Miettinen, 1999). But unlike dialectic, actor–network theory's brand of relational materialism does not assume that such relationships lead to development, increased complexity, or unity. Quite the opposite! And as we'll see below, it does not assume that such changes are irreversible, as dialectic does. Rather, these relationships are metaphorically described as *alliances*, alliances among humans and nonhumans that can be negotiated, compromised, unraveled, or betrayed. Actor–networks, in short, are rhizomes (Latour, 1996a), and the first stroke or "elementary stitch" (Latour, 1988c, p. 29) in an actor–network is alliance.

Mediation

Actor–networks are mediated but in a very different way from activity networks. In activity networks, mediation comes between humans and their objects or communities. It is represented by the lonely corners of the activity system's triangle. But in actor–network theory, mediation involves coming between two actants – whether human or nonhuman – and creating a relation between them. Every actant is also a mediator. "The assumption is not that a machine is a true actor in a humanist sense; rather, the assumption is that only by taking the *active* roles of all these entities into account can we hope to understand the functioning of the work practice and the interrelations between its constituents" (Berg, 2000, p. 489; cf. Law, 1992, p. 382). And the intermediations – the compromises and negotiations among actants, whether human or nonhuman – lead to their mutual adaptation (Akrich, Callon, & Latour, 2002b; cf. Serres, 1982).

For an example, let's turn to the tourist industry (Callon, 1991). Consider Mr. Smith, who wants to go on vacation. He uses a travel package provided by Club Med, "a mixture of humans and non-humans, texts, and financial products that have been put together in a precisely co-ordinated sequence" (p. 139). These actants include "computers, alloys, jet engines, research departments, market studies, advertisements, welcoming hostesses, natives who have suppressed their desire for independence and learned to smile as they carry luggage, bank loans and currency exchanges" (p. 139). This actor–network might be complex, "but in principle it works just like any other intermediary. If Mr. Martin uses a fork to mash potatoes this is just another (albeit simpler) intermediary" (p. 139). And intermediation is reciprocal. Just as the hostess or smiling native serves as an intermediary for Mr. Smith, he serves as an intermediary for them. "*Actors define one another by means of the intermediaries which they put into circulation,*" Callon says in the italics that he liberally uses to emphasize his key points, and "*the social can be read in the inscriptions that mark the intermediaries*" (p. 140). Is a given thing an actor or intermediary? It depends on "where the buck stops" – what you're trying to study – because all actors are also intermediaries (p. 142).

If everything mediates everything else, agency must be seen as distributed (Law, 1992, p. 383). This insight allows actor–network theory, like activity theory, to escape the subject–object dichotomy that leads us to ask questions such as: Do guns kill people or do people kill people (Latour, 1999b, Chapter 6)? Do sailors navigate or do their tools do this work for them (Law, 1986b)? Do medical personnel perform their work or does the carefully crafted system in which they work (Berg, 1999)? What failed in the Rex incident, the people or the system? But whereas activity theory escapes this dichotomy by viewing the subject–mediator relationship as a dialectic that *changes* preexisting entities, actor–network theory handles the problem by seeing subjects and mediators as network effects: subjects and objects, actants and mediators *emerge* from the assemblage rather than preexisting it. "The agent – the 'actor' of the 'actor–network' – is an agent, a center, a planner, a designer, only to the extent that matters are also decentered, unplanned, undesigned" (Law, 2002b, p. 136). Which is another way of saying: the first stroke is a splice.

Actor–networks tend to be unstable, the way that political alliances are, because actants' interests tend to drift. So any actant can deliberately or accidentally become a "traitor," as Rex did, turning away from the settlement or renegotiating it. But, like a political settlement, an actor–network can become more stable as it brings more actants on board. The more intermediated an actor–network is, the more stable it is (Callon, 1991): the more relations, the more dense the interconnections that lock actants into place, the more *sedimentation* of settlements on top of settlements (Latour, 1999b, Chapter 5; cf. Deleuze & Guattari, 1987, Chapter 3). In this view, a history of change is a history of negotiations that have become sedimented.

In actor–network theory, mediation involves mutual transformation of the assemblage, and this transformation has four parts or moments (Latour, 1999b, Chapter 6): translation, composition, reversible black-boxing, and delegation.

Translation

Translation[7] is actor–network theory's Machiavellian explanation of power applied to change (Law, 1992). It provides an account of historical change in that a translation analysis allows us to trace through particular moments of these negotiations (Latour, 1999b). Every change in a series of transformations makes a difference. This account is not woven but spliced: it is a history of negotiations in which the same "token" can be made equivalent to different things simultaneously (Law, 1999, p. 8) and in which surprising alliances can emerge.

In translation, a cascade of intermediaries is set up to create standing sets of transformations. These intermediaries interdefine each other (Callon, 1992), and as a result, their relations lead to composite goals different from the preexisting ones (Latour, 1999b). That is, negotiations between actants lead to a *drift* in the original goals and then (if successful) a compromise that makes the settlement stable – that all the actors can live with. The actors take detours to achieve their goals (Latour, 1999b). We can see why *translation means transformation*: cascades of intermediaries, including rerepresentations, transform actants in ways that facilitate this compromise work (Callon, 1992; Latour, 1999b). Actor–networks, then, represent standing sets of transformations – although in a rather different sense than activity networks do.

I said that translation provides a historical but nondevelopmental understanding of change. Actor–network theorists tend to describe historical change in terms of sedimentation (Latour, 1999b) or temporal differentials (Latour, 2002; Serres & Latour, 1995). That is, translations represent settlements that are built on top of other settlements, with each settlement being made of heterogeneous parts from different temporalities. Actors *give* a history and identity to the world they construct or define (Callon, 1992). (We'll see an extended example in Chapter 4.)

Translation is a multilateral settlement involving four moments: problematization, interessement, enrollment, and mobilization (Callon, 1986b).

Problematization

What must be accomplished or negotiated? The situation has to be turned into a problem so that the actant becomes indispensable, an obligatory passage point through which stakeholders must pass if they are to meet

---

[7] Translation is articulated somewhat differently in successive ANT works. I draw primarily on Callon's 1986 articles. In *Pandora's Hope*, Latour (1999b) reworks translation as part of mediation.

their own goals. Those stakeholders can include nonhumans as well as humans; researchers are seen as negotiating with the phenomena they study as well as with the people involved in the research. They emerge from the relations of the network. In Callon's study of a research project involving scallops, for instance, the scallops take their place next to fishermen and the scientific community as stakeholders with which researchers must negotiate (1986b). Any actant can problematize, not just a Machiavellian Prince – or, to put it another way, any actant can be regarded as a prince since every actant has a hand in the negotiations (Latour, 1988c).

Interessement

What stakeholders are involved in the negotiation? Interessement involves defining the stakeholders and splicing them in (Latour, 2006), locking them into place, inviting them to the negotiations. "To be interested," Callon says, "is to be in between (inter-esse), to be interposed" (1986b, p. 208; cf. Law, 1986a) – and interessement involves finding ways to interpose oneself between stakeholders and their goals, to make oneself an "obligatory passage point" (p. 196) that others must traverse to reach their goals. Interessement knots together different actors: it "emphasizes the existence of a bundle of links which unite the object to all of those which handle it.... [T]he model of interessement sets out all of the actors who seize the object or turn away from it and it highlights the points of articulation between the object and the more or less organized interests which it gives rise to" (Akrich, Callon, & Latour, 2002a, p. 205). This work is done, not by a single controlling force, but through the relationships in the assemblage.

Enrollment

How do these stakeholders relate – how do they negotiate? Enrollment is the device by which interrelated roles are defined and attributed to actors who accept them. Interessement, if it is successful, achieves enrollment: defining the stakeholders involves assigning roles and relationships in the problem space. "The definition and distribution of roles ... are a result of multilateral negotiation during which the identity of the actors is determined and tested" (Callon, 1986b, p. 214; cf. Callon, 1986a). That negotiation is often performed through texts, particularly narratives (Callon, 2002). If it is successful, it redefines the actors' interests in such a way as to provide a shared problem space and it therefore simplifies their world (Callon & Law, 1982). Again, these actors are nonhumans as well as humans: nonhumans push back as much as humans do, providing their own constraints and doing their own enrolling (Akrich, 1993; de Laet & Mol, 2000).

Mobilization
How can the stakeholders be persuaded to link up and accomplish the objectives? In mobilization, stakeholders agree on a cascade of intermediaries that reduces the number of interlocutors by providing a single representation (or a limited number of representations) of their interests (Callon, 1986b; cf. Latour, 1999b). Mobilization is a way of accomplishing a collective solution, a collective representation, and it is a way of policing the stakeholders to make sure they play their roles appropriately.

The translation account of change, as I said, is spliced rather than woven: it highlights contingencies, alliances, and multiplicity of meanings, not development over time. Rather than taking parties and ideas as abstractions with their own unities, it highlights these actors as rhizomatic actants that can be redefined, reproblematized, reinterested, and remobilized. And these splices can unravel, as we'll see below.

Composition

Translation, when successful, leads to the composition of a relatively coherent assemblage of actants. The actants are mobilized to commonly achieve a goal that accomplishes the accumulated goals of the various actants. In so doing, the assemblage becomes an actant itself. "Who performs the action? Agent 1 plus Agent 2 plus Agent 3. Action is a property of associated entities," both human and nonhuman (Latour, 1999b, p. 182). In this sense, actor–network theory parallels activity theory's understanding of mediation. When Telecorp reinstates telephone service for Rex's owner, it's a joint accomplishment by a mobilized set of actants whose different goals or subprograms have been reconciled. This reconciliation involves finding and sticking to a mutually agreeable path, treading the straight and narrow, leading the camel through the eye of the needle.

"Action is simply not a property of humans *but an association of actants*" (Latour, 1999b, p. 182; cf. Berg, 1999, Law, 1986b). In this case, the actants were mostly (but not entirely) parts of Telecorp: employees, phone lines, switches, etc., but also BigTel technicians, equipment, and databases. The more actants are brought into a composition, and the more tightly interconnected they are, the stronger it tends to be: the many goals or subprograms are folded together, reducing degrees of freedom and allowing the assemblage of actants to cohere as a single actant.

Reversible Black-Boxing

The more tightly an assemblage coheres as a single actant, the more easily it is to treat it as such. That is, an especially coherent composition can be "black-boxed" (Latour, 1999b) or "punctualized" (Law, 1992, 2002a), turned into a single thing – an object, a procedure, a concept, a technique – that resists decomposition and that therefore functions as a reliable building block for other work. "Techniques are not something around which there is a society. It is society considered in its obduracy. It is society *folded*, society made durable, society made complicated in order to resist more tensions by enrolling more non-humans" (Latour, 1993a, pp. 379–380). This complication is needed, paradoxically, to ensure enough simplicity for a settlement to function: complex activities require a complexity of work practice without an increase in complexity in individual actions (Berg, 1999; Law, 2002a).

Relationally speaking, any actant is a black box that has resulted as a stabilization of relations among other actants. The more stable a black box becomes, the more we can forget about the actants that compose it. But – and here's an important difference with dialectics – black-boxing is entirely *reversible*. Any settlement can be undone, any black box can be opened, and any composition can unravel. In Chapter 2 we saw how easily this could happen and how quickly the black box of Telecorp could become Pandora's box. When Telecorp is a black box, it's possible for a customer to say, "I'll call X." But if service is interrupted, the customer might make a series of statements in which Telecorp's black box is progressively opened to reveal the many actants that sustain it: "The phone's not working." "The line is dead." "I called Telecorp and they'll send someone out." "Telecorp didn't tell the BigTel technician there was a dog in our yard." It's not that opening the black box shows us what's "really" going on; it just entails reversing or unraveling the settlement that allowed us to treat the assemblage as a single entity (Law, 1992).

Unlike dialectics, in which interactions result in inalterable changes, the sociology of translation describes settlements that can always be reversed. We can talk about irreversibility in *relative* terms, defining it as

(a) the extent to which it is subsequently impossible to go back to a point where the translation was only one amongst others; and

(b) the extent to which it shapes and determines subsequent translations. (Callon, 1991, p. 150)

But "all translations, however apparently secure, are in principle reversible" (p. 150). No matter how widely it is accepted that Earth is flat, or that spontaneous generation occurs, or that mankind is only 6,000 years old – and no matter how many other things are built on these beliefs – they are reversible; they can be undone. And so are the things that replace them. Facts can be walked back. But some facts are harder to walk back than others: the longer a network is, the stronger it is, because more settlements depend on its translations being stable. Irreversible translation is normalization (p. 152) – but irreversibility is "a fight that is never definitively won" (Callon, 1992, p. 89). We may accept that Earth is round, but we still say that "the sun is going down."

Delegation

Delegation involves "crossing the boundary between signs and things" (Latour, 1999b, p. 185). It's not just that goals and functions can be shifted but that *expression* can be changed as well (p. 186). "Think of technology as congealed labor," Latour suggests (p. 189), sounding a bit like the Marxists he likes to provoke. We tire of directing traffic and piloting airplanes, or we find that these jobs test our resources and capabilities, so we delegate them to traffic lights and autopilots. Rex's owner similarly erected a fence because he couldn't monitor his dog all the time.

In situations like these, tasks are delegated, but so is *morality*. If we want drivers to stop speeding dangerously through our residential streets, we might institute traffic calming devices such as speed bumps; drivers begin to behave more morally, and although they might be motivated to save their vehicle's suspension rather than to save lives, the outcome is the same (Latour, 1999b, p. 186). Similarly, Rex's fence acts as a moral barrier, keeping the dog safe and out of the neighbor's flower beds. On a larger scale, the telephone system (currently) acts as a building block of democracy, constituting and enabling the free exchange of information among citizens (see Chapter 4). When actor–network theorists hew to the principle of symmetry, they do so in part because delegation works so well – because the boundary between signs and things is so porous and because things can increase the morality of a society by imposing restrictions that make morality work. As Rex's owner might argue, good fences make good neighbors.

Summing Up

Actor–network theory is a complex, sometimes loosely drawn approach to understanding scientific and technical knowledge. Based on relational sociology, it emphasizes the sorts of things that its Machiavellian roots emphasize: alliances, relationships, reversals, and betrayals. But unlike Machiavelli, it applies these principles to nonhumans as much as humans, and in doing so it expands from a political theory to an ontology. In this account, every actant defines and mediates others, and thus every actant is a potential agent; it is a symmetrical account. Actor–network theory provides a sophisticated set of theoretical and methodological tools in service of this account, although those tools are not as coherently assembled as activity theory's.

Actor–network theory barely touches on issues of weaving, that is, education and development. And when it does explore these issues, as in Callon's (Callon, 1991, 1992; Callon & Rabeharisoa, 2003) discussions of expertise and apprenticeship, it bases its explorations on a *spliced* understanding: a rhizomatic, relationist explanation of how actants define each other, form alliances, intermediate and translate each other, and betray each other. This account does a remarkable job of exploring the political–rhetorical work that makes technical mediation possible. But it does this by deemphasizing the issues of development, learning, and cognition, and consequently it offers very little to explain or address these issues.

GENUINE DIFFERENCES

We saw some false differences at the beginning of this chapter, confrontations in which members of each camp did not engage each other's arguments. Many of these, I think, are due to an *assumed* equivalence that leads to the discovery of *apparent* contradictions.

In *Alice in Wonderland*, the Cheshire Cat compares his behavior with that of dogs and concludes that he is mad: dogs wag their tails when they are happy and growl when they are angry, but cats "growl" (purr) when they are happy and "wag" (switch) their tails when they are angry (Carroll, 2003, p. 33). The conclusion follows if the events are indeed equivalent – but they are not. Similarly, actor–network theory seems quite deficient if you assume it to be a theory of learning; activity theory seems deficient in turn if you assume that it should function as an ontology.

Yet, as I said in the introduction, these two approaches are coming into contact more and more frequently as they are being applied to similar cases. And they undeniably lead to different insights. Quite aside from the false differences, there are genuine differences on which we can base a real dialogue and a real argument. Table 3.1 summarizes these differences.

These genuine differences have real implications for understanding how the two approaches can interact. For instance, since activity theory addresses developmental issues and issues of competence and cognition, it is in a much stronger position to explain how workers learn and how they develop resources. At the same time, actor–network theory's splicing account is stronger, leading us to examine how relationships among actants define

TABLE 3.1. *Differences between activity theory and actor–network theory.*

Activity theory	Actor–network theory
The first stroke is a weave	The first stroke is a splice
Developmental	Political–rhetorical
Competence, cognition	Negotiation
Dialectic	Rhizomatic
Genealogical	Antigenealogical
Asymmetrical	Symmetrical
Structural	Relational
Irreversible	Reversible
Contradictions	Translations
Epistemology[8]	Ontology

those actants themselves and how changes in relationships lead to change in those actants.

At the same time, the differences seem almost insurmountable when opposed as I have done above. So let's look at the common ground they share.

COMMON GROUND

So was the parley a success? I believe so. We now know what the fight is about and we can separate the real disagreements from the apparent ones. That doesn't mean the fight ends – articulating the differences doesn't obviate them – but we can reach stasis in the argument and use that stasis as a starting point for further negotiations.

The parley has shown us that despite their differences, activity theory and actor–network theory have some common ground (cf. Kaptelinin & Nardi, 2006, pp. 196–198). They are both monist, materialist approaches to understanding activity. They are both applied to technical mediation. As we saw in Chapter 1, they both theorize mediated activities in terms of networks, posit multiplicity within those networks, examine texts as mediational means that sustain these networks, and allow for different operant social languages in different parts of these networks. As we saw in Chapter 2, they both see networks as heterogeneous, multiply linked, transformative, and black-boxed. And as we saw in this chapter, although

---

[8] An epistemology is a theory of knowledge. Although Ilyenkov positions dialectic outside of both epistemology and ontology, he repeatedly cites Lenin's assertion that dialectics, logic, and the *theory of knowledge* are one and the same (see 1977, Chapter 9).

these common tenets originate in very different understandings, they do represent points at which the approaches can inform each other. It's going to be important to remember both aspects as we continue to examine Telecorp's net work.

So with this discussion in mind, let's get back to examining that net work. In Chapter 2, I discussed Telecorp's peculiar stance as an organization that is all border and no interior, an organization in which hidden passes potentially connected every person to every other. How did this stance come to be? In Chapter 4, I'll examine the history of Telecorp and its industry, applying two accounts of change to see how networks can be historicized: activity theory's *contradictions* and actor–network theory's *translations*.

4

How Are Networks Historicized?

Now that we've established a theoretical and methodological grounding, let's get back to Telecorp. In Chapter 2, I invoked Machiavelli to discuss how Telecorp's workers were nearly all "massed at the border," nearly all in constant communication with people external to Telecorp as well as with those inside the company. Machiavelli is an apt figure to invoke here, not in terms of war but in terms of strategy – for Telecorp had to lay out a strategy for growth and expansion, and that strategy had to take into account market, regulatory, legislative, and technological conditions. These conditions were like historical accretions forming hills and mountains around which Telecorp had to negotiate. Telecorp's structure, in which its employees were nearly all "massed at the border," was a direct result of its negotiations over this terrain.

To understand how Telecorp acquired this strategic posture – which is to say, its shape at the level of cultural–historical activity – we have to examine the history of the telecommunications industry. But as we saw in Chapter 3, activity theory and actor–network theory disagree on what constitutes history and how to examine it. Activity theory sees history as developmental and linear and examines it through examining the contradictions that form in activities. Actor–network theory sees history as settlements that accrete and sediment and examines it through translations. Each provides insights for us that are potentially valuable. So let's apply them both to the case before us.

THE CASE OF UNIVERSAL SERVICE

Occasionally, when a critical mass of new employees built up in Customer Service, NOC, Sales, and Provisioning, Telecorp held two-week training sessions to introduce the new employees to the telecommunications

industry. These were led by Abraham, the experienced manager of Customer Service. As I sat in on one session in September 2000, Abraham
explained each item on the average phone bill. He made no secret of his
distaste for one of them: the Federal Excise Tax. This 3 percent luxury tax,
he explained, was instituted during the Spanish-American War in 1898. The
war lasted less than six months, but the excise tax is still there on every
phone bill, alongside other historical accretions: the subscriber line charge,
the federal and state Universal Service Fund surcharges, the Local Number
Portability charge, and almost a dozen others. The Federal Excise Tax is the
oldest of these layers of sediment, persisting even though its reason for being
has disappeared and telephone service is now considered a *basic necessity*
rather than a luxury.

A basic necessity? Yes. And that isn't just the industry's perspective. The
principle of universal service, first articulated by Theodore Vail at AT&T
in 1907, is (generally speaking) the commitment to provide reasonable and
widespread telecommunications services to all communities. Universal service was operationalized in the Telecommunications Act of 1996 in various
ways. One of these ways was as subsidies provided by providers to K–12
schools, libraries, and similar nonprofit parties at discounts of 20 percent
to 90 percent. The discounts were set based on "poverty level, as measured
by school lunch eligibility" (Aufderheide, 1999, p. 100) – a startling connection, particularly in contrast with the Federal Excise Tax. Who ever heard
of a service that was simultaneously a necessity and a luxury? Simultaneously subsidized and taxed with a luxury tax? For Telecorp, this connection
means that Accounts Payable has to keep track of customers, separate out
schools and libraries that receive discounts, calculate discounts for each of
these, bill them the discounted rate, and bill the Universal Service Administrative Company (which administers the Universal Service Fund) for the
remainder. It's a complicated arrangement, one in which regulation, politics, technology, and the market lose their distinctions and become a set
of accretions that have hardened into operational procedures. Indeed, as
Thomas P. Hughes (1993) argues, these are in a practical sense inseparable
(although, as Andrew Pickering [1995] points out, Hughes is forever trying
to separate them anyway).

But this complicated arrangement is itself the result of a series of accretions. The term *universal service* has meant demonstrably different things
over the past century. Milton L. Mueller has written a fascinating history of
the term (1997), and in the first three sections below, I draw primarily on
that account. Mueller persuasively argues that universal service, though it
is portrayed anachronistically as the principle of providing affordable basic

telecommunications services for all (i.e., 100 percent market penetration), began as a very different argument: the argument for interconnecting competing telephone networks. He further argues that this shift was a deliberate strategy to prop up AT&T's status as a regulated monopoly – a crude Machiavellian trick that didn't work but that took on a life of its own after the Bell System was broken up. What Mueller labels anachronistic is indeed so, but the term elides the weaving and splicing that go on as "universal service" is transformed in response to certain contradictions – or as it undergoes necessary translations – to accommodate new actors and new relationships. In this case, certainly a concept called "universal service" developed historically, but the contemporary meaning becomes read back into the history, making it seem as if the kernel of the meaning has been there all along. The layers of sediment are folded in on themselves. And as I said earlier, these layers of accretion make up the landscape on which Telecorp has deployed itself. So let's take a "core sample" of this terrain over which Telecorp's net has been thrown.

ARTICULATION 1: UNIVERSAL SERVICE AS THE PRINCIPLE OF INTERCONNECTION

Mueller tells us:

> Universal service entered the vocabulary of American telecommunications in 1907. The slogan "one system, one policy, universal service" was coined by Theodore Vail, president of AT&T, and propagated in the company's annual reports from 1907 to 1914. Its appearance came at the peak of a fierce struggle between the Bell System and thousands of independent telephone companies. The idea of universal service served as the linchpin of the Bell System's argument for transforming the telephone industry into a regulated monopoly. (1997, p. 4)

Alexander Graham Bell patented the telephone in 1876. Until the patent expired in 1894, the Bell System had an exclusive patent on telephony – although rival systems cropped up continually, requiring Bell to take continuous patent action. The technology was very useful and not difficult to manufacture, but the infrastructure was relatively difficult to erect. Bell couldn't be everywhere. When the patent expired, an independent telephone movement sprang up almost immediately, in many cases retaining the names of the abortive companies that had been earlier shut down by patent action (Mueller, 1997).

Competing companies decided to pursue separate, closed systems, each of which had its own subscriber universe (Mueller, 1997). The value was perceived to be in the subscriber universe itself – you bought a brand of phone service because of the other people already on that system. If Person A wasn't on your system, you couldn't call them.[1] Consequently, a subscriber in a densely penetrated area might subscribe to two or more networks to reach everyone he needed to. (I say "he" here because the main target of telephone service in those days was businessmen [Mueller, 1977, p. 40].) Home phones were rare, so rare that when the 3 percent temporary Federal Excise Tax was levied on telephone service in 1898 to raise revenue for the Spanish-American War, it was considered a luxury tax. The systems were not only separate, they weren't even colocated: if your business had service with three companies, you had three sets of phone lines coming into your business, like separate spigots at a soda fountain.

Naturally, the Bell System left vast areas unserved, concentrating on high-density areas and the long distance service in between. The local exchanges were served by operating companies that Bell licensed when its patents were still enforceable; the licenses bound the operating companies to terms that lasted far beyond the life of the patent. That left Bell the ability to construct long distance service. And if a licensee tried to break away from the Bell system, Bell could isolate it – cut off connections to the outside world (Mueller, 1997). This strategy allowed Bell some control over the industry because it held a virtual monopoly over long distance, and that monopoly bound the local exchanges to it. If they wanted to connect with other local exchanges, they had to go through Bell.

This setup, however, left competition opportunities for local exchanges, and companies sprang up to fill the gaps. They began building infrastructure particularly in rural areas, and they began forming interconnection agreements with each other in opposition to Bell. In rural areas where not even the independents would go, farmers would set up party lines to keep their communities connected. Soon telephone service became desirable for homes as well as businesses. And the competition began to hurt Bell.

That competition was exacerbated because the telecommunications industry was unlike other industries. The principle of economies of scale did not apply. It *seems* that the more subscribers your company has, the more efficient the overall system will be. Yes, you can achieve *economies of*

---

[1] This may sound extraordinary to us today. But we have seen similar trends with newer information technologies. For instance, I run two instant messaging clients so that I can access both of their subscriber universes.

density that way – it is indeed more profitable to serve more subscribers in a high-density urban area[2] (Mueller, 1997). But a more general economy of scope or scale doesn't apply because each connection is a distinct service (Mueller, 1997). The more subscribers you have, the higher your costs mount: you need to erect more poles, string more cable, wire more exchanges, troubleshoot more lines, trim more overhanging branches, hire and manage more operators (particularly in the days before automated switching). Many independents failed to grasp this: they would start by offering service at costs lower than Bell's, they would rapidly expand their subscriber base, and then they would go out of business as they raised their rates to compensate. So the industry was beset with rolling waves of competition with Bell acting as a relatively stable player.

The value of telephone service in those early days was not in its rates, then, but in the stable subscriber universe that a service could provide. Bell and the independents both resisted interconnection because it could destroy this advantage (Mueller, 1997). Instead, they competed to pull subscribers into their own subscriber universes, using leverage such as the strategic shapes of their networks (cf. Hughes, 1993).

So what happened to move both parties to interconnection – that is, to the original sense of universal service in which any telephone user could reach any other? Mueller says that

> the networks competed on the basis of their scope, or the size of their bundle of access units. That kind of competition gave the networks strong incentives to tap new user groups, enter undeveloped areas, lower access prices, and interconnect with noncompeting networks. Caught up in this dynamic, Bell and the independents were propelled into a race to achieve universality. The dramatic expansion of telephone service did not occur because of altruistic motives, grand social visions, or governmental policy, but was literally forced onto the contestants by the dynamics of access competition. (1997, p. 54)

Bell had built a nationwide network, but it was a network primarily in and between high-density areas serving businesses. (Remember Bowker's [1994] observation that a network is thrown over large areas of space; the interstices simply don't matter. In this case, competitors had made sure that Bell's interstices *did* matter.) So in its pursuit of national service, Bell had developed in geographically uneven ways and left gaps in local and regional telecommunications (Mueller, 1997). Soon Bell had to start filling in those gaps, penetrating markets that the independents already served.

---

[2] It's easy to see why this is so: think in terms of the ratio of materials to subscribers. How many telephone poles and feet of copper wire are needed to support one subscriber?

From 1898 to 1907, dual service expanded into most rural areas: Bell and the independents began to overlap with more and more frequency, and Bell began interconnecting more frequently with noncompeting independents. At the same time, independents tried to make inroads in areas that had traditionally been Bell's territory (Mueller, 1997).

"As the other tactics failed," Mueller tells us,

> Bell managers saw that its own underdevelopment was the root of the problem of independent competition. Increasingly, they understood that Bell's main competitive advantage was its ability to offer comprehensive service within a given region. Although independent exchanges and telephones often outnumbered Bell in a given territory, Bell still had more exchanges than any individual independent company. With its coordinated business management and superior access to capital, it was in a better position than the independents to expand, interconnect, and integrate the operations of many dispersed exchanges. In effect, Bell began to try to beat the independents at their own game. The "opposition" had bested the Bell System by offering access to a larger number of local and regional points. Now Bell would expand and integrate its operations so that it could offer its customers an even larger bundle of regional connections than the independents. (p. 71)

So in the new strategy, "the real source of competitive advantage was comprehensive coverage of a particular region corresponding to the interest of a majority of telephone users.... [T]he best way to satisfy all possible users was to create a comprehensive, universal network" (p. 72). Mueller doesn't quite say: *the physical network is an argument*, one that worked in a way that previous arguments did not (cf. Hughes, 1993; Latour, 1996a; Suchman, 2003; Thevenot, 2002). This notion of universal service was a new argument, a new logic, that turned the old enterprise logic of restricted subscriber universes on its head. More effective than rate cuts, court challenges, strategic service offerings, or advertising, the new argument won out.

It was a little more complicated than that, of course. Local exchange access was still terrifically expensive due to the fact that every connection was a separate service. To deal with this problem, Bell began subsidizing local service through higher long distance rates – something that it could do, since long distance service was a premium service used by businesses rather than home users and since Bell still had the best developed long distance infrastructure thanks to its long-standing strategy of becoming a national telecommunications provider. These cross-subsidies blunted the cost of local service and gave Bell enough advantage to expand. Bell also began to sublicense more frequently and interconnect with more noncompeting independents (Mueller, 1997).

And finally, in 1907, we hear the first mention of the term *universal service*. AT&T President Theodore Vail began to promote the idea of "one system, one policy, universal service" (Mueller, 1997, p. 96). Universal service was opposed to *dual service*, the old logic of nonconnecting, competing telephone services (p. 92). As Vail articulated it, universal service was a coherent business strategy – not a temporary ploy for advantage nor an altruistic vision of ideal service (pp. 96–97). It had four components:

Network Externality
"The value of telephone service grew as the number of subscribers grew." And "his emphasis on the value of unfragmented telephone access reveals a profound understanding of the growing interdependence and impersonality of industrial society" (p. 97).

Centralization of Control
"Universal intercommunication required centralized control and coordination. Service should be provided by, or under the control of, a single firm" (p. 98).

The Imperfection of Competition in Telephony
"Competition between telephone networks is always imperfect competition" (p. 99). That is, separate networks will always be heterogeneous: they will always offer some significant difference in quality or features. "Consequently, competition requires either a duplicate subscription . . . or restricted access" (p. 99).

Regulation as the Alternative to Competition
Vail made clear that he would accept government regulation of rates and services in exchange for a private monopoly (pp. 99–100).

"What set the Bell policy apart," Mueller summarizes,

> was its commitment to interconnect all telephone users into one big, centrally managed, nationally integrated system. The real debate was between competition and monopoly, between [fragmentation and unification]. Vail's doctrine of universal service represented an extremely powerful case for the latter. (1997, p. 101)

In the wake of the articulation of this policy, Bell liberalized its policy on interconnecting with other telecommunications companies. And it worked. Municipalities felt the contradiction between the desire to maintain competition on one hand and the impulse to unify the system on the other

(p. 114). Interconnection, which in theory favored independents by giving them access to the vast Bell system, in fact destroyed them (p. 117). As Bell's network became longer and stronger, it walked the knife's edge, trying to provide universal service as a regulated monopoly while evading government ownership (p. 129). The result was the Kingsbury Commitment of 1913, which AT&T used to forestall the application of the Sherman Antitrust Act. The Kingsbury Commitment is widely seen as a landmark, but Mueller says it's merely a feint: "the commitment had no impact whatsoever on toll interconnection" (p. 130). Whatever it was, it kept antitrust activity from AT&T as it consolidated its new position as provider of universal service. Mueller adds that AT&T didn't accomplish this in the face of fierce opposition. In fact, the voters, city councils, and statewide referenda wanted universal service rather than dual service; they preferred a regulated monopoly (p. 134), a so-called natural monopoly (cf. Duesterberg & Gordon, 1997). The new enterprise logic had proven to be a successful argument. And by the mid-1920s, universal service had been achieved – in its original meaning, that is (Mueller, 1997).

ARTICULATION 2: UNIVERSAL SERVICE AS TOTAL MARKET
PENETRATION

After establishing the principle of universal service in its first articulation, Bell settled into a long life as a regulated monopoly. Bell didn't allow any non-Bell equipment to attach to its network, a policy so draconian that even the Hush-a-Phone – a plastic cup that attached to the receiver to keep conversations quiet in busy offices – was considered a threat to network integrity! (AT&T finally lost the Hush-a-Phone case in the D.C. appellate court in 1956, and it did in fact become a threat to AT&T's network, since it laid the groundwork for attaching fax machines, answering machines, and other devices to the network. See Aufderheide, 1999; Temin, 1987.) But that monopoly was threatened in the 1970s due to a series of decisions that AT&T and the Federal Communications Commission (FCC) had made throughout the history of the public monopoly.

AT&T had blunted the high costs of local service by cross-subsidizing it through revenues from the long distance side.[3] As long as AT&T controlled long distance, this arrangement worked brilliantly. But as Duesterberg and

---

[3] Despite the antitrust activities and the increase in competition that resulted, the profitability of long distance persists. In 1997, Qwest's President and Chief Executive Officer, Joseph R. Nacchio, said, "Long distance is still the most profitable business in America, next to importing illegal cocaine" (Brull & Elstrom, 1997, p. 43).

Gordon (1997) argue, "an enormous subsidy burden was building" through-out AT&T's monopoly from the 1930s–1970s, a burden that "would haunt later regulators and enormously complicate their attempts to introduce competition as it became apparent that little or even none of the industry any longer exhibited natural monopoly characteristics" (p. 32). Once a competitive model was introduced, AT&T's strength became its weakness. As Patricia Aufderheide (1999) says, "In 1969, MCI won the right to attach to the AT&T network in order to offer what then were merely private network services for corporations" (p. 22), and that attachment was free of universal service requirements. "The decision fundamentally challenged the old logic of cross-subsidy. AT&T charged the upstarts with 'cream skimming' – taking the high-dollar clients and leaving AT&T with the large, expensive network to service" (p. 22). That is, AT&T was attempting to function as a regulated monopoly akin to a public utility; competitors were trying to function as, well, competitors.

In 1959, Microwave Communications, Inc. (MCI) began offering new long distance services. And these services severely undercut AT&T's prices *because the independent long distance companies had no incentive to levy the charges that AT&T had to levy to cross-subsidize local service.* Their long distance connected directly to Bell's subsidized local service. With long distance competition, Bell's advantage in local service was turned into a severe disadvantage.

But that wasn't all. Microwave transmission has a relatively low economy of scale (Crandall, 1991). Imagine being in AT&T's position: you've spent an enormous amount of money on your "long lines," your miles and miles of copper wire strung along wooden poles, connecting different parts of the country. If anyone wants to compete, they have to be willing to duplicate your network, an extremely expensive proposition not just to set up but to maintain. Then suddenly MCI comes along with two microwave towers, placed in two different cities on one of your most profitable routes, and sets up an instant long distance connection – no poles, no lines, no maintenance of miles of copper, no tree pruning or line splicing! The old enterprise logic that led to the first articulation of universal service had rested on the fact that economies of scale were impossible in this industry: each customer represented a separate service, a separate twisted pair of copper wire that had to be strung and maintained and managed. Microwave technology lowered the cost of providing those separate services. But it only made sense along particular long distance routes, and only if the provider was willing to degrade the voice quality of the network (since microwave transmissions didn't have the fidelity of line transmission). It didn't make sense for AT&T,

which was committed to serving all long distance customers with unified service, uniform voice quality, and a comprehensive system.

So Bell had to make some adjustments too. By the early 1970s, AT&T's representatives and advocates had rearticulated universal service as the obligation to provide basic telephone service to as many people as possible (i.e., complete market penetration) – and rearticulated cross-subsidies as a way to keep local service low so that this altruistic goal could be achieved. The preamble of the Communications Act of 1934 – which had nothing to do with either definition of universal service – was anachronistically represented as the origin of the concept (Mueller, 1997). Mueller puts it forcefully:

> During the crisis of the Bell System in the mid-1970s, universal service was redefined as an industry–government commitment to put a telephone in every home. That second-generation universal service policy invented a mandate from the 1934 Communications Act and claimed credit for making telephone service available and affordable to nearly all Americans. Both claims, as we have seen, are myths. (p. 166; cf. Duesterberg & Gordon, 1997)

Despite Mueller's understanding, evidence suggests that this rearticulation was not simply cynical: Bell's "members saw themselves as engaged in a holy mission of service" (Temin, 1987, p. 59), and certainly their positioning as a public utility had been encouraged by legislators and regulators at every level. But the pendulum began to swing the other way in the 1970s: *away* from telecommunications as a public utility, *toward* telecommunications as a competitive business. The U.S. Department of Justice (DoJ) filed an antitrust suit against AT&T in 1974. By 1983, it became apparent that the case was not going well, the rationale of competition did not provide criteria under which AT&T could win, and the best it could hope for was a divestiture that preserved AT&T's vertical structure. In December 1981, AT&T's CEO Charles Brown asked the DoJ to write a modification of final judgment for the 1956 Final Judgment (Consent Decree). Language from a Senate bill was spliced in, and the principals negotiated extensively over the phone before coming up with an acceptable outline for divestiture (Temin, 1987). Although the presiding judge resisted the settlement, resulting in several compromises, the basic agreement held. AT&T divested seven regional Bell operating companies and repositioned them to function as competitors. Ironically, Bell, which had started out by using its monopoly long distance status to consolidate the competitive regional markets, was now split into regional monopolies that could connect to each other through competing long distance companies. In a second irony, the divestiture broke the Bell system along board-to-board lines; despite the rejection of board-to-board theory in *Smith v. Illinois Bell*, it had prevailed in a rather material way (Temin, 1987).

But at the same time, the second articulation of universal service took hold, picked up and embraced by lawmakers and citizens alike. "Although AT&T's political objectives did eventually fail, its historical revisionism was an overwhelming success," Mueller says trenchantly (1997, p. 164). That success spread beyond the U.S. telecommunications industry, as universal service in its second articulation went on to justify telecommunication's role as a public utility. In its first articulation, "universal service" summarized AT&T's new strategy for crushing its competition; in the second, the term was translated across the Atlantic and Pacific into "non-commercial objectives" suitable for public service:

> The so-called "Universal Service Obligations" of telecommunication operators, which has been a common feature of telecommunication regulation in most countries, is an example of such a requirement. Usually these obligations constitute a requirement to provide basic telephone service to all who request it at a uniform and affordable price even though there may be significant differences in the costs of supply. (Xavier, 1995, p. 13)

Individual countries pursue additional means to provide universal service, and these means are by no means identical (Xavier, 1995). In any case, however, the author notes that universal service has traditionally been maintained by cross-subsidies (e.g., keeping local costs low by charging more for long distance costs). But "recent rapid changes in telecommunication technology and policy which has liberalised markets in an increasing number of countries have given rise to concerns about the sustainability of universal service policies based on cross-subsidisation" (Xavier, 1995, p. 14). No kidding. When cross-subsidies support universal service by borrowing from other segments, competition in those segments can destroy cross-subsidies by charging market rates rather than inflated rates (Xavier, 1995). So countries that attempt to offer universal service are caught in a bind. If they liberalize markets and continue to finance universal service through cross-subsidies, they risk cratering the whole enterprise. But if they impede competition, they give up all the benefits that come with it – and "since competition can yield significant benefits for at least some aspects of universal service, prohibiting competition could serve, in fact, to impede progress toward universal service" (Xavier, 1995, p. 15). The author goes on to advocate competition rather than monopoly, as long as "appropriate arrangements" are in place (Xavier, 1995, p. 15; cf. Paltridge, 1995).

Internationally, policy makers were dubious about liberalizing telecommunications, worrying that competition and universal service were incompatible goals. In a 1993 survey, "the most common reason cited for excluding infrastructure competition was the objective of universal service" (Paltridge, 1995, p. 16). "Seemingly inherent in the argument against liberalisation was the notion that competition was a threat to universal service and the presumed economies of a single network" (Paltridge, 1995, p. 17). This is quite similar to AT&T's argument in the lead-up to the antitrust suit the DoJ brought against it in the 1970s. Paltridge's report spends most of its time trying to debunk that argument, drawing on market liberalization data from a variety of countries. The key assumption of the argument – that universal service in its second articulation is a value that should underpin policy – is uncontested, which demonstrates how embedded this second articulation of universal service had become.

Nevertheless, the notion of universal service faced some key challenges in the United States, where it had been accepted as a policy goal but without any solid legal backing: universal service was held up as a universal good, but it was not enshrined anywhere in federal law. At least, not until the next articulation.

ARTICULATION 3: UNIVERSAL SERVICE AS UNIVERSALLY
OBTAINABLE SLATES OF SERVICES

"In a weirdly posthumous political victory," Mueller concludes, "the mythology of universal service created by the old order had become the law of the land" (1997, p. 166). The second articulation of universal service was picked up and enshrined in the Telecommunications Act of 1996, "clearly articulated" (p. 167) and made concrete enough that regulations could be based on it. It was operationalized in Section 254, Subsection b (cf. Duesterberg & Gordon, 1997, p. 52). But it was also *rearticulated* in this third phase, just as telecommunications itself had been rearticulated from a luxury into a public utility. In this third phase, universal service expanded even beyond the definition that AT&T had articulated in the 1970s:

> The language makes it clear that universal service obligations need no longer be confined to traditional telephone service. Universal service is to be an "evolving level of telecommunications services," and the definition must take into account advances in telecommunications and information technology. The FCC must include, at a minimum, any

telecommunications service to which a substantial majority of residential customers subscribe. It must also revise and update the definition periodically. (Mueller, 1997, p. 167; cf. Hughes, 1996, pp. 202–203)

This new articulation of universal service destabilizes the industry significantly. In the old days, telephone service was relatively homogeneous. Quality and subscriber universe might vary, but the basic service was the same in any network: voice telephony, also known as plain old telephone service (POTS) (Mueller, 1997). Today, you can choose from a wide slate of services, including call-waiting, caller ID, dial-up Internet, ISDN, DSL, voice mail, and on and on.[4] Rival companies regularly roll out new services as a way to keep ahead of competitors. *The Telecommunications Act of 1996 essentially says that any of these services can be considered part of basic service once they achieve a certain level of market penetration.* A telecommunications company has to keep up with competitors, not just because of market pressures but because it has to be prepared for popular features to be mandated. Services can't be unbundled; rival networks can't pursue niche markets wholeheartedly.

Beyond this requirement, telecommunications companies must provide "quality services" at "just, reasonable, and affordable rates" (Mueller, 1997, p. 167). Affordability was a post hoc rationale, Mueller reminds us, that was "enshrined" in law (p. 168). But, post hoc or not, it became a policy goal. That goal was achieved in various ways. Universal service was operationalized in the Telecommunications Act of 1996 as subsidies provided by providers to K–12 schools, libraries, and similar nonprofit parties at discounts of 20 percent to 90 percent, administered in the federal Universal Service Fund by the Universal Service Administrative Company. The discounts were set based on "poverty level, as measured by school lunch eligibility" (Aufderheide, 1999, p. 100) – a wonderful illustration of how different sociotechnical networks can be spliced together. And the exigence for this complex splicing – that which underpins the argument for this third articulation of universal service – is the assumption that access to up-to-date telecommunications services is now *the material basis for individuals' effective participation in a democratic society*[5] (Lenert, 1998, p. 11)! It's a *cornerstone of democracy* – one for which we continue to pay a *luxury tax*!

---

[4] For a fascinating view of how some of these more recent services have been adapted and coordinated by consumers, see Huatong Sun's (2004) study of mobile phone users.

[5] In a really interesting case study, Paul de Armond (2001) describes how protesters at the 1999 World Trade Organization summit in Seattle coordinated using mobile phones, which enabled decentralized, democratic decision making. As Yochai Benkler argues, "Freedom depends on the information environment that those individuals and societies occupy" (2006, p. 169).

This rationale of the public good is felt at the local level as well. In 1983's Modification of Final Judgment, the regional Bell operating companies (RBOCs) had been granted limited monopolies in local service. But with the Telecommunications Act of 1996, competitive local exchange carriers (CLECs) were allowed to compete. Ideally, these companies would build their own infrastructure; realistically, the price of entry was far too steep. So the Telecommunications Act mandated that in the short run, RBOCs must provide their services at a discount to the CLECs, which could then repackage that service and resell it to consumers at competitive prices. Eventually, the act envisioned the CLECs bootstrapping themselves: building their own physical facilities, providing hardware-to-hardware or facilities-based competition (Aufderheide, 1999). The act "leaves to the FCC and to states (in an unclear formulation) the determination of what price is fair for resale"; mandates number portability; disallows mandated access numbers; and sets up payment arrangements for calls that traverse multiple competitors' networks (Aufderheide, 1999, pp. 63–64). Of course, once again the competitors cream skimmed. By 1998, CLECs controlled 1 percent of local lines, but those lines represented 3 percent of local phone revenues because the CLECs aggressively pursued business rather than residential lines (Aufderheide, 1999; cf. Heldman, Heldman, & Bystrzycki, 1997; McMaster, 2002).

Finally, we see some really interesting fallout of this articulation in the current state of telecommunications. Since interconnection is mandated by law, no company can gain competitive advantage by being a bottleneck for local service. Local exchange carriers cannot prohibit or limit the resale of their services. Interconnection has to be open and nondiscriminatory (Mueller, 1997), resulting in service that is transparent – when you pick up a phone, your service will be the same no matter what company (or companies) effect the call. (This principle ensures universal service, but it also makes "slamming" possible: the illegal practice of switching a consumer's telephone service without her knowledge. "Slamming" is usually detected only when the new bill comes in.)

Most importantly, the new articulation of universal service requires deep interconnections and interpenetrations among rival companies. In the current environment, workers at telecommunications companies are mostly massed at the company's borders, working closely with their counterparts in other companies; the integrity of the boundaries between companies is not strong. *Like Telecorp, other telecommunications companies have no interior.* How can they? Three different articulations of universal service bind them together and force them to interoperate as a single utility even as they compete with one another.

Although the Telecommunications Act of 1996 enshrined a version of universal service in law, that third articulation had already been enacted in state laws. For instance, Texas embraced this articulation of universal service as a policy goal in 1993, on the basis of even earlier policy actions. The articulation worked because of a general shift in the perception of telecommunications services; it was not just an anachronistic concept that took on a life of its own, it was an evolving argument, as we'll see below.

LOCAL ARTICULATIONS: UNIVERSAL SERVICE IN TEXAS

Given the national history, it's evident that telecommunications made a journey from luxury to business tool to de facto public utility, and universal service took various shapes through this transition, providing various justifications at each articulation. It's also evident that universal service wasn't firmly operationalized until the Telecommunications Act of 1996 (although it began to take shape in the form of cross-subsidies much earlier, as we've seen). That's the national picture. But there were also local articulations, complicated by the fact that telecommunications in the United States are regulated by three sets of bodies with overlapping jurisdictions: the FCC, the U.S. Appeals Court for the District of Columbia (in the wake of the Bell breakup), and state public utility commissions (Crandall, 1991). And here, Texas is an interesting case, because the telecommunications industry was all but unregulated at the state level until Texas established a public utilities commission (PUC) in 1975 – the last state PUC to be established in the United States. Here, I discuss the local conditions that obtained and how the regulatory environment changed in the intervening years.

First, some background. Although Bell was characterized as a monopoly, its reach was not absolute. By the 1960s, AT&T provided 80 percent of the service in the United States, with independent companies such as GTE and Continental Telephone serving most of the rest. Subscriber-owned telephone cooperatives served some of the most remote rural areas. These figures were mirrored in Texas: "Bell System companies continued to serve four out of five telephones in the state, while independent companies served over half the state's 250,000 square miles of certified service territory" (Handbook of Texas Online, 2005). Telecommunications providers acted as local monopolies: service areas did not overlap and subscribers were not able to choose the company that provided their service.

That lack of choice had considerable ramifications given the regulatory environment. Texas was the last state in the United States to establish a PUC, something that posed considerable problems for its telecommunications policy and environment. As Charles Wilson describes in a 1971 interim committee's report to the Texas Legislature:

> Texas is the only state without a public utilities commission to regulate telephone services. We have, instead, a haphazard system of "local regulation" consisting of negotiations, often one-sided, between the telephone companies and nearly 900 city councils. (1971, p. 25)

One-sided indeed. As Wilson tells it, the telephone companies were well organized and well run, and the city councils were no match: underinformed, underorganized, and underfunded. The problems were endemic in the system:

> Even if this system functioned with perfect efficiency, it would still leave unregulated two important aspects of telephone service:
>
> (1) Monthly subscription charges in rural areas. No one, under our present system, has jurisdiction to set rates or insure high-quality service in unincorporated, rural areas. Residents of these areas do not even have the nominal protection of a city council to "bargain" with the utilities on their behalf. No governmental agency – federal, state or local – has the legal power to intervene and assist them in obtaining fair negotiations.
> (2) Intrastate long distance rates. "Local regulation" in Texas extends only to local service in the incorporated areas; it does not – and legally cannot – extend to regulation by the city councils of the rates charged by Southwestern Bell for long distance calls made to other points in Texas. The Federal Communications Commission regulates all interstate calls, and in every other state, a state commission does the same for intrastate calls. In Texas, there is no regulation whatever of the rates Southwestern Bell may charge for intrastate calls. The company, indeed, refuses even to disclose its profits on such calls. They have refused to let any governmental body – federal, state, or local – see how much they make on this important aspect of their service. (Wilson, 1971, p. 25)

The local monopolies were really allowed to run the table in Texas. Vast swaths of the state were left entirely unregulated. And the regulated portions were regulated by municipalities, which had neither the information nor the financial resources to regulate telephone service in a thorough way. "Only Houston and Dallas make even a token effort at regulation. The smaller cities do not have the financial resources to hire the rate experts and attorneys necessary to argue their citizens' case against the numerous specialized, highly-paid telephone company representatives" (Wilson, 1971, p. 26). The report goes on to describe Nacogdoches's futile battle against the vast resources of Southwestern Bell (pp. 26–27 and Appendix A), using it as a case study in favor of establishing a PUC.

The Nacogdoches case was an extreme illustration of the rate inflation that had dogged the entire state. Across Texas, "businesses are being burdened with intrastate leased-line charges that are between 200 percent and 400 percent higher per-mile than comparable interstate leased lines subject to F.C.C. regulation. The discrimination is obvious" (p. 23). And the average monthly rates for consumers were higher in Texas than the national average – across all sizes of telephone exchanges (p. 3).

Rates weren't the only problem. Rural service was poor, leading to unsatisfactory workarounds: "The constable in the east Texas town of Zavalla reported that his patrol car's two-way radio frequently must serve as the only communications link for telephone subscribers whose equipment has broken down during the weekend" (p. 23). Remember, rural service is more expensive to provide and rates are lower. No wonder service wasn't provided at par when there was no regulatory oversight for rural areas! Furthermore, jurisdictional disputes between Southwestern Bell and GTE resulted in other sorts of problems for consumers. "This infighting among utility monopolies reached its most ludicrous extreme at the Ramada Inn in Nassau Bay, where a call from the barber shop to the front desk was a long distance, toll call" (p. 23).

The report recommends, sensibly, that statewide regulation be introduced. The regulation it proposed essentially transformed regulated monopolies into de facto public utilities (p. 28). No more half measures – the local monopolies had to be made to work in the public interest (p. 29). This work led in 1975 to the creation of the Texas Public Utilities Commission, which "sets rates for all local exchange companies... in accordance with the Public Utility Regulatory Act (PURA)" (Rhodes & Hadden, 1995, p. 44).

Texas's PUC was designed to deal with regulated monopolies such as Southwestern Bell's and GTE's. In the intervening years, the regulatory environment has become more complicated: Though Southwestern Bell (now part of SBC) and GTE (now part of Verizon) still provide the majority of local service, the 1983 Modification of Final Judgment allowed long distance competition and the Telecommunications Act of 1996 allowed CLECs. And Texas's regulatory changes followed, and in some cases anticipated, the national changes. The PUC still gives special attention to regional monopolies such as SBC and Verizon, but the regulatory environment has shifted to encouraging competition rather than regulating monopolies.

One way that the PUC anticipated regulatory changes on the national scene was in terms of universal service. The PUC explicitly adopted universal service (in its third articulation) as a policy goal in 1995 (Rhodes & Hadden, 1995), the year before the Telecommunications Act of 1996 defined it in this way. The PUC provides a good breakdown of the current definition of universal service: "Two main features characterize universal service: availability and affordability" (p. 26). That is, people should have service in their area and they should be able to pay for it. The first feature is defined in terms of "telephone penetration": the percentage of households with phone service (p. 26). Telephone penetration was at 94.2 percent nationally and 91.5 percent in Texas in 1993. (Of those without access, 40 percent reported that they would like phone service but couldn't afford it [p. 75].)

Affordability is measured by "a comparison of the annual average rise in the price for telephone service with the average price for all goods and services (represented by the consumer price index)" (p. 27), and evidence suggests that telephone service has become more affordable. Rhodes and Hadden credit this to the introduction of new technology, which has caused marginal costs to decline.

Beyond these two features, Rhodes and Hadden identify three principles underlying universal service. Notice the differences from the national articulations:

1. **Equality of opportunity.** The idea is that citizens must be able to communicate with each other to make reasoned political choices. (This certainly is not what Vail had in mind!)
2. **Quality of life.** The telephone is a "lifeline" for disadvantaged segments of the population such as the elderly, poor, and disabled.
3. **Economic efficiency.** "The rationale underlying this argument is that people place more value on the telephone network the more people are connected to it. But individuals and companies rarely have enough of an incentive to make sure that different networks are compatible and that complete strangers are hooked up" (p. 27). (Compare this reasoning to Mueller's discussion of subscriber universes.)

If phone service was once viewed as a luxury, then as a utility, these principles appear to move it into the civic sphere as public policy at the local scale. Rhodes and Hadden sensibly ask: "If telecommunications services are evolving, how should the notion of universal service evolve? There is no single solution to this puzzle, and as a result universal service has been defined in several different ways" (p. 28). And these different articulations tend to keep accumulating, just as charges from different eras continue to accumulate on one's phone bill. Just as the luxury tax from 1898 still survives, even though phone service is now regarded as a civic necessity, the previous articulations of universal service survive, though brought into a new relationship with each other. The meanings are not replaced, they accrete both in policy and on the phone bill.

So what necessitates this local articulation? Telecommunications services have grown increasingly heterogeneous, and POTS is arguably no longer an adequate standard for universal service. If (for instance) voice mail or Internet connectivity is an overwhelmingly standard service, then denying it to a segment of consumers violates all three of the principles above. According to Rhodes and Hadden (1995), the Texas PUC listed the following as basic services: "voice-grade dial tone service, access to dual party relay service, access to local calling areas, tone dialing service, access to operator services, access to toll services, and access to 911 or enhanced 911 service as requested by local authorities" (p. 29). More on this in a moment.

Universal service used to be funded by AT&T from its profits – part of the price of being a regulated monopoly. But with its breakup, the universal service burden fell directly to subscribers, who pay a subscriber line charge (SLC), set at $3.50/month in 1995 (Rhodes & Hadden, 1995). As universal service is rearticulated, and as its criteria become fuzzier, it becomes less of an abstract principle and more of a policy goal that must be operationalized. How does the rubber meet the road (to borrow a metaphor from a different infrastructure)? Quite concretely, it turns out: Texas established its own Universal Service Fund in 1987:

> Texas is unique in that it has a Universal Service Fund (USF), which is financed by all telecommunications utilities in the state based on toll usage of the telephone network. The USF pays for the Tel-Assistance discount and the Dual-Party Relay Service, a program that allows hearing- and speech-impaired Texans to communicate through specifically trained operators. The fund also covers the costs of the Department of Human Services and the PUC, in addition to any other costs that are necessary to administer the fund. The discount provided under the more recently established Lifeline program is absorbed by the local exchange companies and not the Universal Service Fund. Total monthly gross USF assessments have recently averaged close to $500,000. (Public Utilities Commission of Texas, 1999, p. 15)

Even in 1987 we see the shift toward the third articulation of universal service. But it co-existed with the second articulation: the Public Utility Regulatory Act of 1995 strengthened

> the eligibility that local exchange companies (LECs) must meet, requiring LECs to offer service to every consumer within its certified area and render continuous and adequate service within the area or areas. In addition, the pending legislation includes the proposal to establish a Telecommunications Infrastructure Fund. This $75 million fund will be administered by a nine-member board and financed by telecommunications providers. The board will award loans and provide necessary equipment and infrastructure to promote telecommunications services that the board finds are directly related to a distance-learning activity that is or could be conducted by an educational institution in Texas. (Rhodes & Hadden, 1995, pp. 30–31)

Still later, a new Texas Universal Service Fund was created in 1999; it supports local exchange carriers in rural areas (Public Utilities Commission of Texas, 1999).

How does the concept of universal service get translated into actual policy? The answer is breathtaking. Universal service, which started out as the principle of interconnecting competing networks to form a single subscriber universe, had changed so much that by 1995 it required an increasingly lengthening laundry list of initiatives, agencies, charges, acts, and funds. *And since the latest definition of universal service made it a moving target, we can expect to see these multiply in the future.* The more telecommunications companies innovate, the more their innovations are likely to become standard, thus basic, and thus the more likely they are to come under the purview of the PUC. This articulation, in effect, mandates a continuing proliferation of services and corresponding regulations and practices. That means that telecommunications is going to continue to internetwork with other trades, disciplines, industries, and technologies.

"Texas is unique," Rhodes and Hadden indicate (pp. 30–31). The unique solution of the USF indicates a local articulation of universal service. What is universal service? Not so much an essence or principle as it is a "handle" for a broad set of concrete practices and mechanisms. What a great illustration of what actor–network theorists like to argue: the inseparability of the social and the technical – in this case, the technological innovations meant to attract new subscribers, which eventually translate in a fairly direct way to new regulative and legislative activities.

EVEN MORE LOCAL ARTICULATIONS: UNIVERSAL SERVICE
AT TELECORP

At the turn of the twentieth century, Bell's early competitors looked for interstices in Bell's network – rural areas that Bell wouldn't serve. But at the end of that century, competitors like Telecorp, which moved into telecommunications after the 1983 Modification of Final Judgment (MFJ), had to find different kinds of interstices. They had to compete in areas that Bell already served.

Telecorp took advantage of market liberalization, entering markets shortly after they were opened for competition. It entered the long distance market shortly after the MFJ in the mid-1980s, initially reselling AT&T service as it began working on its own infrastructure and connecting it to the infrastructures of other regional independents. And shortly after local service was opened for competition in 1996, it began selling BigTel service while constructing its own local loops. It also signed an agreement with a national wireless carrier to provide wireless service. At the time of the study in 2000–2001, Telecorp had developed an extensive network serving retail and business customers across the southwestern United States through purchases of some telecommunications companies and strategic partnerships with others.

By 2001, Telecorp offered a wide array of products and services reflecting the current state of telecommunications – which is to say, hypercompetition through diversification. Products include local dial tone (both its own and resale); long distance (both its own and resale); toll-free services; calling cards; Internet services (dial-up, dedicated LAN, ISDN, xDSL, T1, T3); paging services; telephone systems; point-to-point services; frame relay; ATM services; prepaid phone cards; conference calling; and mobile phone service through a national provider. The wide array of services reflected the increasing competition in this industry as well as the increasingly broad set of activities, sets of expertise, types of education, and literacy that had to be spliced into Telecorp (see Chapter 5).

The range of services presented significant challenges. Jean in Accounts Payable kept a spreadsheet handy for calculating schools and libraries discounts, a hand-me-down genre from the previous worker in this position:

> And then, um, and now I'm in the regulatory clerk position and I bill the schools and libraries for their discounts and then bill USAC [the Universal Service Administrative Company, which administers the federal Universal Service Fund] to get refunded back. And we pay into this fund,

I guess. I'm still kind of learning what we're doing, but it almost sounds like a vicious circle of you kinda pay in discount and then you get paid back or whatever. So it's kind of new. I've only been doing it for a week now.... I had three mornings [of training] with the girl that was doing the schools and libraries, and the rest of it's gonna come from a couple of different people. And that's why I'm kind of in limbo now because they're letting me learn one thing first. And as soon as I get that figured out, then they're gonna start throwing other things at me.

Jean oversaw a "vicious circle," perhaps, but one that was necessary to bind together the many nodes of the sociotechnical network of which Telecorp was a part. Schools and libraries, school lunch programs, telephone lines, spreadsheets, regulators, legislators, currency, clerks, and in-house training were all connected with unlikely but persistent links. This network was more than a little jury-rigged, but it bound together the contradictory articulations of universal service; it embodied a relatively coherent argument about what universal service was and should be. More to the point, this "vicious circle" – this regulated cross-subsidy – is the only thing that keeps local service feasible while addressing universal service. In fact, in rural areas, the gap between high provider cost and low consumer price for local service is really abysmal, which is why Congress reserves the right to *require* local exchange carriers to remain in rural areas as carriers of last resort (Hughes, 1996). Jean didn't understand all this, but she understood enough to keep things running, thanks to her spreadsheets and collateral genres:

Well, I'm invoicing the schools and libraries that are going to this universal service ... for schools for the ... universal service administrative center [*sic*]. So we show what we discounted the schools and they in turn send us back a statement type invoicing when they give us credit back for what we've already discounted the schools off of their phone bills. So this here is just a form of invoicing them and you can only put one school per form.

Such genres have proliferated to support this work, taking apart, reassembling, rearticulating, and recirculating information across the network. As I said in Chapter 1, these texts tend to weave and splice together parts of the network. Just as articulations of universal service have accumulated, just as charges accumulated on the phone bill, textual genres have accumulated to help perform this coordinative work.

Now that I've provided a history of universal service in the United States, in Texas, and at Telecorp, let's perform two analyses: one based on activity theory's contradictions and one based on actor–network theory's translations.

WEAVING UNIVERSAL SERVICE: AN ACTIVITY THEORY ANALYSIS

As we saw in the previous chapter, activity theory understands history as development driven by *contradictions* that develop within and among activity systems. In this woven understanding, activities become more complex over time and forge increasingly wide networks with other activities, periodically forming and then dealing with contradictions. In dealing with these contradictions, activity systems transform themselves and their networks. Here, history develops linearly, unrolling like a scroll and bifurcating like a tree.

In an activity–theoretical reading, the different articulations of universal service were responses to contradictions in the developing activity network of U.S. telecommunications, and each articulation set the stage for the next contradiction. The telecommunications activity network periodically extended to deal with each contradiction, linking to other emerging activity systems such as legislatures, regulatory bodies, fields, and disciplines, and generating new activity systems as divisions of labor hardened and became more distinct. And as the network expanded, the potential for more contradictions increased. As Engeström (1996a) reminds us, contradictions are engines of change, providing opportunities for expansion. That's exactly what happened in the telecommunications industry.

The activity network shared a single object, the telephone system, which developed steadily through the interactions of the linked activity systems. But these overlapping or interpenetrating activity systems, as multiple parallel contexts (Engeström, Engeström, & Kärkkäinen, 1995), construed this object in different ways and sought very different things from it. Contradictions in their understanding and construction of the object led to changes in the object itself, changes in the activity systems and their relations, and the addition of other activity systems, each of which *also* construed the object differently and introduced new contradictions. Contradictions engender changes, so the object changed radically as it dialectically adjusted to the changes in the activity network that sustained it. But as Ilyenkov (1982) argues, the internal relations of the object remain fixed; the telephone system is still a recognizable, bounded object throughout these changes.

Contradiction 1: Exclusivity or Interconnection?

For instance, before the first articulation of universal service (as the principle of interconnection), Bell faced the problem of how to retain its domination of the industry after its patents ran out. This question was pressing not just because Bell was motivated to make money but because telephone service had no appreciable economy of scale – telephone service was viable for small companies or for overwhelmingly dominant ones, but not for those in between. And by 1907, Bell controlled only 49 percent of the telephone market. Other providers faced the same issues: they periodically assumed that they could achieve an economy of scale then grew too large to sustain their businesses. And municipalities grew tired of the unrest in the market as well as the attendant headaches: granting right-of-way for new lines, granting licenses for new companies, wondering whether they would be best served by this provider rather than that one. As telephone service became more pervasive, it also became more generally useful, more of a public concern, and less of a luxury.

In 1907, recognizing the shifts in the market, Bell abandoned its previous business strategy of withholding interconnection and adopted a new strategy of "universal service" or universal interconnection. This strategy, which began as a *rule* of the Bell system, became embedded as an aspect of the object of telephone service. This rule was mediated through interconnection agreements and other artifacts as well as the rationale of natural monopolies that justified it. Eventually, through acquisitions and interconnection agreements with noncompete clauses, Bell merged with most of its competitors and formed a unified telephone system. The many woven systems were spliced together.

In the process, the object was transformed: rather than telephone *systems*, it became a universally interconnected, spliced telephone *system* in which any user could connect with any other, cheaply and effectively. To achieve this transformation, different activity systems had to be linked: telephone companies, civic authorities, equipment manufacturers, and others. These activity systems were spliced together through the common object of the telephone system, which was construed and constructed differently in the different nodes (activity systems) but still recognizably the same object across all nodes. The object developed considerably, but its internal relations held.

Without substantial competition, Bell was able to mitigate the lack of economies of scale through cross-subsidies: more profitable service areas could subsidize less profitable ones.

Contradiction 2: Business or Public Utility?

But though the old contradiction was eased, a new contradiction formed. The principle of interconnection led to a monopoly on a service that was quickly becoming as essential as water or electricity. Was it best achieved by a private, regulated company, as Bell wanted it to be? Or as a public utility, like water and electricity? The telephone system had entered the realm of public policy, and this connected it to other activity systems: legislatures and regulatory bodies, representatives and referenda. These had their own developmental histories, but in taking on the object of the phone system, they became spliced into the weaving, developing activity network of telecommunications.

I mentioned that an activity network's object is construed differently by the component activity systems. This polycontextuality made itself felt throughout the next several decades. In becoming a monopoly, Bell had taken on severe regulation and governmental oversight; to avoid the Sherman Antitrust Act, which had dismantled so many of its contemporaries, Bell had to think and act as a public utility. At times it was even run as a public utility – for instance, in World War I, it was run by the postmaster general (Temin, 1987). At all times its profits were regulated, its costs were inspected, and even its billing procedures were micromanaged by the legislature and the courts. This contradiction in the object of the telephone system became exacerbated as time went on. Was it to be treated as a business or as a public utility? Was it answerable primarily to stockholders or to the government? This contradiction led to the development of the object: universal service became rearticulated as an aspect of the object, a *policy* that addressed both sides of the contradiction. The new articulation of universal service as affordable total market penetration meant that Bell could address the public policy mission (by serving more and more citizens as an indispensable utility) while also addressing the business mission (by expanding as well as monopolizing the market). In areas where local regulation was weak, such as Texas before 1975, the business mission tended to win out; in more heavily regulated areas, the public service mission did. But the transformation of the object also necessitated further development across the activity network: within Bell and other telephone companies, it spurred more complex rules and divisions of labor; within related activities, it resulted in increasingly complex regulations, laws, and technical specialties. That is, these spliced activities reacted to the splicing by weaving further, by further bifurcating and changing.

What made the whole enterprise work, of course, was the increasing tangle of cross-subsidies that were themselves made tenable by Bell's monopoly status. So when MCI and other long distance competitors came on the scene, unencumbered by the rearticulated rule of universal service and armed with new technologies that could achieve economies of scale, Bell's monopoly enterprise became untenable. Furthermore, regulatory support for Bell's monopoly status had weakened: although the FCC could initially be counted on to squelch competition as harmful to Bell's de facto public utility, by the 1970s that was no longer the case. The notion of natural monopoly had fallen out of favor, and the government increasingly began to see competition as a way to achieve policy goals rather than as an impediment to them. The contradiction between business and public concerns, which had become increasingly tense over time, had reached a breaking point, resulting in another transformation of the object.

When I say "breaking point," of course I mean that *Bell* had to be broken up. And as Temin points out, Bell's breakup meant immediate competition among the regional Bell operating companies as well as competition between AT&T and the other long distance companies – which began to proliferate at a startling rate. The activity network had suddenly expanded, forming a number of new contradictions, and these necessitated a transformation in the common object: universal service had to change so that it could be supplied by a confederation of telecoms rather than a monopoly.

The telephone system had functioned as a de facto public utility for a long time, and the public service mission was still an important part of the object. So although the long distance market had been opened to competition, the telephone system still had to function as a single construct. That meant that the competing telecoms had to forge ever-increasing splices at various levels; they had to conspire to provide customers with the illusion of unified service, and to do that, they had to learn to connect with each other, to hand off customers and service, and even to train their competitors' workers. They had to splice. And at the same time, regulatory agencies had to protect local service, which had been operating with profits well below costs for decades thanks to cross-subsidies that had only been tenable under a monopoly; mechanisms such as the subscriber line charge, access charges, and federal and state universal service funds sprang into being to replace (or sometimes supplement) the tangle of cross-subsidies that had developed during the Bell monopoly. Activity systems clustered thickly around the object of the telephone network, crowding and interpenetrating each other.

The industry experienced more complexity, more specialization, more parallel contexts, and consequently more aspects of the common object. But the object remained essentially the same: you pick up a phone; you call anyone else who has a phone. The object remained the same in its internal relations, but it evolved and increased in complexity.

Contradiction 3: Competition or Public Good?

Around this time, universal service was rearticulated again. Whereas the first articulation (interconnection) was eminently achievable, and the second (total market penetration) was nearly so, the third articulation was an infinitely receding horizon. Competition was harnessed, leading to universally achievable slates of services that changed as new services and technologies became available. This rearticulation began in various markets but was written into the Telecommunications Act of 1996, along with the liberalization that allowed competition in local service. The contradiction between competition and public good took on new dimensions as telecoms faced the question of how to gain competitive advantage through technological innovations and new features while consolidating these gains enough to feasibly offer them as universal services if they became popular enough. And still telecoms had to compete with each other but in ways that provided an apparent unity of service: total interconnection, the illusion that customers are using a single seamless network.

The object has developed, but each articulation assumes and recapitulates the last. This latest articulation has led to a proliferation of splices between activity systems, including many new tools and practices to mediate their activities. For instance, "slamming" was not possible in the age of the local monopoly, but it is now; telecoms must therefore keep extensive documentation, including voice recordings of customers who formally agree to switch their phone service. Similarly, the explosion of telecommunications features means that people from very different fields and disciplines must interact in new ways. Recall that Telecorp's Network Operations Center workers train with BigTel and interact with their BigTel counterparts more than they do with their own sales representatives. At this point, do activity systems represent organizations or disciplines?

Summary: What Do We Learn from a History of Contradictions?

This brief activity theory analysis emphasizes the dialectical changes in the activity network. Contradictions form, develop, and eventually lead to large-scale transformations of the entire network, and these transformations become the stage for the next contradictions and the next set of transformations. Each transformation is both social and material; it is durable and irreversible. Objects, actors, and activities persist over time; they have trajectories. Activity theory provides a strong historical account of how activities weave and develop and how they splice with other developing activities that share the same object, forming activity networks. It provides a woven understanding of activities, which become more complex and eventually can split into a network of related activity systems. But it also provides a spliced understanding of how these might link with other activities. We get to see how these spliced activities transform the object – and each other – dialectically, through contradictions that are periodically addressed with systemic changes.

At the same time, the account privileges development to such an extent that it only touches on the multiplicity of the object. As we saw in Chapter 3, even a concrete artifact such as the Zimbabwe Bush Pump has unclear, indeterminate boundaries. How much more so does an object such as the national telephone system! Activity theory assumes that such an object has stable internal relations that hold it steady. But those relations are hard to nail down here, particularly as the telecommunications activity network expands and brings in different trades, texts, and technologies. Indeed, the more thickly activity systems are spliced, the more difficult it is to tell how the object is enacted. Telecorp's Network Operations Center workers, for instance, train with BigTel, work closely with BigTel reps, and use BigTel's social language. Are they working within Telecorp's activity system, BigTel's, or their trade's? The "parallel activity contexts" hardly seem parallel – they thoroughly interpenetrate.

SPLICING UNIVERSAL SERVICE: AN ACTOR–NETWORK THEORY ANALYSIS

An actor–network analysis of the same history looks quite different. In contrast to activity theory's dialectical account of history as a series of contradictions, actor–network theory's rhizomatic account is that of translations. This account is not developmental, as activity theory's is, although it is still material and transformational. It provides a spliced understanding, one that highlights contingencies and stabilized-for-now settlements. Here, actants are continuously being defined (i.e., they are continually defining each other) and continuously converging, intersecting, and splicing. This splicing strengthens the network by locking actants into roles and stabilizing them, so the longer the network becomes the stronger it becomes. Of course, there is always the potential for treason: any actant can pull out of the settlement and necessitate a renegotiation.

Unlike an activity network, an actor–network does not assume a common object or motivation. What keeps an actor–network together is the way in which a situation is problematized and the ways in which actants are defined, enrolled, and mobilized within that problem space. This negotiation is always tentative and somewhat unstable, and therefore it is always reversible (in theory, at least). But as we saw in Chapter 3, these alliances accumulate like layers of sediment: it becomes harder to undo a settlement when other layers of settlements have accumulated on it.

Such settlements become folded in on themselves. As Serres argues (Serres & Latour, 1995), history unfolds less like a scroll and more like a crumpled handkerchief. Heterogeneous entities from different times are juxtaposed to form the present:

> The hammer that I find on my workbench is not contemporary to my action today: it keeps folded heterogenous temporalities, one of which has the antiquity of the planet, because of the mineral from which it has been moulded, while another has that of the age of the oak which provided the handle, while still another has the age of the 10 years since it came out of the German factory which produced it for the market. (Latour, 2002, p. 249)

In this line of thought, history is not a series of bifurcating decisions (Serres, 1995) but an accumulation of material propositions with varying temporalities. These propositions do not necessarily cohere. Five hundred years after Copernicus and Columbus, most of us accept that Earth orbits the sun, but at dusk we still say that "the sun is going down." And similarly, a hundred years after Vail first articulated the principle of universal service, we find aspects of each articulation in how the telecommunications system has been implemented. Let's examine how this works, drawing primarily on Callon's (1986b) account of translation (cf. Spinuzzi, 2005).

Translation 1: From Disunity to Unity

Let's start with Bell, not because it was the Machiavellian Prince that pulled the strings of the other actants, but because in retrospect its actions were most successful.

In the late 1800s, Bell faced a set of problems. How could it hold on to the market once its patent on the telephone ran out? How could it defeat the problem inherent in the enterprise, the problem of no economy of scale? But others faced problems as well. How could local areas get reliable phone coverage? How could individual users get a single phone line so that they could expect simple, even, and affordable service? How could the government turn this luxury service into something that would be useful to the nation? How could independent phone companies manage their growth and prosper, avoiding the boom-and-bust that had overtaken so many unsuccessful companies? But let's not forget to be symmetrical. How could phone lines reach each other rather than being isolated in rural areas? How could they manage to throw their signals over broader areas? How could actants prosper?

Unlike activity theory, actor–network theory doesn't posit a persistent object that can be used to define entities. Rather, in the *problematization* of phone service, these actants all defined each other. As Law (1992) argues, the actants are network effects, not originators. Whereas activity theory's object allowed us to trace back to existing activity systems full of existing actors, actor–network theory's problematization actually *creates and isolates* the actants. Actants define each other and invite each other to the negotiations. Here, we could divide actants in any number of ways: humans and nonhumans, regions, political affiliations, etc. But in this case, actants include Bell, other telecoms, municipalities, and the federal government, not (for instance) stars, microbes, scientists, Masons, churches, or cats – because the problematization invites particular actants and particular *types* of actants.

The problematization, in this case, was the first articulation of universal service. With this articulation, Bell problematized in terms of interconnection, making itself an obligatory passage point; interconnection simply couldn't be done without Bell, the largest telecom and the only one that had strategically built long distance network capacity. But others were not just sitting on their hands. The independents helped define Bell just as much by concentrating on their own areas and differentiating themselves competitively against Bell. (That's especially true of the ones that built local service in areas that Bell initially didn't serve.) The municipal governments similarly defined Bell and the independents, insisting on granting access to some and not to others.

Once the actors defined each other, they found ways that they could *interesse* each other, ways in which their interests were congruent. They locked each other into place as allies, opponents, etc. They consolidated and redefined each other's processes. In a word, they *spliced*. They were interested in different things, but they determined a common way to get to those goals – universal service, in its first articulation as universal interconnection of telephone service.

In particular, once Bell and the other actants had problematized the industry, these actants became locked into place. The independents, accepting their role as defined against Bell, had to interconnect or risk missing out on the subscriber universe, spelling failure for their enterprises. Bell had to interconnect with them – as long as they signed appropriate agreements – to expand into untouched local markets and to consolidate its hold on the national market. Municipalities had to insist on interconnection as well if they wanted to escape the boom-and-bust cycle of new telecoms periodically discovering that the telecom market had no economy of scale. Everyone wanted interconnection to meet their own goals, and Bell had made sure it was the obligatory passage point.

This brings us to *enrollment:* "The group of multilateral negotiations, trials of strength and tricks that accompany the interessements and enable them to succeed" (Callon, 1986b, p. 211). Methods of enrollment included various sorts of agreements and divisions meant to further differentiate and segment the actants: interconnection agreements, both pre- and postpatent; guarding of long lines, cutting off those without interconnection; subscriber universes; the division of market into long distance and local. Once the industry had gotten to this stage of translation, Bell consolidated its role as obligatory passage point by functioning as a coordinator; municipalities, in turn, ceded their ability to choose other companies and accepted the rationale of the natural monopoly.

If an interessement is successful, actants accept interrelated roles. That's what happened here. During the "multilateral negotiation," the actants came to divide their work roles. Independents accepted their roles as Bell partners; Bell accepted the role of a natural monopoly acting as a de facto public utility; municipal and federal governments accepted the roles of regulatory authorities. These roles were defined, negotiated, and made durable largely through texts: legislation, regulations, compacts, bills, contracts, cross-subsidies.

Such texts were also key in the last stage: *mobilization.* Who represents whom? Who speaks in whose name (Callon, 1986b, p. 214)? Universal service was a business strategy, but it also was framed as a public good: as a way to avoid boom-and-bust cycles and to stabilize the industry, as an alternative to endless new infrastructure and the headaches that went with it, as a bow to the iron law of the natural monopoly. The more actants were mobilized under the banner of universal service, the more real it became, made progressively more real through representations such as maps, user statistics, network diagrams, and other instruments.

Finally, once the stakeholders accepted their roles, they had to agree on intermediaries that yielded collective representations. There were many such representations. For instance, the Bell system was seen as a single company, though it was made up of semiautonomous regional operating companies. Regulatory documents, court cases, strategic decisions, technical metaphors, and endless other representations continued to define, separate, and lock in actants. The first articulation of universal service was a settlement, and each new year brought in new layers of representations that served to reduce the reversibility of this settlement.

Perhaps this changing, sedimenting settlement sounds like it is *developing* historically. But in this account, change is better understood as *accumulation* rather than development. Just as laws and institutions can accumulate in a nation but be swept aside by a cataclysm such as a revolution or invasion, historical accumulations can similarly collapse. There is always the potential for betrayal and reversal; it's always possible for actants to pull out of the negotiations, to fall apart, to strike out on their own, or to give way to new actants negotiating new settlements. And since everything could be reversed – though, granted, reversing a massive settlement is not a piece of cake – the settlement is never quite stabilized. Its existence is an ongoing achievement, one that is not indefinitely sustainable.

Translation 2: From Unity to Universality

The telephone system was universally interconnected, but at the cost of continual adjustments and interdefinitions. In particular, Bell had to continue negotiations with the national and state governments and regulatory agencies in order to consolidate its monopoly. And that brings us to the second articulation of universal service.

This second articulation was *problematized* as total market penetration at "reasonable" prices. Bell's initial work had been so successful that it had defined most competitors out of existence: they had either been absorbed into the Bell system, gone out of business, or held out in utterly unprofitable areas (such as the party lines run by farmers' cooperatives). But success brought its own pressures; actants such as Congress became more active and defined, and new actants such as the FCC emerged. To continue to be the obligatory point of passage for telephone service, Bell had to keep its status as the dominant provider without being defined out of existence itself – that is, without being nationalized or broken up. And to achieve that balance, Bell took on many of the characteristics of public utilities, including a mission emphasizing public service – the essence of the second articulation of universal service.

To achieve universal service in its second articulation, Bell and the other actants had to *interesse* each other: they had to interpose themselves between each other's goals and make themselves vital to the others' interests. Bell turned out to be exceptionally good at this splicing work, partially because it could promise universal service in its second articulation. It was in the position to offer infrastructure and expertise that no other actant could offer; it used cross-subsidies to subsidize local service, keeping rates low and making phone service affordable; it kept voice and service quality uniform across the nation. Moreover, it maintained a close interactive relationship with regulatory agencies. Through these promises, Bell successfully locked in legislators, the DoJ (which always seemed poised to strike under the auspices of the Sherman Antitrust Act), and the FCC. In doing so, it invited these actants to the negotiations, collaboratively defining goals so that everyone has an interest in maintaining Bell.

Well, almost everyone. Some actants resisted. Independent telephone companies such as GTE persisted in certain areas. New long distance companies such as MCI took advantage of new technologies and changing regulations to launch services that were unfettered by Bell's cross-subsidies and voice-quality commitments, undercutting service severely in profitable market segments – and creating powerful new actants, business customers in specific cities, who were suddenly differentiated from other customers. And finally, the DoJ eventually did strike, breaking up the Bell monopoly. From Bell's perspective, interessement eventually failed: actants defined each other and rejected Bell's settlement. Soon Bell had to agree to a new settlement, one that involved decomposing itself regionally and generating new actants.

But in the happy decades before the agreement unraveled (happy for Bell, anyway), the actants were *enrolled* in different ways. Bell played the role of a public utility, keeping public costs low and ensuring network integrity and jealously guarding its role as monopoly telephone company. The FCC provided regulatory backing to support Bell's monopoly status in order to keep the telephone system stable, and sometimes it pursued this duty to an extraordinary degree: in the Hush-a-Phone case, for instance, the FCC accepted Bell's implausible argument that a plastic cup threatened network integrity. But the FCC's decision was reversed by the courts, which themselves constituted actants that became more significant and harder to enroll as time went on. The Hush-a-Phone decision had the effect of counter-enrollment: it changed the FCC's stance toward Bell and led to later regulatory defeats (such as the Carterfone decision, which led to fax machines and modems). New actants, such as MCI, appeared and refused the roles that Bell tried to assign them. And the DoJ, although initially amenable to its role as collaborator in Bell's program, eventually "turned traitor" and enrolled Bell's regional companies and long lines in its own program.

Finally we get to *mobilization*. From 1907 to 1983, Bell mobilized the actants in various ways. Bell itself spoke for the phone system, arguing for a particular understanding of economics (the "natural monopoly"), billing, service, voice quality, and progress. It even argued successfully for artificially high long distance prices during World War II. But Bell retained its ability to speak for the phone system because it aggressively bargained with other actants – the FCC (which spoke for consumers), the DoJ (which spoke for the Sherman Antitrust Act), Congress (which spoke for citizens), and many other large and small actants. Bell didn't simply manipulate the other actors; it became to an extent what those other actors needed it to be; it compromised, just as they did, during the ongoing negotiations. And that ongoing compromise was represented in innumerable texts, from court decisions to regulations to phone bills to advertisements.

How bitter for Bell, then, that the settlement didn't hold! The unraveling of this delicate settlement meant the unraveling of Bell itself in the wake of the 1983 MFJ. But aspects of the settlement, particularly the second articulation of universal service, held.

Let's pause to note that in this translation analysis, the emphasis is on bargaining and contingency, not development as it was in the contradiction analysis. Yes, we can put together a historical account, and yes, some settlements remain relatively stable during different parts of the history. But this view is quite different from that of history as irreversible development. Any settlement is contingent and, in principle, can be reversed. On the other hand, a settlement can outlive the actants that were originally involved in forming it. And that is what happens with this story – sort of. I insert the qualifier because universal service was rearticulated and renegotiated after Bell's breakup.

Translation 3: From Universality to the Rising Tide

The rising tide lifts all boats. And the third articulation of universal service attempted something similar, an arrangement whereby universal service would steadily improve. No longer was the goal a fixed one: POTS for every household. In the third articulation, the tide could rise indefinitely, with new features turning into standard services accessible on every phone line.

This third articulation begins with a new *problematization*. How do you keep the democracy healthy? How do you keep telecommunications as a public good – now a cornerstone of democracy, no less – while still maintaining competition? As Marc Berg points out, "democracy" has become associated with "access to information" and notions of direct participation (1998, p. 479). Once that association is made, how are the material institutions to embed that morality (Latour, 2002)?

This problematization, with its focus on democracy, leads to segmenting and *interesting* certain actants: citizens, consumers (and these may be nearly congruent sets but not the same actant), legislators, incumbent and competitive local exchange carriers, long distance providers, public utility commissions, wireless companies, public advocacy groups, technology providers, and an ever-widening circle of others. Now that Bell is no longer an obligatory passage point, more actants can emerge and negotiate.

Those actants lock in and *enroll* each other through various agreements: legislation, regulation, competition. These agreements are dynamic: the third articulation of universal service means that part of enrollment involves continually reframing and re-enrolling.

The most significant limiting factor in this enrollment, perhaps, is that the many members of the industry share the same interconnected network. It's not the "same" Bell network, since it constantly decays and is renewed, constantly expands across new pathways. But it is governed by the same principle of interconnection established in 1907, the first articulation of universal service. And it must be maintained and expanded further due to the second articulation of universal service – which is still operative and forces incumbent local exchange carriers to serve even unprofitable areas as carriers of last resort. Finally, it must be updated due to the third articulation of universal service, and that means an increased emphasis on new services and technologies, leading to even more actants – including trades, texts, and technologies – becoming enrolled.

Finally, these actants are *mobilized* through various representations. The Telecommunications Act of 1996, federal and state regulations, local rules, and local conditions do some of this work. Even at the level of the individual transaction, the decision to switch phone service must be made in front of a witness who (like a witness of a wedding or a will) can stand up in court and represent the parties if necessary. Furthermore, actants represent each other. BigTel may be Telecorp's rival, but it also represents Telecorp during maintenance calls. Telecorp in turn represents BigTel by reselling its phone service. And, of course, texts proliferate: databases, forms, folders, voice memos, agreements, and many other texts summarize, represent, and circulate the interests of the different actants.

Summary: What Do We Learn from a History of Translations?

What do we learn from a translation account that we don't learn from a contradiction account? We start to see the practical benefits and difficulties of its ontological stance. By allowing actants to define each other, actor–network theory decouples actants from an evolving object and opens the possibility of seeing new actants emerge through negotiation – even overlapping actants (like citizens who are also consumers or NOC workers who have interests as BigTel collaborators, Telecorp employees, and trade members). By keying actants to *interests* rather than *objects*, actor–network theory embraces interlinked (interpenetrated, overlapped, multiroled, spliced) activity rather than trying to put it back in the box, as activity theory tends to do. And by seeing history in terms of political–rhetorical settlements and negotiations, the translation account opens up the possibility of examining phenomena nondevelopmentally.

On the other hand, actor–network theory does this by dropping any articulated understanding of development. Furthermore, as you can see if you review this section closely, it's quite difficult in practice to perform a symmetrical analysis! Humans' interests and agency, collectively and individually, are far easier to identify than nonhumans'.

WEAVING AND SPLICING TELECORP

Finally, we return to Telecorp. At the beginning of this chapter, I suggested that Telecorp's structure – with its workers all massed at the border – was a strategic response to the terrain it inhabits. The technological, legislative, regulatory, and economic terrain has made it not just advantageous but necessary to keep everyone at the border, giving them contact with others: regulators, government bureaucracies, workers at rival telecommunications companies, customers, vendors, and each other. Telecorp is a competitive business, but it has to work closely with its competition to provide universal service in all articulations: the industry, in effect, has to function as a single public utility. And that means that the network must be lengthened and strengthened, texts have to circulate far and wide, and divisions become unclear.

This is why Telecorp has no "interior." The telecommunications industry is, by law, deeply interpenetrated. And that means everyone must be massed at the border. Furthermore, the third articulation of universal service combined with the increased competition means that more and more disparate technologies and services must be spliced in and integrated into standard slates of services. No wonder we see the growth, the interpenetration, the increased need for communication across all areas, and no wonder the tensions are becoming so strong. This is an industrywide phenomenon, arguably an economywide one. The industry has to act as a stable, unified utility – a confederation of companies working toward the same goal, universal service – even as these same companies compete with one another in pricing, service, and features. That basic tension between competition and universal service manifests itself at all levels of the industry.

One result was that Telecorp, which once had a rudimentary division of labor comprised of customer service, the Network Operations Center, and administration, had expanded by 2001 into 20 distinct functional groups (see Figure 1.1).

These functional groups reflected several kinds of splicings and weavings related to the mission of universal service:

New Services
The third articulation of universal service had the effect of requiring telecoms to continually develop and deploy new services – almost always services that involved new technologies and therefore required new expertise to be spliced in from different fields and trades. Telecorp tended to bring these in as separate functional groups. For instance, Internet service required new expertise, so Data Network Products was created to encompass DSL, ATM/frame relay, Internet administration, and the Internet help desk. Such services required very different sorts of expertise from the long distance resale work that Telecorp had begun doing in the 1980s, and the workers in such groups tended to bring in specialized social languages and genres to help them enact that work. Ricardo, a local operations switch technician, described the Tower-of-Babel effect caused by this meeting of very different trades:

> Mainly it's – like, the other groups really don't understand how our part of it works. And I'm pretty sure that, you know, we don't understand how some of their stuff works. I mean, they start talking about the ASRs, the provisioners, and FOCs . . . I have no idea what they're talking about. Now, when I go out in the field and we work on something and we're seeing like an, you know, an AIS condition for a circuit and what have you, they don't understand what we're talking about. So sometimes we can actually word it a different way so they can understand what we're talking about. I would say the lingo is the main thing, main problem as far as why we get the communications wrong.

Ricardo's description echoes that of many who worked in the technical trades and who found difficulty describing their work to the other functional areas. But these difficulties were not just in the technical work. Another example was the marketing group: a specialized marketing group had not been needed until mid-2000, since Telecorp had traditionally relied on an advertising agency, and the two people in that vestigial group had sales rather than marketing experience. They had to rapidly learn about marketing and begin to develop a marketing plan – that is, they had to assimilate the logic and genres of a different trade. This continual splicing reflects the increased competition in the telecommunications sector, even as the sector has to act as a single utility.

New Divisions of Labor

And to act as a single utility, Telecorp also had to weave new divisions of labor to handle the rapid scaling of its customer base. Some functional groups strongly reflected a continuation and development of previous work. For instance, the customer service data entry group formed in mid-2000 to address the increasing data entry burden in customer service – to ensure that details did not fall through the cracks as Telecorp handled more and more calls. Similarly, some reflected the shift in administrative work that came from growing in size and serving new markets: sales, for instance, began shifting administrative work in its group from salespeople to administrative assistants, finding that dedicated administration tended to result in fewer incorrect orders and more face time with customers. This continual weaving reflected Telecorp's fortunes, of course, but it also reflected how the demands of universal service required new ways to manage attention to detail. The entire telecommunications industry must act as a single utility, after all, and such an enterprise requires extraordinary coordination.

New Relationships within Groups

The continual expansion into new regions meant that the functional groups themselves often became fractionally coherent as companies were continually spliced into Telecorp. Salespeople who had worked for years for smaller telecoms, for instance, suddenly found that their telecom had been bought by Telecorp. They were required to learn about new services and new ways to interact with the functional groups that supported them.

New Relationships with Other Telecoms

Finally, since the industry had to function as a single utility, Telecorp's technical workers found that they often had to work with and train at other telecommunications companies. NOC and CLEC Provisioning workers continually spoke with workers from other telecoms, picking up their social languages and learning how to switch from BigTel terminology to Telecorp sales terminology. LD Provisioning workers attended training sessions with a variety of national long distance telecoms, learning their terminology and coming back with thick binders of reference material. Alarm Management workers established new relationships with tiny network providers in a neighboring state, training them in the fine points of connecting with other networks and mapping the new connections with the help of Yahoo! Maps. And local operations technicians cautiously documented their work on circuits they maintained with BigTel.

Each of these changes required adjustments and interlinkings; as I said in Chapter 2, there was no way to close the black boxes. Telecorp was internally interlinked in what could be described as an "all-channel network," in which every node was potentially connected to every other through multiple communication technologies (Arquilla & Ronfeldt, 2001a). But it was also connected via multiple links directly to other entities: competitors, customers, regulators, corporations. This thick interlinking was a strategic response to the terrain on which Telecorp had to operate, the terrain that had been sedimented by the successive articulations of universal service.

CONCLUSION

In this chapter, we've examined the telecommunication industry's history through activity theory's and actor–network theory's accounts, and we've discussed how history has informed Telecorp's strategic stance. In the next chapter, we'll look at the consequences for Telecorp's net work. We'll examine how Telecorp's work is organized, how that organization represents the broader knowledge economy, and how its net work is enacted. We know what Telecorp's strategic stance is; now we'll look at its tactics.

5

How Are Networks Enacted?[1]

We've seen how work at Telecorp is deeply interpenetrated and how this has historically occurred. Telecorp has taken a strategic stance, as I argued in Chapter 4, but it's a stance into which many other companies and organizations have also shifted. In such organizations, everyone is at the border; everyone can link up with anyone else inside or outside the organization. This is what I've been calling the *net work*, the coordinative work that weaves and splices divergent work activities and that enables the standing sets of transformations that characterize such work. This coordinative, polycontextual, cross-disciplinary work, which makes this interpenetration hold together, has been noted in scholarship focusing on what is variably called the "new economy," the "knowledge economy," the "control society," the "politics of informatics," the "support economy," and the "hyperlinked organization."

But if everyone is massed at the border – if the organization is not arborescent but rhizomatic – how does the company work? Isn't that different from traditional work?

Sure it is. The modular understanding of work that we get from chained activity networks and from similar understandings of work – both Marxist and Taylorist (Braverman, 1974; Ehn, 1989; Marx, 1990) – isn't adequate for explaining what is going on at Telecorp or any other deeply interpenetrated organization, particularly those performing knowledge work. Given that, how is this net work done? That is, how are networks constructed and repaired, how are new nodes added, and how do workers collaborate? How are collaborators recruited and persuaded to help? How are poor collaborators routed around? In this chapter, I'll examine these questions by looking at routine and unusual interactions among different functional groups at

[1] Portions of this argument appear in Spinuzzi (2007a).

Telecorp and between Telecorp workers and workers at different companies. I'll particularly examine ways in which workers recruit new collaborators; rhetorically connect their teams with other teams; and ascribe motivations, values, and beliefs to those other teams. In the previous chapter, we looked at Telecorp's *strategic* stance; in this chapter, we'll explore its workers' *tactics*, the recurring mediated actions in which they engage.

But first, let's talk about an understanding of work that doesn't particularly help us in Telecorp's case: *modular work*.

MODULAR WORK

By *modular work*, I mean the understanding of work organization grounded in the Industrial Revolution, the understanding that has enabled industrial and managerial capitalism. Karl Marx argues that manufacturing takes two forms: *heterogeneous* and *organic*. Heterogeneous manufacturing is like watchmaking, in which different streams of supplies eventually come together (1990, p. 461); think of supply chains in which multiple vendors supply parts that are eventually assembled by a manufacturer. Organic manufacturing involves progressively transforming material, isolating the different stages of manufacturing and yielding a chained division of labor (p. 463) in which work that had been accomplished in one place, by one person, can be distributed in space and time (p. 464). Think of an assembly line. This division of labor is further discussed on p. 456, where Marx really begins to analyze how industrialism had changed labor; he argues that each option becomes crystallized into an exclusive function of a particular worker (also see p. 457).

Organic and heterogeneous arrangements both divide labor progressively across space and time. Work is encapsulated and developed (i.e., woven), and manufactured products develop linearly by being moved from one station to another, from one job to another. Both arrangements are also highly managed: line workers are unable to see the overall shape of the product they are assembling. In both arrangements, modular work entails standardizing parts, materials, and actions. It also entails *deskilling*, in which tasks are broken down into easily learnable and repeatable components, decision making is reserved for management, and automation becomes prevalent.

Chained activity networks, as discussed in Chapter 3, essentially assume and model this mass production configuration. By separating activities and conceptualizing their relationships in terms of production and consumption, chained activity networks portray complex work as a process, a series of spatial and temporal moves that progressively develop the network's cumulative object. Relations among activities are circumscribed, black-boxed, with links limited to maximize control and enforce the process. Workers are focused on the object of their own activity system. This understanding of work leads us to expect singularity rather than multiplicity, monocontextuality rather than polycontextuality, hand-offs rather than conversations, arborescent rather than rhizomatic logic. That is, it is geared to a different strategic stance; it has little explanatory power for the events we've seen throughout this book. Its underlying assumptions, its warrants, don't apply to net work.

NET WORK

As indicated above, *net work* is the coordinative work that enables sociotechnical networks – standing sets of transformations – to hold together and form dense interconnections. Net work is deeply interpenetrated, deeply rhizomatic: it has multiple, multidirectional information flows. Yes, work may resemble a process, as in Figure 2.1. But within the black box, work is performed by assemblages of workers and technologies, assemblages that may not be stable from one incident to the next and in which work may not follow predictable or circumscribed paths. These assemblages are spliced settlements that can quickly unravel and just as quickly reform. Under these circumstances, singularity/monocontextuality is impossible to sustain at any significant scale; multiplicity/polycontextuality is inevitable. Trades are not strictly delimited. Neither are organizations.

As the discussion of activity networks in Chapter 3 suggests, overlapping activity networks have developed in part to provide insight into how deeply interpenetrated work can be theorized and studied – to get a handle on the developmental paths that workers travel. Its metaphors (netWORKing, knotworking) deal with the interlinking that is prevalent in this sort of work. Nardi, Whittaker, and Schwarz argue that

> new economic conditions and ways of working require that we expand our theories. A core concept in activity theory is the subject. The unproblematic assumption of a subject works well in classical activity theory which took the perspective of the individual (Leont'ev, 1974). However, if we want to study joint activity, which is essential for understanding the networked nature of today's workplace, the development of a collective subject is important. It has probably been pertinent all along to study collective subjects, but current conditions make this omission even more obvious. It is time to ask questions such as: How and why do people get together for collective activity? How do people find and communicate with one another for purposes of joint work? Can we rely on notions

of "teams" and "communities of practice" to understand collectivities in today's workplace? Our data suggest that these concepts are *insufficient* to account for important forms of collective activity in the modern workplace. (2002, p. 207, my emphasis; cf. Kaptelinin & Nardi, 2006, pp. 26–28)

Yes, insufficient! A unitary subject, a singularity, is adequate if work is kept corralled in the heterogeneous or organic relationships that Marx describes, Taylor prescribes, and chained activity networks inscribe. But arguably it was never quite sufficient for understanding even those circumscribed sorts of activities (Blackler, Crump, & McDonald, 2003). And in an organization like Telecorp, whose strategic stance requires that every point be connected to every other, a unitary subject is entirely inadequate. Rather, we're faced with collective subjects, composite subjects whose stability is punctuated by changes in the assemblages that constitute them, *cyborgs* (Haraway, 1991; Ronfeldt, 2007, pp. 22–23).

Telecorp is, in this respect, similar to other organizations that do what is often called knowledge work. These organizations are shifting from modular, hierarchical forms of organization to networked forms. Below, I discuss this shift in terms of economics, broad cultural trends of organization, and power issues associated with networked organizations.

Net Work and Informational Capitalism

The shift from hierarchical to networked organization is discussed in economic terms by Manuel Castells in *The Rise of the Network Society* (1996). Castells argues that capitalism has been profoundly restructured as "informational capitalism":

Capitalism itself has undergone a process of profound restructuring, characterized by greater flexibility in management; decentralization and networking of firms both internally and in their relationships to other firms; considerable empowering of capital vis-à-vis labor, with the concomitant decline of influence of the labor movement; increasing individualization and diversification of working relationships; massive incorporation of women into the working force, usually under discriminatory conditions; intervention of the state to deregulate markets selectively, and to undo the welfare state, with different intensity and orientations depending upon the nature of political forces and institutions in each society; stepped-up global economic condition, in a context of increasing geographic and cultural differentiation of settings for capital accumulation and management. (pp. 1–2)

Castells argues that the traditional, hierarchically organized form of work is eroding (p. 268). Employment now is characterized by decentralized data entry (p. 248); the concentration of higher-level operations in the hands of skilled workers (p. 248); multiskilling of jobs (p. 251); the individualization of responsibility (p. 251) and labor (p. 265); and segregation by education (p. 251).

Telecommunications and digital technologies play a critical role in enabling networked organizations, and vice versa:

> [W]hat characterizes the current technological revolution is not the centrality of knowledge and information, but the application of such knowledge and information to knowledge generation and information processing/communication devices, in a cumulative feedback loop between innovation and the uses of innovation. . . . The uses of new telecommunications technologies in the last two decades have gone through three distinct stages: automation of tasks, experimentation of uses, reconfiguration of applications. In the first two stages, technological innovation progressed through learning by using. . . . In the third stage, the users learned technology by doing, and ended up reconfiguring the networks, and finding new applications. (p. 32)

He concludes, "The new social and economic organization based on the information technologies aims at decentralizing management, individualizing work, and customizing markets, thereby segmenting work and fragmenting societies" (p. 265).

Castells offers a straightforward assessment of this shift. Some in the business literature have discussed the implications for work organization in more detail and with considerably more optimism. For instance, in *The Support Economy*, Shoshana Zuboff and James Maxmin argue that work organization is about to experience a fundamental paradigm shift in which control is distributed across customers, just as ownership is currently distributed across stockholders. They argue that this shift to distributed capitalism will be enabled by digital technologies but also through individual consumption (the desire for unique identities and experiences); the resulting increase in relational value; and the desire for unique support (stable and trustworthy relations among consumers and producers providing these experiences). In this new distributed economy, the existing enterprise logic is no longer operative; supply chains are dismantled; and "advocates" – professional relationship workers – assemble temporary "federations" of suppliers for each transaction or service (cf. Castells, 1996, pp. 154–168; Malone, 2004, p. 31). (Notice that this description of *federation* sounds quite similar to the sorts of brokering that telecoms perform as they negotiate lease rates for lines and bring other telecoms into their networks.) In distributed work, the emphasis shifts from predictable, monodirectional flows of information and services to unpredictable, multidirectional flows (cf. Boczkowski, 2005), and services and products are constantly adjusted or "co-configured":

> Co-configuration work occurs at the interface of the firm, the customer, and the products or services. It requires constant interaction among the firm, the customer, and the product. The result is that the product continuously adjusts to what the customer wants. Co-configuration creates customer-intelligent value in products or services, where the lines between product and customer knowledge become blurred and interwoven. (Victor & Boynton, 1998, p. 14)

Examples of co-configuration range from the complex and exclusive (e.g., open-source software development) to the simple and inclusive (e.g., user-generated content such as the popular reviews feature on Amazon.com).

Net Work and the Information Age

While Castells and others focus on the economic aspects of net work, others examine the organizational aspects in the context of broad organizational trends across human cultural development. For instance, in their book on networked organization, Lipnack and Stamps (1996) argue that "the network is emerging as the signature form of organization in the Information Age, just as bureaucracy stamped the Industrial Age, hierarchy controlled the Agricultural Era, and the small group roamed in the Nomadic Era" (p. 3). They argue that networks have five key organizing principles: unifying purpose; independent members; voluntary links; multiple leaders; and integrated levels (p. 18). Networks, they say, exist at the top of "organizational sediments" that include the previous forms (bureaucracies, hierarchies, and small groups) (p. 35). In this latest phase, the Information Age, "relationships are the dominant reality" (p. 42) and links across agents increase dramatically, leading to greater horizontal complexity across and within organizations. Those links convey the benefits of flexibility, power, and speed (p. 70), but only if the complexity can be managed.

Drawing on Lipnack and Stamps as well as others in this vein, Ronfeldt (2007) argues that in Information Age networks, "people who are far removed from each other can connect, coordinate, and act conjointly across barriers and distances" – and although membership can also serve tribal identity, that's not the point: "this form is suited to enabling people to address modern, complex policy issues that may require efforts from many directions at the same time" (p. 22). In such networks, Ronfeldt says, what matters is not bloodline but ideas; members have "fluid, multiple identities"; and networks themselves have "blurred, indefinite boundaries" (pp. 22–23). Ronfeldt goes on to argue that

> the information revolution strengthens and favors network forms of organization. The new information and communications technologies – all that make up the Net, the Web, the Grid – are enabling dispersed, often small, once-isolated groups and individuals to connect, coordinate, and act conjointly as never before. Power and influence are migrating to actors who are skilled at developing multiorganizational networks and operating in contexts in which such networks are common, as evidenced by the rise of transnational networks of environmental, human-rights, and other [non-governmental organizations] that represent civil society – not to mention terrorist and criminal organizations that represent uncivil society. It is also evident among businesses that form strategic partnerships, and among interagency mechanisms that operate at many levels of government. All are pursuing network designs, although non-state actors remain generally ahead of state actors at adopting them. These trends, projected into the future, seem to augur major transformations in how the world's advanced societies will be organized – or, if not societies as a whole, then at least key sectors of their governments, economies, and civil societies. (pp. 9–10)

Such changes are certainly not universally positive.

Net Work and the Informatics of Domination

Various commentators have warned about the potential and actual threats of transitioning to networked forms of organization. For instance, Gilles Deleuze (1995) argues that whereas the twentieth century was primarily marked by *disciplinary societies* (in Foucault's terms), the twenty-first will be dominated by *control societies*. He foregrounds the drawbacks of "the ultra-rapid forms of apparently free-floating control that are taking over from the old disciplines at work within the time scales of closed systems. . . . With the breakdown of the hospital as a site of confinement, for instance, community psychiatry, day hospitals, and home care initially presented new freedoms, while at the same time contributing to mechanisms of control as rigorous as the harshest confinement" (p. 178). Deleuze argues that this control society poses a threat that rivals that of the disciplinary society Foucault described.

In the disciplinary society, factories produced a body of workers that could be controlled en masse by management, as well as an avenue of mass resistance via unions. But in the control society, a linear, static, modular type of work (e.g., factories producing goods) gives way to a nonlinear, shifting, interconnected arrangement (e.g., businesses producing services). In this new control society, individuals relate to each other, compete against each other, and their wages fluctuate continually, "bringing them into a state of constant metastability punctuated by ludicrous challenges, competitions, and seminars" (p. 179). The result is a sort of "endless postponement" rather than a defined avenue of development; workers travel in continuously changing "orbits," they "undulate," they find themselves switching jobs and careers and positionalities (p. 180). The factory is gone, as are unions and lifetime employment; the best way to get a raise is to switch jobs. Capitalism in a control society becomes distributed and "essentially dispersive": "it's a capitalism no longer directed toward production but toward products, that is, toward sales or markets" (p. 181). Capitalism in a control society promises more freedom and empowerment for workers, but critics charge that it often does not deliver (Clark, 2007; Gee, Hull, & Lankshear, 1996; Longaker, 2006).

Like Deleuze, Donna Haraway outlines the threats of what she calls the "informatics of domination": the systematic deskilling of workers and their resulting vulnerability; the "homework economy" in which the workday is no longer limited and work is no longer confined to the workplace thanks to new technologies; the decentralization of state power, with increased surveillance and control; and the massive intensification of insecurity (1991). In shifting from monodirectional to multidirectional information flows and from limiting to proliferating links among heterogeneous entities, net work has shifted from the Panopticon to the Agora, which is to say, from surveillance by an authority figure to mutual, distributed surveillance and critique – as popular works have begun to highlight (Hewitt, 2005; Locke et al., 2001; Reynolds, 2006; Tapscott & Williams, 2006). Black boxes are undone and redone. We monitor ourselves and each other.

This shift is not restricted to the economic sector, however. Even warfare, which has long been the domain of the state and implemented through strong hierarchies, is being radically reconfigured through initiatives that emphasize decentralization; spontaneous self-organization; information technologies; and recombinant alliances among militaries, governments, and nongovernmental organizations (Arquilla & Ronfeldt, 2001b; Atkinson & Moffatt, 2005; Boot, 2007; Edwards, 2000; Ronfeldt & Arquilla, 2007).

Al Qaeda is, of course, a networked organization. But one good example of a spontaneously forming network is that of the passengers of Flight 93, who turned on their mobile phones after being hijacked, only to find out what had happened to the other planes on that terrible day. With this information, they swarmed the terrorists, defeating them – though at an awful price (see Reynolds, 2006).

In such an environment, it's no wonder that people have begun to adapt techniques and technologies from office life to manage their home life as well (Allen, 2003; Covey, 1990; Geisler, 2003). Time management gurus Stephen R. Covey and David Allen separately declare that they see no practical difference between home and work life; Cheryl Geisler finds in her studies of personal digital assistants that although a difference does remain for some PDA users, it appears to be eroding. Other technologies meant for the business environment, such as text messaging, have flourished in informal social networks and facilitate far-flung social connections (Sun, 2006). At the same time, work has become more fragmented, leading to a wealth of research on how workers manage and organize the surfeit of information (e.g., Czerwinski, Horvitz, & Wilhite, 2004; Gonzalez & Mark, 2004, 2005; Hutchings et al., 2004; Johnson-Eilola, 2005; Mark, Gonzalez, & Harris, 2005) and in an explosion of time management and "lifehacking" resources. Similar trends can be seen in journalism (Boczkowski, 2005), warfare (Arquilla & Ronfeldt, 2001b), and education (Paretti, McNair, & Holloway-Attaway, 2007).

In net work, digital technologies play a vital role in forming, interconnecting, and even dispersing nodes; consumption is individuated as the desire for unique identities and unique experiences; relationships between customers and businesses become more important, even as the distinctions between them become unclear; and customers look for stable beneficial relationships among consumers and producers that support these individual experiences (cf. Sless, 1994). These needs are supplied not by large, vertically integrated companies but by temporary "federations" of suppliers for each individual transaction. These federations are endlessly recombinant. Lifelong employment is replaced by what Zuboff and Maxmin call "lifelong learning" – what Donna Haraway calls "continual deskilling and retraining," and Castells calls "multiskilling" – as workers cope with continually changing arrangements.

In this shift toward net work, negotiation becomes an essential skill. Trust becomes an ongoing project (Benkler, 2006). Organizations become looser aggregations held together by alliances, and agility entails constantly having to work to reaffirm and redefine alliances (Alberts & Hayes, 2003;

Atkinson & Moffat, 2005). *Rhetoric becomes an essential area of expertise*; direct connections mean that everyone can and should be a rhetor (Carter, 2005). Taylor gives way to Machiavelli.

We can see the signs of a shift toward net work in the service sector, in the outsourcing of technical support, and in places like eBay and Craigslist. But we can also see it in the rise of homeschooling, the emergence of telecommunication-based distance education models, the weakening of unions, the shift from stable identity politics to unstable political subsegments, the popularity of automobile customization, the increasing importance of content management systems, and the early success of Howard Dean's campaign. We see it in social networking software, from the early message boards studied by Shoshanna Zuboff (1988) to later iterations such as blogs, del.icio.us, Flickr, and Facebook. We certainly see it in the open-source movement.

In this context, organizational, spatial, and temporal boundaries become less important than the fluctuating networked connections. Organizational charts are maps that do not show the hidden passes of the organization. Net work involves establishing and negotiating those hidden passes, organizing work through weaving and splicing. It means making connections and circulating things: texts, money and its many representations, heterogeneous resources, and people. It means bringing different trades and activities into contact: massive influxes of social languages, genres, and chronotopes (Bakhtin, 1981, 1984, 1986) that then have to centripetalize and organize. It means interrupted development, stochastic development (Bateson, 1979). It means multiplicity. And consequently, it means that everything is transformed, including the workers who transform everything else; in activity theory's terms, workers are part of the activity's composite *object* as well as its composite *subject*.

This phenomenon is described in actor–network theory as "polycentric" actor–networks (Callon, 1992, p. 83) and in activity theory as "polycontextuality" and "border-crossing" between activity systems (Engeström, Engeström, & Kärkkäinen, 1995). Callon argues that "in a sense actors do not really exist outside texts and the sequences of actions these suggest" (2002, p. 199). So let's look at how these texts weave and splice net work.

THREE SENSES OF TEXTS

Here, I mean "texts" broadly speaking: literature, instructional materials, printed forms, Web sites, computer interfaces, hash marks on sticky notes, and checks and annotations on lists, just to name a very few. Let's use King and Frost's broad definition: "the creation of a concrete representation on some medium (e.g., paper) of abstract symbols that refer to something concrete – in the world of things, ideas, feelings, and so forth" (2002, p. 5). The number and variety of texts have increased dramatically with increasing literacy rates and with the proliferation of text-based information technologies. Texts enjoy a special place in both activity theory and actor–network theory because of their mediatory properties. Here, we'll review texts and connect them with the problem of conducting net work.

As we'll see, texts (from *textere*, to weave together) both weave and splice networks. We've seen indications of this point in previous chapters, including the e-mail and database messages in Chapter 1, the trouble tickets in Chapter 2, and the phone bills in Chapter 4. Actor–network theory and activity theory both provide ways for us to think about texts.

Texts weave and splice so successfully because they are *inscriptions*, concrete traces that represent phenomena in stable and circulable ways. They appear in *genres*, regular responses to recurrent situations that can connect activities in continuous, developmental ways while accommodating changes and that function ecologically. And they are *boundary objects*, artifacts that serve as mutual reference points across different activities while retaining different meanings within these activities. As I argued in Chapter 1, we can trace the trajectory of genres as they circulate through and build networks of human activity.

Inscriptions

Texts are *inscriptions*.

In his studies of scientists, Latour notes how central inscriptions are in performing their work. The key, Latour argues, is in transforming the substance to be studied into an easily manipulable representation that is usually about the size of a desktop or smaller. "No matter what the (reconstructed) size of the phenomena, they all end up being studied only when they reach the same average size" – galaxies and chromosomes both become represented on similarly sized sheets of paper (Latour, 1990, p. 45). Once they reach that size, they can be mastered: "There is nothing you can *dominate* as easily as a flat surface of a few square meters" (p. 45). In this conversion, the materiality of the process gets deleted (Bowker & Star, 1999; Star & Griesemer, 1989), allowing the texts' readers to work with abstractions. (Recall how this worked for Gil in Credit & Collections, as described in Chapter 1.)

Inscriptions are "relatively immutable media that resist transport" (Callon, 1991, p. 135). This resistance leads some actor–network theorists to call them "immutable mobiles": referential inscriptions that can circulate from one locale to another while resisting deformation (Latour, 1987, p. 227). These circulating rerepresentations undergo standing sets of transformations, weaving and splicing together the material assemblage that is the sociotechnical network.

They also create realities – sort of. In representing phenomena, inscriptions link those phenomena to particular activities. And, John Law argues, multiplying inscriptions *multiplies the realities that they describe* (2004a). That's not as counterintuitive as it sounds. Recall Annemarie Mol's study of atherosclerosis that I cited in Chapter 1. Health care workers from different fields look at the same phenomenon in different ways, using different inscriptions, and come up with very different understandings of the phenomenon. This doesn't mean that the different medical fields are solipsistic, but it does mean that their different practices and inscriptions produce different kinds of knowledge, understanding, and belief about reality. Realities, statements about realities, and inscription devices are all produced together (Law, 2004a). As Law argues, "Multiplicity is the product or the effect of different sets of inscription devices and practices . . . producing different and conflicting standards about reality" (p. 32). And these different realities overlap and interfere with one another (p. 61).

Genres

Texts belong to *genres*.

Inscriptions provide a way to fix, record, and dominate phenomena by capturing representations. But for these inscriptions to circulate more widely and regularly, and for them to interact in predictable ways with other inscriptions, they can't be entirely idiosyncratic. Types of inscriptions tend to develop over time within particular activities to meet recurrent needs. These *genres* provide a developmental, stabilizing influence on human activity. For instance, people in different locations, disciplines, and cultures read maps in similar ways because the genre of the map has become regularized enough to sustain stable interpretive strategies. Genres tend to be living, constantly adapting and hybridizing with other genres in order to fit more particular and restricted situations while providing regularity and stability. Genres are, then, *woven* or developed over time to respond to recurrent situations but also *spliced* or hybridized to adapt to local conditions and intersecting activities. And *tracing* them allows us to examine how they circulate through and build networks of activity (Spinuzzi, 2003b).

Genre, in the sense that I am using it here, is a behavioral rather than a structural construct, a tool-in-use. As Schryer, Lingard, and Spafford define it, "Genres are constellations of regulated improvisational strategies triggered by the interaction between individual socialization, or habitus, and an organization or field" (2007, p. 31; cf. Russell, 1997a; Spinuzzi, 2003b). It is a way of talking about how people regularly interpret and use texts. Such texts, including computer interfaces and related technological artifacts, can be and have been productively examined in terms of genre (e.g., Antunes & Costa, 2003; Orlikowski & Yates, 1994; Spinuzzi, 2003b; Yates & Orlikowski, 2002; Zachry, 2000). A genre analysis of a particular technological artifact can be useful for understanding how the artifact is typically interpreted and used, but any given artifact is typically used in concert with others. That is, genres are used in assemblages or complexes; few if any technological activities use just one, and most use great clouds of them.

Genre theorists have discussed extensively how genres tend to work within assemblages, usually conceptualized as sets, systems, repertoires, or ecologies (see Spinuzzi, 2004, for a review). For instance, a worker at Telecorp tends to draw on multiple genres simultaneously to make sense of a case, organize her work, coordinate with others, and solve problems: database entries, phone conversations, F1 notes, lists, stacks of paper, and dozens of other genres collectively mediate her activity. And like the individual genres, these genre ecologies tend to be both woven (developing over time into stable configurations that can be conveyed to others) and spliced (rhizomatic, including opportunistic additions, innovations, and comediations). They provide, as I said in Chapter 1, stability-with-flexibility. The stability comes from the *associations* developed among genres through long practice: workers in the Network Operations Center (NOC) knew, for instance, how to coordinate "winpops" (instant messages) with their phone conversations and database records. The flexibility comes from the *substitutions* that workers are able to make in the genre ecology: if "winpops" aren't available, NOC workers could shout their messages to the room or pass handwritten notes. (These associations and substitutions are reminiscent of the sociotechnical graphs discussed in Latour, Mauguin, & Teil, 1992.)

Boundary Objects

Texts function as *boundary objects.*

Star and Griesemer define boundary objects as "objects which are both plastic enough to adapt to local needs and the constraints of the several parties employing them, yet robust enough to maintain a constant identity across sites" (1989, p. 393). Boundary objects are material links between two or more activities, functioning differently in each activity, providing a productive difference and often a coordinative role.

Boundary objects can be texts, but they are often other objects that take on a representational function. For instance, in their seminal article, Star and Griesemer describe how trappers and collectors obtained animal carcasses that then made their way into Berkeley's Museum of Vertebrate Zoology. The carcasses certainly weren't texts, but they did perform representational functions for each actor involved in the collection process. Those representations weren't identical: their differences were productive differences, differences that caused them to circulate toward the museum.

Boundary objects are mediated by other representations, which often must accompany them on their journey across boundaries. "Without a label," confides one of Star and Griesemer's zoologist friends, "a specimen is just dead meat" (p. 401). So a boundary object is often an *assemblage* of related texts (inscriptions, genres) that collectively plays different roles in overlapping activities. These different roles allow boundary objects to support what Etienne Wenger calls "boundary practices," which constitute "a form of collective brokering" among domains (1998, p. 114).

But the different roles are often papered over to provide the illusion that the boundary object works the same everywhere. As John Leslie King and Robert L. Frost (2002) argue, the Roman Catholic Church and the creation of constitutional government both used "ambiguating technologies" to manage distance work. King and Frost discuss two types of immutable mobiles – texts and money – in ways that brilliantly point out the necessary ambiguities and slippages that make the system work. Such ambiguities, they demonstrate, were necessary to manage distant relationships across time and space.

So texts are *inscriptions* that represent phenomena, belong to *genres* that construct relatively stable relationships, and function as *boundary objects* that bridge among different activities. Texts create circulating rerepresentations: representations that themselves become represented by other representations (Latour, 1999b). In doing so, texts help define the groups that they weave and splice together. Circulating texts means circulating relatively similar text types (genres) that splice activities by forging a connection where one did not exist and weave activities by serving as a boundary connection in a developing activity.

Below, I primarily focus on genres as they characterize texts and relations and as they function as boundary objects circulating among activities.

FOUR CASES OF NET WORK

Genres are intermediaries. As Callon (1991) describes it, actors are drawn into relationships through intermediaries; "an intermediary is anything passing between actors which defines the relationship between them" (p. 134). They include inscriptions ("relatively immutable media that resist transport"); technical artifacts; human beings (with "the skills, the knowledge, and the know-how that they incorporate"); and money (p. 135). These intermediaries "describe their networks in the literary sense of the term. And they compose them by giving them form" (p. 135).

With this in mind, let's trace the genres, examining their trajectories to see how they splice and weave together the network of activities at Telecorp. We'll look at four cases as we follow an order, follow the money, follow the substitutions, and follow the workers.

CASE 1: FOLLOWING AN ORDER

Let's follow an order to get a sense of how texts circulate – as inscriptions and as genres – and to see how circulating rerepresentations, or series of transformations, weave and splice together Telecorp's activities. For simplicity, we'll use the functional groups from Telecorp's organizational chart to delineate these activities.

A phone service order could start in many places, but let's follow an order originating in Customer Service. Figure 5.1 is a flow diagram (Beyer & Holtzblatt, 1998), in which worker roles are depicted along with the textual artifacts they use to transfer information to each other.

Priscilla, an experienced Customer Service worker, received a call from a customer who wanted to switch to Telecorp's local service. First, she pulled up the AS/400 window and entered the customer's phone number to determine his current service. Next, she filled out an application form, prompting the customer for information that she needed for each blank on the form. She looked up the customer's information on BigTel's database, to which Telecorp has access, and then she began to fill out credit check information on Telecorp's intranet. After hanging up, she finished filling out this information, then brought up the resulting file order confirmation (FOC) form and printed it, filing the printout in an alphabetizer on her desk. She saved

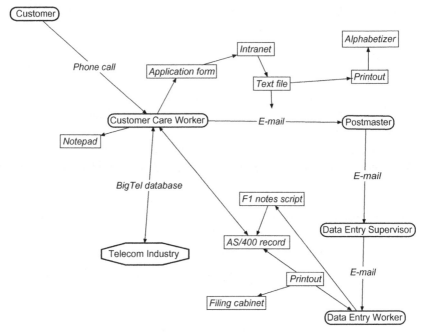

FIGURE 5.1. A flow diagram of an order being placed.

it as a text file under the customer's first and last name. Then she retrieved the printout and filed it. Eventually, she e-mailed the saved text file to the postmaster, who routed it to the appropriate group for further data entry.

The data entry group was formed just after I began my observations; until that point, data entry had been done by Customer Service workers between phone calls. This group consisted of workers who were completely new to Telecorp and generally new to telecommunications. Its data entry sessions doubled as training sessions. Here, workers received FOCs from their supervisor via e-mail, printed them out, and used highlighters and pens to mark them up – initially in similar ways, then more idiosyncratically, and eventually almost not at all. They entered the relevant (usually highlighted) information into the AS/400 then checked each other's work for errors. They also entered F1 notes describing their changes, using the script mentioned in Chapter 1.

And let's stop there. We could go further by tracing the work into CLEC Provisioning, where the next available phone number is obtained from a set of unassigned numbers provided to Telecorp by an industry organization, where the billing address and premises address are separated, and where

911 information is entered into the database – and from there to CLEC Design, where the circuit is actually designed; the CLEC switch, where the circuit is actually entered; and Billing, where the billing information and account activity are brought together in monthly printouts. But we have enough work to examine already!

I've illustrated this work in Figure 5.1 as a flow diagram (see Beyer & Holtzblatt, 1998), which does a nice job of illustrating how worker roles were connected through the circulation of documents. But in emphasizing flow, Figure 5.1 elides some important information about how this net work is being done.

There Was No "Order"

First, there was no "order." The inscriptions collectively constituted the order, or rather aspects of it. The "order" was a black box containing several related texts, on- and offline, within and without Telecorp: a relatively stable set of transformations through circulating rerepresentations. What the customer thought of as the order, the set of information s/he gave to the Customer Service worker, was atomized and sent to different parts of Telecorp to be processed. Like the atherosclerosis that Mol (2002) described, the order was articulated differently by the different functional groups. As Law suggests, when Telecorp's workers multiply inscriptions, they multiply realities (2004a).

This multiplicity continued as orders progressed into other functional groups. In CLEC Provisioning, for instance, workers entered orders into a Microsoft Access database. They distinguished between that database, which they characterized as order tracking, and the AS/400, which they characterized as customer history. However, the Access database was not well maintained: provisioners complained about its reliability and assumed that other functional groups did not need to see how orders progressed through CLEC Provisioning. Instead, provisioners developed a system of manila folders with order information, including a detailed checklist for processing orders and tracking their progress, and circulated these folders from desk to desk. One provisioner, Joshua, remarked: "Each person has a little bit of information on that order. And that's why we need to track down each person." And since each order was really a set of interrelated inscriptions bound together in a folder, when workers from other functional groups (such as the NOC or Bill Verification) wanted to check on an order, they had to call CLEC Provisioning and track down the worker who currently had the folder.

This problem, incidentally, was shared by the entire rapidly changing industry. As Joshua told me:

> Getting people to put people to put all of the information in the same place so the next person can come in and see okay, this is what's wrong about the order...I find that that's also a problem with other CLECs and other LECs. For instance, BigTel has that exact same problem with tracking remarks, tracking comments, tracking notes. They have a difficult problem with that, so when we call to get information from them, they don't have [it] because so-and-so didn't put it in their order where they were supposed to. So I think that's kind of an industrywide kind of problem.

There Was No Transportation without Transformation

Second, there was "no transportation without transformation" (Latour, 1996a, p. 119). The inscriptions circulated, but they did so by going through standing sets of transformations to meet different needs. For instance, when Data Entry workers received the e-mailed FOCs, they needed to enter information on only a handful of lines from the FOCs to do their work. (One trainee, Karl, told me that the other information was not relevant to him, but it was to others such as "the people throwing the switch.") To filter out the unneeded information, they would print out e-mails, then use up to four colors of highlighters to indicate important information. They also often used pens to circle and annotate information. And although these highlightings and annotations were similar enough that one worker could read another's notes, they were idiosyncratic and change frequently. And as a given worker grew more experienced, she would highlight less frequently, use fewer colors, and annotate less heavily. "You get weaned from the colors," Charity explained, echoing comments made independently by Priscilla, Amanda, Susan, and Maura. Workers became more experienced in reading these printouts, internalizing the ways of reading information that were once externally mediated through the annotations. Figure 5.1 shows the circulation of inscriptions, but it doesn't show the heterogeneous annotations, accretions, and variances that accompanied and enabled this circulation, the rerepresentations that made it work: the ongoing transformations that localized boundary objects (Swarts, 2004; Wolfe, 2002). Genres lent interpretive stability to the activities in which they circulated, but to share a genre, to make it a boundary object that can properly mediate their work, workers had to find ways to tailor it.

There Was a Surplus of Information for Supporting Workers' Discretion

Third, there was a surplus of information for supporting workers' discretion within these inscriptions; they were not just about the order. For instance, one F1 note told Renee in Customer Service that she should not let anyone change a particular account: the customer's wife was alcoholic and may attempt to make unauthorized calls. Other notes, Renee said, were to record experience with customer: "this customer was not nice."

This latter information was important across the company. As Damon at the Internet Help Desk told me:

> Plus we talk. We talk about what the customer... what you're gonna be in for... I mean, you gotta be in the mind-set to handle that, you know... some old dude, screaming, half drunk or something. And they do call in like that. You gotta be in the mind-set to handle that.

This surplus of information allowed texts to reach into different activities, making linkages possible by supporting multiple activities. These texts could be marshaled for a variety of purposes inside and outside Telecorp, as we'll see below.

There Was No Single Genre

Fourth, there was no single genre of inscriptions being circulated across functional units, even if inscriptions were being read and treated as belonging to the "same" genre. As discussed in Chapter 1, even something as restricted as an F1 note was articulated quite differently across the different functional groups. In Customer Service, F1 notes became more enforced, more rigidly defined, and more focused on helping other workers interact with the system and the customers. But in the Network Operations Center, F1 notes have two goals: (1) to cover the worker and Telecorp by providing documentation for every action, and (2) to provide a problem-solving history for any worker who reads the note. NOC workers reported that the NOC manager had hammered the first point home, emphasizing that if an action was not in the notes, it could not be proven. As one NOC worker summarized, "documentation is representation." NOC workers' F1 notes were thus constructed to circulate to problem-solving co-workers, to management, and even to lawyers to be used as evidence in possible lawsuits. Consequently, workers by their own accounts used a narrative structure; wrote in plain language, using generally recognized terminology; and

DATE	TIME	USER	REMARKS
——	—	—	————————
07/26/00	09:32:00	FRED	TICKET ADDED
07/26/00	09:58:00	FRED	CUST BILL SMITH CALLED STATED THAT A BIGTEL TECH WAS AT THE PREM TO INSTALL 2 ISDN LINES AND GAVE THE CUST THE NUMBERS TO THE LINES AS 555–0609 & 5550611. CUST IS NOT ABLE TO USE THE LINES AND CANT LOG ON TO THE SYSTEM. IN AS400 WE ARE NOT SHOWING AS ISDN LINES WE HAVE A FEW AS MODEMLINES NOT ISDN LINES. NUMBERS DID NOT MATCH
07/26/00	11:41:00	EDDIE	ARNOLD/CUSXX DOES NOT SHOW ORDER COMPLETED AND WILL DO SOME CHECKING
07/26/00	11:42:00	EDDIE	RESOLUTION CHANGED FROM TO PEND
07/26/00	12:26:00	EDDIE	REFERRED OUT TO CHANGED FROM CUSXX TO BIGTEL
07/26/00	12:26:00	EDDIE	ARNOLD/CUSXX CALLED IN AND STATED TKT WAS OPENED WITH BIGTEL PROBLEM ON THE LINES. THEY HAVE HANDED IT TO THE CO. FOR A FURTHER INFO ON THIS CALL 555*5555909 AND REFERENCE 33.IBJD.000296 OR ORDER N975725
07/26/00	13:06:00	ADAMW	THE ABOVE # DAN/BIGTEL GAVE IS DISCONNECTED ADAMW
07/26/00	13:23:00	ADAMW	SPESKING WITH KARA/BIGTEL LSP AND SHE STATED THE DUE DATE ON THIS WAS 7/14
07/26/00	13:34:00	ADAMW	AND LOOKS LIKE IT WAS MISSED. SHE IS RESEARCHING THIS NOW.

FIGURE 5.2. A series of F1 notes written by NOC workers.

noted contacts that the workers made with customers and other vendors. (How easy were these for laypeople to understand? You be the judge; see Figure 5.2.)

In other words, a note was not just a note. F1 notes were written in different functional areas to perform different goals and to be read by different people. They were usually written with an explicit understanding of who the audience would be. And furthermore, as we saw in Customer Service, the genre expectations for F1 notes had changed radically, but those expectations could remain local to functional areas; new trainees may have had slips of paper to guide them in writing notes, for instance, but old hands had learned their own way of writing F1 notes and didn't use those slips (see Chapter 6). Even in a single functional area, then, we find differences in how workers were trained to circulate knowledge of an account.

This multiplicity of F1 notes built in adaptation but also robustness. The genre, though relatively stable, drifted over time and across divisions of labor, as it had to if it was to support activities that diverge as much as these functional groups did. As it drifted, localized features of the genre developed to support links that could be activated with still other activities (e.g., the legal system).

Summary: Following an Order

Texts, as I said, weave and splice networks. In their circulation, they tie together, mediate, and relate the functional areas that work together to collectively accomplish the order.

In Case 1, such texts were cast in relatively stable genres, and thus worked as boundary objects that can be shared across functional groups. To the degree that they were stable, they *wove together* these functional groups: they provided relatively stable points of communication and collaboration; they ensured some degree of codevelopment, since shared texts still had to be interpretable by the groups that shared them; they ensured that out of a sea of inscriptions, new workers would be able to isolate and artic-ulate just the inscriptions that they had to circulate to other groups, an especially important function given Telecorp's high turnover; and in the case of Customer Service and the Data Entry group, shared texts reflected and affirmed the shared heritage of these two groups, which had very recently split. Similarly, the FOCs provided stable boundary objects that workers could share, even as they annotated these texts in order to localize them.

At the same time, these texts served as one way to associate historically disparate and heterogeneous activities, *splicing* them together. This action is most easily seen in the F1 notes, where alcoholic wives, lawyers, vendors, dogs, lines, rival companies, and disparate functional groups are strung together and articulated. But it is also seen in divergences in genres, which marked varying temporalities and linkages. One example is the difference in F1 notes across functional groups such as Customer Service and the NOC. Another is the *historical* differences in F1 notes, which reflected Telecorp's significant changes over the years and which could pop up at any time. For instance, Karl in Data Entry reported that he had had trouble decipher-ing older F1 notes (circa 1989), which predated the F1 script and typically comprised just "a couple of words." In Case 2, we'll see another example of this sort of splicing.

CASE 2: FOLLOWING THE MONEY

Orders were, of course, services rendered for money. But money was itself another kind of text that was received and rerepresented at Telecorp. Once an order was processed, Telecorp put the customer on a billing cycle and sent out monthly bills. Customers paid these bills – or not. If the bills were paid, they were processed by Cash Posting; if they were not, the account was sent to Credit & Collections. Comparing the two functional units' work is fascinating.

Following the Money in Cash Posting

In Cash Posting, Carly received customers' envelopes from the mailroom. The envelopes typically contained invoice stubs and checks, but they could also contain cash (including change), notes explaining why a bill had not been paid or partially paid, or even responses to customer surveys and spontaneous praises or complaints. To process these envelopes, Carly did what her co-workers in Cash Posting did: she set up an elaborate system of stacks for unopened envelopes, invoices, checks, cash, and notes. She also got out an adding machine, the kind that prints numbers on a roll of white paper as they are added. Together, these many texts were combined and coordinated (Slattery, 2005) in different ways to ensure that customers had paid.

The stacks that Carly and others used were not in themselves textual genres. But they provided a relatively stable, easily interpreted way of addressing or mediating recurrent situations. They were interpreted and used similarly by workers across the company and indeed in most U.S. offices and beyond. They provided rich interpretive cues that allowed workers to mediate their work. They sequentially coordinated other genres (e.g., a stack of invoices). They differentiated completed tasks from pending tasks (e.g., a face-up stack represented tasks to complete, while a face-down stack represented completed tasks). They kept the workers' place in a complex task (the top item on the face-up stack is always the current task). They signaled progress in a complex task, both to the stack's owner and to other workers (through, e.g., the stack's height). And they separated different types of genres and tasks (e.g., separate stacks for checks, cash, and invoices; separate stacks for different projects). Indeed, stacks were *the* central way for Carly and her

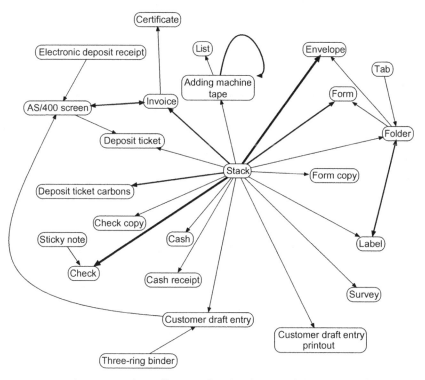

FIGURE 5.3. A genre ecology diagram showing how Cash Posting workers used genres to coordinate each other (adapted from Spinuzzi 2002a).

co-workers to coordinate the many genres they had to progressively recombine on their desktops. See Figure 5.3, which is not a flow diagram but a genre ecology diagram (Spinuzzi, 2003b), a way of visualizing the mediational relationships among genres. The thicker the lines, the more common the observed coordination was across workers.

The stack was a highly developed genre used to transform the other genres by coordinating them. For instance, workers would use stack types in specific orders. In one example, workers who were posting payments would initially form mixed-genre stacks for unprocessed payments, each of which would contain cash, checks, invoices, notes from customers, and so forth encapsulated in envelopes. As they processed the payments, they would form separate stacks for cash, checks, invoices, and other genres, usually topped by adding machine tape that summarized the stack's contents. These separate stacks were distinguished not just by contents but also by spatial arrangement: each worker would place each stack in the same place.

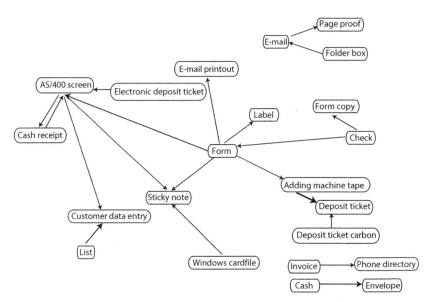

FIGURE 5.4. A genre ecology diagram showing how Cash Posting workers transferred text across genres (adapted from Spinuzzi 2002a).

Such coordination work becomes extremely important in knowledge work as more links to other activities and more heterogeneity intrude, resulting in work fragmentation. To put it another way: if you increase the heterogeneity of texts and the number of links to other activities, you also need to increase standing sets of transformations and black-boxing for handling them. (Beniger [1989] calls this "preprocessing.")

Carly and her co-workers also transformed genres in another way: by transferring text from one genre to another. They wrote cash sums on the envelopes containing the cash; read sums from adding machine tape and wrote them on deposit tickets; and entered cash receipt sums into an AS/400 screen. As these examples illustrate, much of the work in Cash Posting had to do with redundantly calculating and recording sums (Figure 5.4).

Following the Money in Credit and Collections

In contrast, Credit & Collections was categorized and structured primarily by *lists*. Relatively few genres categorized and coordinated each other; of these, lists were the most universal, coordinating workers' interactions with AS/400 screens in all the sessions I observed (Figure 5.5).

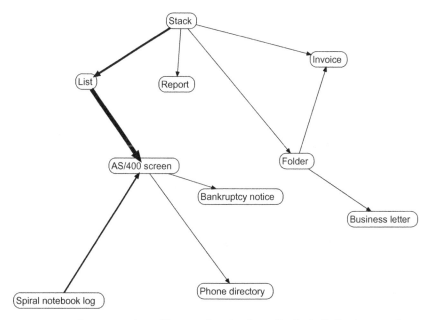

FIGURE 5.5. A genre ecology diagram showing how Credit & Collections workers used genres to coordinate each other (adapted from Spinuzzi 2002a).

Lists were adapted from two sources: a spreadsheet file containing a record of customers to disconnect, and an AS/400-generated report of past due accounts for a given cycle. Although the list sources were different, they coordinated genres in substantially the same way: they were marked up with the same markup system, they led workers to perform actions in the same sequence (top to bottom), and they guided the same set of actions (calling customers, crossing off entries, copying text to AS/400 screens). This coordinative work spliced together heterogeneous inscriptions from heterogeneous activities: banks and courts, for instance, as well as functional groups such as Billing and Cash Posting.

Closer inspection of the observations and the lists suggests that Credit & Collections workers, like their counterparts in Data Entry, had developed a stable, complex system of markings for lists. For instance, in interviews, workers described the system of markings in similar ways, explaining that they were taught the system during initial training and that they used it to interpret each other's progress, even though they claimed these were idiosyncratic. Indeed, on more than one occasion I observed one worker reading another's list to determine the progress and status of his or her

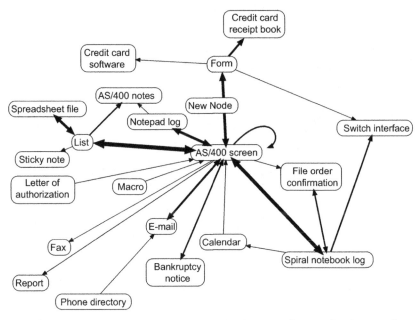

FIGURE 5.6. A genre ecology diagram showing how Credit & Collections workers transferred text across genres (adapted from Spinuzzi 2002a).

work. In transforming these lists, they were able to transform the texts' relationships.

The AS/400 screen was the nexus in terms of transferring text from one genre to another (Figure 5.6). About two-thirds of their work involved copying or transcribing text from one genre to another, and most of these have to do with the AS/400. Credit & Collections workers interacted frequently with customers, and due to the nature of their work, they had to meticulously and redundantly record aspects of each interaction in the AS/400 screen, the spiral notebook log (a phone log), and the notepad log (an action log). They also had to transfer text between AS/400 screens and the list, synchronizing the two so that the list could continue to accurately coordinate their work.

Like other texts, money traveled through circulating rerepresentations: cash, checks, AS/400 entries, adding machine tape, bank account entries, and a variety of other genres. In fact, as we follow money's rerepresentations around, we begin to see them as very similar to the orders in Case 1, and we may even wonder whether there's such a thing as money per se circulating through Telecorp. The cash and checks are eventually taken to the bank, but their rerepresentations continue to circulate and materially affect work; they continue to show up on lists, in databases, in bankruptcy notices and

1-30-01	PER CUST AT COUNTER-HAS PAID COLLECTIONS AGENCY AND PAID
	2 MOS ADVANCE AT COUNTER TO REACT-EMAILED ANNX HILDAX

FIGURE 5.7. A note on an account.

sticky notes, and they continue to be idiosyncratically transformed with scrawled annotations.

We also should remember that the ecology of genres developed in each functional group represented the social languages with which they interacted. For instance, even when workers scrupulously kept notes on the AS/400, knowledge circulation could be disrupted. When Carly received a payment and had to find out how to apply it to an account, she tried to get information on whether an outstanding debt on the account had been paid off and found the note in Figure 5.7.

Hilda was a worker in Collections, so Carly had some idea of how to interpret the note. But she still found it to be unclear:

> Everybody interprets things differently. And I had to ask her [a co-worker in Cash Posting] 'cause she used to be in Collections. And she made it sound like they paid here in the office. But when I read it to somebody else, it sounded like they went downtown and paid a retail merchant. So it just wasn't real clear in the F1 notes whether or not she paid here in the office. Which it turns out she did pay here in the office and the two months for the previous that hadn't billed yet. So it just wasn't real clear if it was here or there. So there was no billed amount, so we put what she paid toward the benefit.

Carly ended up calling Credit & Collections and discussing the problem with Hilda, as often happens, but even this was not as helpful as it might seem:

> Usually we call the person who wrote them. . . . And sometimes you know, they use a lot of abbreviations and so forth that we're not used to, so we do call them and say "What does this say?" or "What does it mean?" But also this happened in January, so even the person that wrote it . . . couldn't even remember giving this to a collections agency.

Abbreviations, specialized terms, and the like marked specialized social languages. And although workers attempted to write in "plain language," as we saw with the example in Figure 5.2, what appears plain to the writer may be difficult for the reader to interpret. At the same time, specialized languages – particularly abbreviations – are necessary because workers had to document thoroughly and quickly in a short amount of time and in a quite limited writing space. NOC workers, for instance, often had four AS/400 windows open at once and would type notes into one account even as they were speaking to customers or vendors about a different account. "Trying to shorten your 20-minute conversation into 10 words is kind of difficult," one former Credit & Collections worker reported with some understatement. Workers tended to pick up social languages within their own functional areas rather quickly, helped by other channels of communication such as interoffice communications and phone calls. "Some [notes and abbreviations] are pretty cryptic but you get used to it," explained Walter, a Credit & Collections worker. But workers in different functional areas, separated from the activity and the constant communication of the area where the note originated, have trouble picking up another area's social language.

Perhaps for this reason, some workers tended to form stable relationships with workers in other functional areas. Those relationships could be positive or negative. For instance, one worker at the Internet Help Desk reported that she had formed a stable working relationship with a worker in Billing Administration: they trusted each other, knew how to talk to each other, and found that their functional areas worked together more smoothly if they functioned as point people. On the other side of the coin, a supervisor in CLEC Provisioning informed an inexperienced provisioner that Fred, a worker at the NOC with whom the provisioner was trying to collaborate, "is such a fuck-up." Similarly, CLEC switch techs described losing trust in one of the salespeople after she gave a collaborating telecommunications company an incorrect list of circuits. Fair or not, these stabilizing relationships provided clues to help workers evaluate each other's contributions, collaborate despite the differences in social languages and activities, and keep texts – and money – circulating.

This issue of trust becomes very important in the shift to net work, in which any node can connect to any other, allowing workers to constitute networks across organizational boundaries. Since Telecorp had no interior, some workers (e.g., workers in CLEC Provisioning, the outside techs, and the NOC) had constant contact with their counterparts in other organizations and had more affinity with their counterparts (in terms of social languages, technical understandings, and assumptions) than they did with others in their own organization. Just as the U.S. Navy is said to be more comfortable working with the British Navy than with the U.S. Army (Alberts & Hayes, 2003), Telecorp workers in technical specialties often found it easier to work with their counterparts at rival telecoms than with their co-workers in different functional groups. Not only did they share a trade and a social language with these competitors, they often even trained at the competitors' workshops. So it was that even though CLEC provisioners distrusted BigTel *as a whole*, they could identify particular BigTel contacts with which they had managed to forge trust. More on this in Case 4.

Summary: Following the Money

Like the order we followed in Case 1, money appeared to be a unitary object but was actually treated as a multiplicity in Telecorp's net work. Its many representations were circulated into related activities, refigured in different genres, and couched in different social languages. And as they circulated, these rerepresentations tied together different functional groups and their different activities. Money's rerepresentations *wove* the activities together by constituting regular ways for workers to relate their activities, standing sets of transformations that developed as the activities of Telecorp developed. But they also *spliced* these activities together by bringing different social languages and different goals into contact.

CASE 3: FOLLOWING THE SUBSTITUTIONS

The NOC, in fact, is an interesting site for the next issue to investigate: the issue of additions and substitutions of genres.

Sociotechnical graphs are an attempt to empirically model assemblages of humans and nonhumans as they associate themselves with each other and intermediate each other. Borrowing from linguistics, Latour et al. (1992) describe these associations as having paradigmatic and syntagmatic dimensions. By *syntagm*, the authors mean the associative dimension, the AND dimension: the human and nonhuman elements that are associated in order to make a statement true. By *paradigm*, they mean the substitutive dimension, the OR dimension: the human and nonhuman elements that can be substituted for each other while keeping the statement true. For instance, let's take the statement "The hotel manager asks his clients to bring their keys back to the front desk" (p. 36). In this example, the statement itself is a syntagm: it assembles a set of heterogeneous units that are associated to make a meaningful and true statement. We can add more units if we like, to make the statement even more specific:

> The hotel manager asks his clients to bring their keys back to the front desk *by checkout time.*

> The hotel manager asks his clients to bring their keys back to the front
> desk by checkout time *and place them in the basket.*

But in addition to associating units, we can substitute them. This is the
paradigmatic dimension:

> The hotel manager asks his clients to bring their *towels* back to the front
> desk.
>
> The hotel manager asks his clients to bring their *maps* back to the front
> desk.
>
> The hotel manager asks his clients to bring their *bags* back to the front
> desk.

Latour et al. (1992) use sociotechnical graphs to parse statements by
users of science and technology and to compare those statements across
users. Doing so allows them to determine, for instance, what actants are
black-boxed (i.e., what clusters of humans and nonhumans are routinely
lumped together by all users), what contradictory accounts exist, and how
stable the associations are across accounts. This approach has its problems,
both theoretically (see Carlson & Gorman, 1992, and Latour's unsatisfactory
response, 1992a) and methodologically (Latour et al. are not terribly clear
on how statements are parsed and do not account for how the accounts
themselves recursively shape the assemblages; see Scott, 1992). But it provides
an interesting model for extending the assemblage work of genre ecologies.
I'll draw on the idea analogically (see Spinuzzi, Hart-Davidson, & Zachry,
2006, for more discussion).

In particular, the syntagmatic and paradigmatic dimensions can be used
to examine genre associations and substitutions in two types of accounts:
observed work and interviews. The two-dimensional examination can allow
us to further explore how genres overlap in particular episodes, how they
mediate individual workers' actions, how they cluster in relatively stable
configurations across workers, and how they are sometimes used idiosyncratically.

In the NOC, workers used a variety of genres to mediate their work. A
very short list of those genres included

> F1 notes, e-mail, "winpops," phone lists, list of worker's active tickets.

Without this string of associated heterogeneous genres (or appropriate
substitutes), the work wouldn't get done. F1 notes provided a detailed history
of the ticket; "winpops" provided a way to broadcast messages to the entire
room; phone lists provided contact information within and without the

company; and the list of active tickets let the worker know what to work on and how long it had been active. All five genres interconnected: workers could use any of these in combination with any of the others, not sequentially but jointly.

But sometimes circumstances intervened. For instance, workers sent what they called "winpops," or short text messages broadcast to all terminals in the NOC, with a program called "winpopup." All workers could receive "winpops," but only those at Windows 98 terminals could send them; those at the newer Windows NT terminals couldn't. So, for instance, when Jack was seated at a Windows 98 terminal, he would send "winpops"; but when he was at an NT terminal, he would instead shout to the entire room: "Ticket 17, CLEC!" This was an explicit substitution, as he demonstrated in a little joke: "26 is CLEC. Nathaniel? You gettin' my winpops?" So we can envision the substitution in the string of associated genres:

F1 notes, e-mail, *yelling at the room*, phone lists, list of worker's active tickets.

Fred also worked at an NT machine, but rather than yelling he wrote his "winpops" on a piece of paper and handed them to specific people. That's not Fred's only substitution. In a more involved example, Fred decided to use a spreadsheet to store his frequently called numbers and his list of active tickets (another example of innovation that transforms existing information). By importing both genres into a spreadsheet, he was able to hybridize them (Spinuzzi, 2003b) with the conventions of the new space, assigning different colors to different pieces of information, for instance. So Fred's string of genres looked more like this:

F1 notes, e-mail, *handwritten notes, spreadsheet phone list, spreadsheet of active tickets*.

Nathaniel, who usually sat next to Fred, became interested in the innovation and had Fred e-mail the file to him. But Nathaniel decided not to use the spreadsheet for his list of active tickets – after all, it entailed entering information that had already been printed out, taking precious time – so he modified the spreadsheet to just contain the phone list:

F1 notes, e-mail, "winpops," *spreadsheet phone list*, list of worker's active tickets.

Table 5.1 summarizes these strings, not in a flow or genre ecology diagram, but in a modification of Latour et al.'s sociotechnical graphs. Observing the associations and substitutions in these strings, as Latour points out, allows

TABLE 5.1. *Viewing genres syntagmatically and paradigmatically: Solving problems in the NOC*

		Syntagmatic dimension
Paradigmatic dimension	General NOC	F1 notes, e-mail, "winpops," phone lists, list of worker's active tickets.
	Jack	F1 notes, e-mail, *yelling at the room*, phone lists, list of worker's active tickets.
	Fred	F1 notes, e-mail, *handwritten notes, spreadsheet phone list, spreadsheet of active tickets.*
	Nathaniel	F1 notes, e-mail, "winpops," *spreadsheet phone list*, list of worker's active tickets.

us to see not only the volatile parts of a network but also the stable ones, the "black boxes." That's an important function because an actant is itself a network (or analogically, a genre intersects, interpenetrates, and "digests" other genres; see Bakhtin, 1981, 1986). Seeing relative stability allows us to black-box actants and treat them as unified wholes; it lets us stop what could become an endless, recursive process of unpacking those black boxes or following those "sticky threads" that, Donna Haraway (1996) tells us, connect everything to everything else. For instance, we can note that workers seemed to treat F1 notes in the same way, without substituting for parts of them, and thus we don't have to examine the narrative and categorical genres that make them up; we don't have to examine F1 notes themselves as an ecology. Instead, we can focus on the substitutions, which tell us about how workers had "componentized" their work and how innovations might change those components.

For instance, we see that Jack used "winpops" when feasible. When not, he settled on a genre that similarly allowed him to broadcast information, and he formulated his pronouncements in very similar ways. Fred settled on a different genre that allowed him to target information, but he still formulated them like a "winpop." Noticing the differences in the substitutions leads us to examine "winpops" more carefully, and we notice that some of them were to the entire room while others were meant for specific people:

Broadcast: "whoever has tkt 2 for today, first 2101 is for you."
Specific: "did you ever ask Fred about tkt 1234?"

Unlike F1 notes, then, "winpops" can be separated syntagmatically into at least two separate genres, each of which addressed a component or recurring purpose in the work. A more detailed study of substitutions could yield more differences among genres.

Such substitutions were quite common: workers individually and collectively drew from the ecology of available genres to adjust their work, and in doing so, connected that work to other activities. In Alarm Management, Oscar began to use Yahoo! Maps to find and plot the lines of local telecoms that had signed agreements with Telecorp. In Network Coordination, Candi used a spreadsheet to track long haul routes, and Leann used Microsoft Access as a simple tool to convert tabular data from one format to another. And in CLEC Provisioning, as we saw earlier, workers used Access to track orders in place of the AS/400 – and then used a system of paper folders and checklists in place of Access. As these genres were adopted and adapted to substitute for other genres, they brought in new capabilities – and new connections to other activities.

Summary: Following the Substitutions

As we follow the substitutions made across these genres, we get a sense of how varied the genre ecology is for these workers. The heterogeneity of genres is potentially put into play by every worker; every worker can now bring new genres into the ecology, hybridize these genres (see Spinuzzi, 2003b), and seek new relations among them. Such genres have developed in different activities and can potentially drag in other genres from those activities and link to these activities' other tools, rules, and social languages, as I've argued elsewhere (Spinuzzi, 2003b). But they can also be spliced in, operating in ways that are utterly unconnected to the genres' developmental histories. When Fred used a spreadsheet to manage phone numbers, or when Leann used Access to convert data, they were splicing.

By viewing genres syntagmatically and paradigmatically, we can get a sense of how these genres are being perceived, used, shared, and transformed. We can see them as black boxes and examine where they come open. We can also see how syntagms – these strings of genres associated with work, which vary widely across workers – become paradigmatically compressed and black-boxed. The genres listed in the syntagmatic–paradigmatic view in Table 5.1 were rarely if ever mentioned in the descriptions NOC workers provide of their own activities; only when I prompted them did they discuss these. And why should they? This sort of splicing work goes on all the time; it is what lets workers manage to keep their work flexible and responsive to changing conditions. At the same time, as workers develop and spread their genres, weaving them into the pattern of their work, they manage to retain relative stability and codevelopment.

But these assemblages' trajectories aren't the last kind of trajectory that we can trace. Workers also have trajectories, and these trajectories carry texts in their wake.

CASE 4: FOLLOWING THE WORKERS

As noted in Chapter 2, workers circulated through Telecorp as well. And as they did, they brought texts with them. Before examining those texts' movements, then, let's look at the workers' many circulations.

Workers circulated *in* quickly: Telecorp was growing rapidly and consequently hired many people, preferably with telecom experience, often without.

They circulated *through* quickly: Workers were permitted and sometimes encouraged to take different positions within Telecorp. Sometimes this was to keep them fresh and provide new challenges (such as Marisela, who moved from Customer Service to Network Coordination, and Rae, who moved from Collections to Accounts Receivable); sometimes to promote understanding among functional groups (such as Sheila, who moved from Customer Service to Sales); and sometimes because a functional group was divided in two (such as the Data Entry trainees discussed in Case 1).

They circulated *out* quickly: Turnover was relatively high, especially in the technical areas, due to the low unemployment in this rapidly expanding sector and due to the demanding nature of most jobs at Telecorp.

And they circulated *among telecoms*, either by training with other companies, by coming to Telecorp from another telecom, by taking jobs at other telecoms (where they still occasionally interacted with Telecorp workers), or by having their employer acquired by Telecorp.

This high level of circulation is typical of knowledge work. In fact, Castells suggests that circulating workers drives innovation (1996), a claim that certainly seems to be supported at Telecorp (as we'll see below). Workers, like the environmental activists studied by Luther Gerlach (2001), functioned as "living links" who circulated through loose networks, lending relative coherence and spreading and rearticulating genres. As we saw in Chapter 2, management planned to encourage and extend this circulation of workers by having some workers spend time in every functional group in order to learn the industry. The problem with this plan, of course, is that the different functional groups were changing, dividing, and drifting so rapidly that this knowledge had a very short shelf life: in the rearview mirror, as it were, the workers' previous functional group would be adopting new genres and practices and making new links. Workers' movements can be depicted by moving their names around an organizational chart, but the chart is just a map; in the actual territory, things looked quite different.

At the same time, circulating a worker isn't like grafting wild branches onto a cultivated tree: the older links are not severed, they decay. As long as they had not decayed completely, any worker could be called upon to reconstitute a previous network – inside or outside Telecorp. (And as we've seen, it's often difficult to tell the outside from the inside.)

Here's a case in point. In Data Entry, Susan was training during my observations in late summer 2000. She was working on a disconnect report when she received an e-mail from the person who had taken over her previous job in the accounting department of an Internet service provider. Evidently that person had difficulty settling into Susan's old position: after reading the e-mail, Susan fumed, "She must have been on crack yesterday!" and called the person, initiating a discussion of accounting tools, procedures, and notes. *Susan was still answering questions about her previous job after two weeks.* Surely Telecorp had no interior if any worker could be called at any time to help reconstitute a previous network – to assist in the work at her previous workplace! Scripture may tell us that we cannot serve two masters, but Susan certainly did – for a time. At the end of the conversation, she reminded the former co-worker politely but firmly that she no longer worked there.

As Alberts and Hayes argue, "With almost universal market penetration, the telephone provided a way, at least theoretically, for anyone in the United States to talk to anyone else" (2003, p. 75). And that *theoretical* capability enabled anyone, like Susan's former co-worker, to reconstitute a previous network at any time. Susan was hardly the only person to be called upon in this way. As I mentioned in Chapter 2, Marisela had moved from her Customer Service job to a Network Coordination job, but she still received calls from less experienced Customer Service workers eight months later. Others were similarly called on in Cash Posting, Sales, and CLEC Provisioning. Workers may have circulated in space, but spatial location was hardly meaningful when everyone had a published phone number and could be (literally) called to reprise roles and fulfill obligations at any moment. As Susan's experience suggests, workers *can* serve two masters, *can* be called upon to help constitute and reconstitute networks that do not appear on any organizational chart, *can* point out and travel the organization's "hidden passes." And since everyone was on the organization's border, all workers had to become boundary workers, use boundary objects, and learn multiple social languages.

Since previous networks could be constituted easily regardless of organizational borders, those borders were difficult to sustain: everybody, as I said in Chapter 2, was on the border. For instance, dialer techs at Telecorp and BigTel spoke the same social language, but as Ricardo at the CLEC switch told me, Telecorp's dialer techs had to change their "lingo" when talking to Sales, CLEC Provisioning, and other groups. The differences in the "lingo" were striking. During his work, Ricardo would effortlessly slip into different social languages, using terms and concepts familiar to the different functional groups with which he worked. These social languages marked different sorts of expertise, different activities, and different ways to understand the work with which Ricardo and others were involved. Ricardo was not the only one to remark on having to consciously switch social languages: workers in the NOC and CLEC Provisioning frequently remarked on having to tailor their speech for functional groups that were less or more "technical" than their own and to interpret F1 notes written in different social languages.

This phenomenon is hardly unique to Telecorp. In the context of military organizations, Alberts and Hayes argue that "stovepipes" – specialized, typically noninteractive functional units from separate parts of a hierarchical organization – lead to

> the lack of systems that support widespread information sharing and peer-to-peer interactions. The result is not a single center but a loose confederation of centers, not one edge but many. Stovepipes greatly inhibit information flows, constrain command approaches, and restrict asset utilization. Stovepipes suboptimize. Worst of all, stovepipes result in cultural differences and tensions between and among different parts of the organization. (2003, pp. 174–175)

Such "stovepipes" form because "the economics of information made it prohibitively costly to support widespread information sharing and peer-to-peer interactions" (p. 175; cf. Beniger, 1989; Malone, 2004). And those interactions become more difficult to foster as stovepipes develop, because "these stovepipe entities evolve their own cultures and languages." So,

> A large percentage of the available energy (peoples' time and commitment) is spent internally to establish and maintain "trust," build and maintain loyalty to the "tribe," and establish and employ cross-cutting relationships (often informal) so that the larger organization's goals can be pursued independently of the formal structure. (p. 216)

As we've seen, such "cultures and languages" and texts formed at Telecorp due in part to functional specialization – though I think Alberts and Hayes don't account for the necessary separations of social languages due to the differences in disciplinary and occupational focuses. The converse also happened. In Sales, Sheila adopted specialized checklists from the sales division of a telecom that Telecorp had recently acquired, making them part of the standard operating procedure in Sales. Just as social languages migrated, so did genres. At any rate, Telecorp's functional units developed tactics to communicate despite these organizational barriers.

In describing this organization, I want to avoid an assumption that occurs to some extent in both the knowledge economy and netwar literature: that a network's nodes are stable individuals with stable capabilities and links (Alberts & Hayes, 2003; Atkinson & Moffat, 2005; Benkler, 2006; Malone, 2004). That assumption does lead to a focus on multiple connections but tends not to acknowledge that the assemblage includes tools, and these tools do more than simply boost the capabilities of individuals. Like the children whose memory improved when they used cards in Vygotsky's study (1962), Bateson's blind-man-with-cane (1972), or Deleuze and Guattari's horseman-with-stirrups (1987), workers were transformed in assemblages, becoming workers-with-social-languages, workers-with-genre-ecologies.

Summary: Following the Workers

Like orders, money, and substitutions, the workers at Telecorp have led us to surprising places as we followed their circulation. Workers picked up genres and social languages from one activity and deployed them in another. But they also found themselves bound to those previous activities, called upon to constitute previous networks, and working to develop connections and trust with those in the current network.

CONCLUSION

At the beginning of this chapter, I said that we would look at the tactics of net work. And at this point, perhaps we have a better sense of the tactical situation. Telecorp's net work is enacted through standing sets of transformations, transformations that include textual rerepresentations in different genres. As we followed the orders, money, substitutions, and workers, we saw that these genres circulated as boundary objects that both wove and spliced functional units at Telecorp. In this rapidly changing, spliced network, development became problematic, especially since the network reached far beyond Telecorp's organizational boundaries. Yet workers did learn and did become part of Telecorp's net work. As I contended in Chapter 1, despite the quotidian disruptions, Telecorp worked well – surprisingly well. Even in this complex, rapidly changing, underdefined, and overconnected environment, workers learned. How does this learning happen in net work?

6

Is Our Network Learning?

We've seen the strategic and tactical elements of net work at Telecorp, particularly in how these allow the splicing and weaving of different activities into a network. But how are networks trained? In an organization in constant flux, with constant turnover and acquisitions, how do workers learn their jobs – particularly jobs that they themselves consider unteachable?

The problem is compounded because, as we saw in Chapter 5, Telecorp was constantly and deeply interlinked with other organizations. At any time, a worker could be collaborating with workers in other functional groups, counterparts in other telecoms, customers, service providers, and so on through a seemingly endless list. And this worker might have had to draw upon various sorts of genres and social languages from wildly different domains. It's notoriously problematic to apply one activity's tools and skills to another, so boundary work – work that potentially any worker at Telecorp could be called upon to perform, since everyone was on the border – tended to involve learning different *sets* of genres and social languages. That is, workers had to keep a foot in each activity, becoming "dividuals" (Deleuze, 1995), workers who were continually – pick your term here: *deskilled* (Haraway, 1991), *reskilled* (Castells, 1996), or engaging in *lifelong learning* (Zuboff & Maxmin, 2004). Learning had become discontinuous and spread across multiple activities and domains (see Drucker, 2003; cf. Johnson-Eilola, 2005). At Telecorp, this learning was rarely done in a coherent, consistent way. Neither *could* it be, arguably, since conditions were changing so rapidly.

In particular, lifelong employment is replaced by what Zuboff and Maxmin call "lifelong learning." More critical scholars have noticed the same trends: Donna Haraway (1991) warns that they lead to continual deskilling and retraining, while Gilles Deleuze points out that individuals find themselves in a constant state of "metastability" (Deleuze, 1995, p. 179) characterized by constant forging and testing of relationships. The result is a sort of "endless postponement" rather than a defined avenue of development (p. 180). Consequently, workers are having to focus far more on boundary spanning or coordination among very different activities, and vocational training typically does not prepare them for this coordinative work (Engeström, Engeström, & Kärkkäinen, 1995; Tuomi-Gröhn & Engeström, 2003).

Nevertheless, Telecorp's network learned.

Training and learning are important issues as we look at the political–rhetorical and developmental aspects of net work. In this chapter I examine the different, often conflicting, and mostly tacit ways in which workers learned at Telecorp, including apprenticeships, computer-based learning, and formal training sessions. Drawing from activity theory in particular, I analyze the learning and training approaches in terms of how they enable – and inhibit – net work at Telecorp.

LEARNING NET WORK: THE PROBLEM OF DISCONTINUITY

At Telecorp, workers were inducted into overwhelmingly complex jobs as quickly as possible, with few black boxes to simplify the work, little or no formal training to help them operationalize the actions they had to perform, and few systematic regulative genres such as scripts and checklists. Generally, they had to learn everything at once, primarily through observation, and keep track of what others do across what seemed to be a complex, un-black-boxable company. Of course they complained about the lack of formal training. But in the same breath, many affirmed that *the best way to learn was through this sort of experience.* As Walter in Collections said:

> The person that was doing it was no longer here. So I sat with the manager. And it started out basic, this is how you look up, figure out where the area code and exchange would route to. And then pretty much kinda *thrown to the wolves,* just learning, you know, a little training here and there, but for the most part, learning hands-on, and *that's probably the best way I learn.* (my emphasis)

Walter's reaction was fairly common among more technical workers such as Network Operations Center (NOC) workers, switch techs, and network coordinators, though it showed up in the comments of workers from other areas as well (see Chapter 5). When describing training, workers used metaphors that conveyed uncertainty, contingency, and risk, often in violent terms: "trial-and-error" (Russel, Network Optimization; Tanika, Marketing; Jake, CLEC Switch); "sink or swim" (Jeannie, Network Coordination); "hide and watch" (Jack, NOC); "we were just thrown into it" (Priscilla, Customer Service; Candi, Network Optimization; Damon, Internet Help Desk); "fast and furious" (Ginger, Administration); "digging in" (Timothy, Sales); "get your hands dirty" (Nathaniel, NOC). They sometimes suggested that "this is a different kind of industry" (Joshua, CLEC Provisioning); that the industry's terminology was like a language that could only be learned through immersion (Susan, Data Entry; Jeannie, Network Coordination); and that some parts of the job were simply unteachable (Tanika, Marketing). As I said in Chapter 2, it *was* unteachable as long as networks continued to grow, divide, and associate without affording a chance for workers to manage that complexity and change. Without relative stability on which sustainable practices could be founded and formalized, workers could only learn by encountering contingencies and tailoring responses to each one of them. Mediational genres developed and spread across the company but not evenly or reliably because the work was too ad hoc and mercurial to make them possible on a broad enough scale.

Mercurial is certainly the word for it, since Telecorp's pace of change made any sort of stability very difficult. Telecorp's training measures were well adapted for a smaller, more static company with more limited interconnections. But Telecorp's conditions had changed. It was rapidly expanding in a rapidly changing, interpenetrating industry (as we saw in Chapter 4). Consequently, its training measures – which emphasized inductive learning to handle unpredictable contingencies, the sort of learning often associated with "agility" (Atkinson & Moffat, 2005) – had become out of sync with the organization. Training was built on the assumption that everything changes: a reasonable assumption, but one that had forced the company into an entirely reactive tactical stance. Telecorp's leadership had recognized this problem by the time I began my study and had begun a search for a training specialist, a search that concluded just before this study ended.

The state of training at Telecorp points to the broader problem in the knowledge economy literature that I mentioned earlier in the chapter. Authors such as Zuboff and Maxmin point out that a networked economy necessitates "lifelong learning": like Telecorp, other organizations in the information economy are characterized by frequent career changes, a lack of lifetime employment, a high number of emerging or hybrid job descriptions, and frequent collaboration across functional areas (Castells,

1996; Drucker, 2003; Zuboff & Maxmin, 2004). In consequence, the concept of "learning" becomes quite problematic when applied to networks, which is possibly why actor–network theory has so little to say about it. The assumption that people generally make about learning and training is that individuals progressively accumulate skills; it's *developmental*. But in a network, it's far from clear that developmental models obtain: the individual herself is called into question, becoming what Deleuze calls a "dividual" (1995) whose work activities are fragmented and interleaved, whose attention is continuously partial (McCarthy & Boyd, 2005; Stone, 2006), whose work takes place in many organizational structures simultaneously (Castells, 1996; Drucker, 2003), whose "activities are increasingly infiltrated with . . . new types of working and learning – of living" (Johnson-Eilola, 2005, p. 31), and whose learning is consequently more self-directed (Senge, 1994; cf. Amidon, 2005) and continual at all levels (Castells, 1996). Under such conditions, associative complexes, which Vygotsky characterized as childish (1962), become the primary way of understanding and learning about work (Johnson-Eilola, 1998, 2005). Indeed, some speculate that childishness – psychological neoteny – is "probably adaptive in modern society because people need repeatedly to change jobs, learn new skills, move to new places and make new friends" (Charlton, 2006, p. 679). Contra St. Paul, if we are to understand net work, perhaps we *cannot* put away childish things. Or to use another metaphor: a house that is *not* divided against itself is too rigid, too static to stand; houses built on shifting sand *must* be divided, must be as easy to fold, move, and reconfigure as tents. An interconnected network (in any of the three senses of network discussed in Chapter 2) disrupts traditional, developmental learning and training. Or as Engeström puts it:

> Learning in co-configuration settings is typically distributed over long, discontinuous periods of time. It is accomplished in and between multiple loosely interconnected activity systems and organizations operating in divided local and global terrains and representing different traditions, domains of expertise, and social languages. Learning is crucially dependent on the contribution of the clients or users. Learning is embedded in major transformations, upheavals, innovations, implementations and movements. It takes place in heterogeneous patchworks and textures of small and large, unnoticeable and spectacular actions, objectifications, trajectories and trails. (2004, p. 5)

Let's go back to Telecorp to see how this happens.

HOW LEARNING WAS HANDLED AT TELECORP: SOME TECHNIQUES

Telecorp's training model had been adequate in the recent past, but in 2000 it was unrealistic. Eddie at the NOC noted that the prodigious increase in customers and services had come with a concomitant training burden, a burden that went unrecognized:

> I basically didn't know this job at all when I first hired. And personally I didn't have to learn Internet, didn't have to learn local service, didn't have to learn dialer stuff when I was first hired, basically it was just long distance. And that was a different call for me! Now, these new people comin' in, they're like, wham, "You gotta learn this, you gotta learn this, you gotta learn this, you gotta learn this, you gotta learn this, you gotta learn this, don't do this!" And I can understand the new people, how they get frustrated. I really do. I think, expectations, because they see other people and say, "Well, that's how fast *they* learned it." Well, when they first got here, we didn't have all of this!

Eddie concluded, "A lot of new people that get hired on get frustrated because they're just overwhelmed."

Training was not simply through immersion. As the workers told it, Telecorp had instituted a number of training measures for workers at various levels, but these were mostly ad hoc and uncoordinated with each other: apprenticeship, formal training, corporate training outside Telecorp, documentation, and computer training. In addition, workers developed and circulated knowledge through trial-and-error and through stories. Let's begin by examining cases of each in order to see how training was done. Then we'll circle back and examine some of these cases in the terms we've been using throughout this book. Finally, I'll suggest lessons for training in net work.

Apprenticeship: "You Never Ever Do a Partial Connection"

As Lave and Wenger (1991) use the term, *apprenticeship* involves people *participating* in an activity, first *peripherally* (on the edges, with minor responsibilities), then in ways that increase complexity and responsibility. This participation must be *legitimate*, that is, sanctioned and validated so that the activity is properly continued. When all three of these are put together, you get "legitimate peripheral participation." That's not as easy as it might sound. Schooling allows learning that is legitimate and peripheral, but not participation. Apprentice meat cutters, as Lave and Wenger demonstrate, engage in learning that is legitimate and participation, but not peripheral. They start with simple tasks such as wrapping, but they are physically separated from the journeymen who actually cut the meat in the back room.

In knowledge work, apprenticeship typically involves genres as well as other forms of participation. And in knowledge work, as Etienne Wenger argues, workers need to participate (and participate in learning) across multiple boundaries. "In a knowledge economy, sustained success for any organization will depend not only on effective participation in economic markets, but just as importantly and with many of the same players, on knowing how to participate in broader social learning systems" (2003, p. 98). The more distributed knowledge work becomes, and the more central knowledge work becomes to the economy, the more important it will be to understand and describe how workers interact – and, specifically, learn – across increasingly porous boundaries. Certainly that was true at Telecorp.

At the level of functional units, workers were often trained by apprenticeship, broadly speaking: shadowing a more experienced worker for an amount of time, engaging in "hands-on" training procedures, or learning innovations from a more experienced worker. This sort of dyadic training happened across the company, and in fact it was the most frequently mentioned form of training (in 51 of 84 interviews) as well as the training mentioned across the most functional areas (20 of 23). It was especially used in certain functional areas: the Internet Help Desk, LD Operations, the NOC, Network Coordination, and Sales.

So how was apprenticeship enacted at Telecorp? It varied, often in the same unit. Some workers were assigned to a more experienced worker, whom they observed, sometimes listening in on customer interactions with a set of headphones. Hilda in Network Coordination explained:

> When I first came here they were really shorthanded. So they're just basically, they come and sit for a few days and watch over the shoulder of somebody doing it, and ask questions, and then "here you go."

And she said that "I still, after a year feel like I don't know what I should know." Observing, she said, meant that workers couldn't catch everything in their notes and didn't know what was in the computer system. Even the basics need training, she said.

Hilda's story was more or less typical. Some workers were trained with more of a progression, while others were given even less guidance;

apprenticeship was not evenly enacted across the company, and experienced workers were not given guidelines for apprenticing new workers. Karina in Administration, who was a manager at the time the study was conducted, recalled that her apprenticeship was minimally guided:

> I wasn't trained. . . . I listened to the people working – I watched what they did. I learned how to cash post, I did cash posting and credits even before I did cust – I did customer care, I went to cash posting. . . . Everything I learned to do, I learned either by watching somebody or by looking at something they've done . . .

Karina didn't reproduce that training experience when she trained Rae during one session I observed. As Rae looked over Karina's shoulder, Karina went through Rae's work for that day, explaining each situation and its background as it came up, then having Rae complete the tasks under close supervision. From my field notes:

> Karina leafs through invoice slips (rubber banded). "Aha! This one's a duplicate so we need to do a correction. . . . To do a correction, real simple – the same thing you just did, just the opposite. Now this is very important, if you do a correction, you back all the way back out and back in. You never ever do a partial correction."
>
> Karina walks Rae through this process on the AS/400. They look at a printout, using a ruler to help them see what line they're on.
>
> Karina calculates the sum on her adding machine. "That's what the balance should have been, but that's not what it is. . . . I am wondering seriously what's wrong with that account and whoever's been posting it, why they haven't noticed it. . . . So we want to call [a worker in another city] – why don't you send her an e-mail . . ."

Certainly Karina gave Rae more guidance than she herself had received. But the training was contingent, guided by whatever work transpired on that day, making it difficult for Rae to extract general principles. And that was problematic because the point of one-on-one introductory training like Rae's was to impart procedural knowledge and conceptual tools for understanding specialized work in small functional groups. Statements of general principle, such as "you never ever do a partial connection," were embedded in encounters within the activity rather than framed broadly and in relation to each other.

On occasion, a worker would train her or his replacement. This sort of apprenticeship usually happened when only one worker held a particular position, and therefore the new worker couldn't rely on a set of other workers for guidance. For instance, Jean in Accounts Payable took over for a worker who had decided to leave Telecorp to have a baby:

> Well, I had three mornings with the girl that was doing the schools and libraries, and the rest of it's gonna come from a couple of different people. And that's why I'm kind of in limbo now because they're letting me learn one thing first. And as soon as I get that figured out, then they're gonna start throwing other things at me.

These sessions were typically more formal than shadowing and included procedural explanations. These sessions typically involved explaining the job and procedures in plain terms, supplemented by examples on screen or diagrams drawn on the spot. Sometimes the replacement would arrive after the original worker had left, and in that case the replacement would have to reconstruct the work from the original worker's notes and from discussions with co-workers.

Recall that workers at Telecorp often characterized their work as uncertain and contingent, impossible to formalize. This uncertainty and contingency was reflected – and reinforced – in the wide use of apprenticeship, in which workers were trained by observing how more experienced workers dealt with contingencies. This training, then, tended to be reactive, as Leann in Network Optimization pointed out: this method was "probably not the best," she conceded, but "everything is changing so fast," making it difficult to establish a more detailed training program. "Probably the ideal would be yes, to train, not just hands on, but a little more in depth as to why you do the things you do."

Formal Telecorp Training Sessions: "Nine Times out of Ten . . ."

When we think of "training," we often think of formal, deductively organized training situations with set curricula, materials, and time set aside for lectures and workshops. For instance, Gee, Hull, and Lankshear (1996) describe training at a "fast capitalist" company in which the trainer followed a set inquiry-response-evaluation (IRE) pattern to lead employees through discussions and role-playing in order to inculcate company values. (For more on this pattern, see Wells, 2001.) But such training was not broadly deployed at Telecorp.

Seventeen workers mentioned formal training in their interviews – but those workers were concentrated in five areas, particularly Sales, CLEC Provisioning, and Customer Service. Those were the areas most served by the occasional two-week training sessions offered by Abraham, the senior manager of Customer Service. These training sessions were meant to introduce new workers to the industry. And I use the term *new workers* loosely here: since the training sessions were held only occasionally, they were often attended by people who had worked at Telecorp for three or four months.

Priscilla in Customer Service described her experience in this two-week course:

> They just went over talking about the phone system and phone lines and what type of phone systems there were and so forth. And then, you know, when we got through with that, Sheila . . . gradually gave me some work to do.

I attended an iteration of the course myself. In a conference room, workers from the NOC, Data Entry, and CLEC Provisioning sat two to a table, each with a thick training book in a three-ring binder. The training book consisted primarily of sample printouts without commentary or explanation. All chairs were oriented to the front of the room, where Abraham had a whiteboard and a computer with a projection unit. Although workers were encouraged to ask questions throughout the session, interaction mostly followed the pattern of inquiry, response, and evaluation that Gee et al. (1996) noted.

What was striking, however, was the number of *stories*: stories about how workers had challenged BigTel's charges on particular services, how Abraham had ordered his own personal phone service, how business owners had complained about their employees' use of the autoredial feature, how an auto parts store had paid more than it needed because it wasn't aware of a specific feature. Even when workers were asked to do exercises (on paper, simulating the computer screens they would be expected to encounter), their results were compared to the results Abraham put on the whiteboard and framed with stories about the situations in which they would be used. Such stories continually contextualized workers' learning within Telecorp, emphasizing the local aspects of the knowledge. For instance, when Abraham described the Federal Excise Tax (see Chapter 4), it was from Telecorp's perspective, frustrated by the bureaucratic nature of the tax and the impact on Telecorp's customers, and emphasizing how Telecorp broke out this tax on the bill in order to distance itself from the cost. The stories emphasized contingencies: trainers, and often workers, offered stories of specific customers facing complex, unique circumstances and testimonials about how these were handled. One of the most commonly used phrases in training was "nine times out of ten, it'll be . . . "

In addition to the formal training workshops that Abraham offered, Telecorp also offered group introductory training when a number of new workers came to a unit. When the Data Entry group was formed, for instance, and when four new salespeople joined Sales. The format was up to the trainer. In Data Entry, the training involved working with actual data and was conducted in a workshop format. In Sales, it took a lecture format. In CLEC Provisioning, a refresher course was held as a two-hour workshop over lunch in which workers discussed difficult orders and how they could be handled. These formal sessions varied dramatically in terms of preparation, activities, and atmosphere, but they all involved a led synchronization of expectations, and all but the sales training relied heavily on stories and the contingencies they represented.

Corporate Training Outside Telecorp: "Nobody Had Time to Learn from Her"

Corporate training was mentioned by 12 workers in 9 areas. Workers who interacted frequently with technical counterparts in the industry – such as workers at Bill Verification, Translations, and Alarm Management – often attended training provided by other telecommunications providers (such as BigTel), equipment manufacturers, and software trainers. They often brought back thick manuals and three-ring binders full of notes from these sessions – along with newly learned terms, genres, and social languages.

Workers generally reported learning a considerable amount from corporate training, including social languages that affirmed and distinguished their fields and trades (as we saw in Chapter 5), creating linkages with others outside Telecorp. As we'll see below, some of the training documentation also affected those who didn't go to these sessions.

However, training often benefited individuals rather than teams: workers had difficulty circulating this knowledge to those who did not attend the sessions. For instance, Gwendolyn in Human Resources reported that her manager had gone to training in Chicago and was "excited" about it, but nobody had had time to learn from her.

Documentation: "I Need to Do It from This Day Forward"

Documentation was mentioned by nine workers in seven areas. Sometimes this documentation was self-generated. For instance, the front desk kept a notebook of procedures that was eventually typed and reformatted as a manual. Similarly, Angelina in Computer Services, who was the sole individual responsible for billing, reported developing documentation to help her as she took over the job from the previous person. That person had been at Telecorp for 10 years and had never made any notes, so in the two weeks before he left, she "made notes like crazy" and developed "runsheets," preprinted tables that she used to record and monitor her work in three-ring binders. Similarly, receptionists at the front desk kept a spiral notebook in which they wrote procedures to convey to new receptionists; this notebook was eventually transcribed as a manual.

Angelina was fortunate. Sometimes a new worker would have to replace someone who had already left, as Oscar in Alarm Management did, and would have to piece together the system of the previous worker by looking at documents and asking other workers in tangentially related functional groups. It was "hard to get ahold of exactly what this position did," Oscar told me.

Documentation could also be a byproduct of other work (cf. Zachry, 1999). Some positions, especially in larger functional groups with high turnover, had done a more thorough job of documenting procedures. Christal in CLEC Provisioning reported:

> Basically, the procedure that I do now, I go into the CLEC handbook and I read up everything because it changes every day, there's something new every day. But basically I kinda go into the handbook and I train myself, "Okay, you know, this is something new, I need to do it from this day forward."

And as I mentioned earlier, sometimes documentation came from corporate training outside Telecorp – although that documentation was not always easy to find. Russel in Network Optimization reported that when he first started, he wanted to see the manual of instructions, but "they didn't have one." After about a month, someone pointed out a manual produced by a telecommunications research and development company. He spent the weekend reading it and came back a "completely different worker." Consequently, he arranged to attend a seminar produced by that company.

As with training, documentation was implemented unevenly and idiosyncratically across Telecorp, and when formal documentation was available, it tended not to be well publicized; workers generally had to rely on the apprenticeship process to discover documentation. Surely this contributed to the overall perception that telecommunications work was idiosyncratic.

Computer-Based Training: "Basically It's Just a Crash Course"

Like corporate training, computer-based training tended to focus on industry-level rather than local concerns and fixed concepts rather than contingencies. Computer-based training was mentioned by four workers in three areas: the NOC, Network Design and Inventory, and CLEC Design and Inventory. Rusty in CLEC Design described this training program:

> On my first day – I was at the corporate office, not here – my supervisor... sent me to the [Network] Control Center and I went through a three, three-day computer course, talking about how each central office is connected, how you go from, what a POTS line is, what a digital four-wire is, and a little bit of history of where the phone systems came from. And also learned about ground starts, loop starts and all that other stuff. Basically it's just a crash course on, a really quick crash course on phone systems and stuff. And how it's come this far. And they had a lesson on Internet and digital and SDSLs and whatever.

The four-hour computer training culminated with an automated test covering terms and history.

In addition to these training measures, workers learned in at least two other ways: through trial-and-error and through listening to stories.

Trial-and-Error: "Willing to Get Your Hands Dirty"

"Trial-and-error" was all about contingencies. "Trial-and-error," or some variation, was mentioned by 15 workers in 11 areas. When workers used this phrase or an analog, they meant attempting to complete a task through self-directed exploration, then applying these lessons to future tasks.

For instance, Nathaniel at the NOC reported that although he was apprenticed to a particular NOC worker, she was not willing to "sit there and give you advice." So his training was "basically just jumping in there and being willing to get your hands dirty." Many of the most memorable metaphors discussed earlier – "sink or swim," "thrown to the wolves" – describe the sort of uncertainty and contingency with which workers had to deal as they learned through trial-and-error. Like apprenticeship, trial-and-error learning magnified contingencies.

At the same time, trial-and-error resulted in some interesting and useful innovations. For instance, Kim in Bill Verification reported that workers helped each other with software: they learned tricks "by accident" then taught these to each other. Leann in Network Optimization found that she could import carrier rates from Excel (a spreadsheet) into Access (a database) then export the text into a text editor so she could assemble it into scripts, allowing her to avoid typing in the information; she conveyed this procedure to the worker she was training. Although it magnified contingencies, trial-and-error learning often did result in stabilized knowledge that could then be routinized.

Stories: "There Was Nothing About a Dog on the Ticket"

Workers generally did not mention stories in their discussions of training and learning, but stories were everywhere, as we saw in the discussion of formal training. The best example, perhaps, was the story told in the NOC in Chapter 2.

The NOC's assistant manager sternly told the story about Rex's death to the entire NOC. "There was nothing about a dog on the ticket," he said. "You *must* note that." This is how the NOC promulgated the rule to ask about pets and locked gates: through stories delivered sternly by a manager to overworked trouble ticket specialists, half of whom were on the phone and typing four notes at once. Through stories circulated among those workers during short breaks as they waited for the next call. Such stories mediated and regulated the network, attempting to manage the multiplicity that came from splicing together actors in an assemblage. Like trial-and-error and apprenticeship learning, they emphasized contingencies and provided resources for dealing with them. But stories were not concrete or durable enough; they didn't circulate broadly enough to stabilize the network sufficiently. That is, there was no guarantee that stories would be passed on, told accurately, or interpreted consistently enough to induce rules.

Summary: Making Sense of Learning Measures at Telecorp

What are we to make of this incoherence in learning?

These different sorts of learning measures are bewildering at first glance. They are not well integrated or coordinated, and they almost all emphasize contingency over continuity, local over universal. They remind us of the critique often leveled against Machiavelli: that so much of his advice boils down to "it depends." But at the same time, as Wenger reminds us, they also represent a developing community. There's a surprising breadth of learning measures here, particularly since workers tended to characterize training as minimal or nonexistent. (Some of the people who described training as impossible were the same ones who were expected to train new workers.) But these procedures were not well integrated, not coordinated, and generally not formalized or documented. In part, this was a function of the spliced organization, in which it became important not just to *learn*, but to identify *who to ask*; the cultivation of social contacts became critical (cf. Nardi & O'Day, 1999; Nardi, Whittaker, & Schwarz, 2002).

I argue that this incoherence is not just a function of rapid growth – or of rapid change. In addition, Telecorp workers were dealing with increased interconnections that made traditional disciplinary, trade, and functional boundaries – and organizational boundaries – impossible to sustain. Consequently, it was sometimes unclear what knowledge an individual was supposed to have or how well knowledge applied from one context to another. This lack of clarity comes out in the frequent variations between Telecorp's official job descriptions and workers' self-descriptions. For instance, the official job description for an NOC trouble ticket coordinator focused on order processing and network surveillance. Trouble ticket coordinators' self-descriptions, in contrast, focused on contingency and boundary crossing.

Contingency tends to be emphasized because people have to cross boundaries or entangle activities, and conditions are constantly changing for each. This entangling is often termed *agility* (Atkinson & Moffat, 2005). But, at least in Telecorp's case, agility was gained at the cost of stability. Notice that services, technologies, and coverage areas were also changing.

Boundary crossing became important, since everyone was massed at the border, as we've seen throughout, and boundary crossing especially included the ability to develop relationships. Continuing relations led to stability while new relationships led to agility. But Telecorp had no good way to aggregate or circulate knowledge on an organizational scale (although some ways existed at the functional group level, such as F1 notes).

Learning becomes a different problem when organizations are less stable, less bounded and hierarchical, more interconnected. In this sort of environment, how do workers learn? How do they become competent? And what do learning and competence mean in net work? Let's apply insights from activity theory and actor–network theory.

THEORIZING LEARNING FOR NET WORK: ACTIVITY THEORY'S CONTRIBUTION

How do we theorize training for net work? Let's acknowledge at the outset that actor–network theory will be next to useless here. Actor–network theory is simply not a theory of learning. The closest actor–network theory has come to addressing the issue is to note some cases of apprenticeship (Callon, 1991; Latour, 2006) without exploring them in any appreciable detail. Actor–network theory's work is splicing work; it tracks movements and associations, not learning.

Activity theory, on the other hand, takes development – weaving – as its work. It has an extensively theorized and researched account of education and development based on dialectics. This is where dialectics really shines, of course: in examining how people formulate and develop concepts, how they assimilate and incorporate new knowledge. From its roots in Vygotsky (1962, 1978) through later Russian work (Leont'ev, 1978; Luria, 1976; Zinchenko, 1996), and "third-generation" work elsewhere (e.g., Cole, 1996; Engeström, 2001; Tuomi-Gröhn & Engeström, 2003), activity theory has been steadily applied to education and has yielded important insights.

Let's use Engeström's recent writings on developmental work research (DWR) to characterize learning at Telecorp. Engeström views development in organizations based on the dialectical "spiral model" of development described by Evald Ilyenkov (1982). Ilyenkov argues that

> this dialectics of all real development, in which the universal necessary condition of the emergence of an object becomes its own universal and necessary consequence, this dialectical inversion in which the condition becomes the conditioned, the cause becomes the effect, the universal becomes the particular, is a characteristic feature of internal interaction through which actual development assumes the form of a circle, or, to be more precise, of a spiral which extends the scope of its motion all the time, with each new turn.
>
> At the same time there is a kind of "locking in itself" here which transforms an aggregate of individual phenomena into a relatively closed system, a concrete integral organism historically developing according to its immanent laws. (pp. 115–116)

This spiral is not circular, with an effect becoming its own cause, because dialectics regards cause and effects as manifestations of "a system of mutually conditioning aspects, as a historically emerging and developing concreteness" (p. 117).

The spiral model is clearly a weaving model. But Engeström and his colleagues complicate the model by introducing *multidimensionality.* As I mentioned in Chapter 3, learning involves a "vertical" dimension of development within a specific domain of expertise:

> [D]ominant approaches to cognition share a narrow and "vertical" view of expertise in which some have more knowledge than others. Characteristically they distinguish between "stages" or "levels" of knowledge and

skill. Such a vertical image assumes a uniform, singular model of what counts as an "expert" in any given field. (Tuomi-Gröhn, Engeström, & Young, 2003, p. 3)

But the authors argue that a "horizontal" dimension of expertise also exists, in which

> experts are viewed as operating in, and move between, multiple parallel activity contexts. These multiple contexts demand and afford different, complementary but also conflicting cognitive tools, rules, and patterns of social interaction. Criteria of expert knowledge and skill are different in the various contexts. Experts face the challenge of negotiating and combining ingredients from different contexts to achieve hybrid solutions. The vertical master-novice relationship, and with it in some cases the professional monopoly on expertise, is problematized as demands for more dialogical problem solving increase. (p. 3)

In Engeström's view, activities can co-exist without merging or synthesizing. In fact, Engeström and his colleagues working in this strand of activity theory have increasingly used M. M. Bakhtin's concept of *dialogue* to talk about how activities can interface, and how people within those activities can cross boundaries, without the activities synthesizing and transforming into higher forms, as one would expect in a strictly dialectical model (Engeström, 1999, 2004). The boundaries that workers cross, the overlapping activities in which they work, constitute the polycontextuality discussed in this strand of activity theory (cf. Engeström, Engeström, & Kärkkäinen, 2005) and result in multivoicedness (Engeström, 2001) or polyvocality (Tuomi-Gröhn, 2003; Tuomi-Gröhn et al., 2003) at every level. Polycontextuality and boundary crossing are iteratively connected (Engeström et al., 1995), then, with the overlapping of activities generating new contexts. Such overlappings have increased with the death of lifetime employment.

In concrete terms, developmental work research provides insights into how Telecorp's network learned. Telecorp's interconnected trades, disciplines, fields, functional groups, competitors, and partners can be analyzed as overlapping activity systems in an interpenetrated activity network. In this activity network, workers acquired trajectories that took them across boundaries and contexts; they were *all* boundary workers, coordinating and coconfiguring work, often knotworking. The many genres functioning as boundary objects helped the workers conduct this work as they continued to develop. In the metaphor I used in Chapter 3, these workers were "astronauts" who crossed boundaries, sustaining their core, developing selves as they worked in different, sometimes hostile and foreign contexts, circling (or orbiting) in developmental spirals.

TABLE 6.1. *Horizontal and vertical learning at Telecorp*

Dimension	Learning context	Techniques
Vertical	Within functional groups	Apprenticeship; formal Telecorp training sessions; trial and error; stories; documentation
Vertical	Within trades, disciplines, and fields	Computer-based training; corporate training outside Telecorp
Horizontal	Across functional groups	Trial and error, stories, apprenticeship
Horizontal	Across organizations	Trial and error, stories, apprenticeship

In Telecorp's discontinuous environment, workers were often involved in the sort of multidimensional learning that Engeström and his colleagues describe – although two dimensions of learning hardly seem enough! Workers developed in several ways at once, through the various learning techniques above, as Table 6.1 illustrates.

When we examine learning techniques at Telecorp in this way, we see that vertical expertise was supported by a mix of formal techniques (Telecorp training sessions, documentation, computer-based training, corporate training) and informal techniques (trial-and-error, stories, apprenticeship). That is, when learning *within* their functional groups, trades, disciplines, and fields, Telecorp workers had a set of resources, some of which provided stable long-term frameworks, some of which were more oriented to contingency. But their horizontal expertise – the cross-boundary coordinative work that is so common and vital in net work – *was supported almost wholly by informal, contingent ways of learning*: workers learned through apprenticeships, stories, and trial-and-error how to perform the boundary spanning that they had to do each day across multiple activity contexts. And, constantly, the *contingency* involved in this boundary work was magnified even more than in the vertical learning, while stable interfaces and procedures were barely discussed outside the context of specific contingencies.

Applying the notion of spiral development provides further insight – because workers often *did not complete* developmental spirals. As we saw in Chapter 5, workers circulated constantly through Telecorp: in, out, and from one functional group to another. Metaphorically speaking, the developmental paths or learning trajectories (Wenger, 1998) were less like spirals and more like *eddies*. The disconnected, divided activities and "heterogeneous patchworks" that Engeström describes (2004, p. 5) meant that these eddies could not complete the cycle and turn into spirals.[1] Just as Eddie

---

[1] In Deleuze's terms, knowledge workers change "orbits," they "undulate" (1995, p. 180).

(i.e., the NOC trouble ticket specialist) complained at the beginning of this chapter, things had changed radically in the two years since he had been hired. Lifetime employment, which afforded stable "vertical" learning pathways and allowed steady developmental spirals, has given way to *lifelong learning*, increasingly characterized by destabilized learning eddies and a consequent need for "horizontal" learning support. As we saw in Chapter 4, this state of flux characterizes the entire telecommunications industry: in its regulations, legislation, technology, and infrastructure, the industry is constantly changing.

Problems with Activity Theory's Developmental Account

"Living in time," Johndan Johnson-Eilola argues, "we think of our history as building us in a slow, steady accretion of experience." But living in space, "we experience things not as depth but on the surface; not a slow accretion but an everything-all-at-once shout. We do not pass tales linearly, but experience them multiply, simultaneously, across global communication networks" (1998, p. 185). And this point presents interesting difficulties for activity theory's account of net work, which involves an accretion of experience along linear time (although not one that is as necessarily slow, steady, or continuous as what Johnson-Eilola describes).

Despite some influx of dialogic theory, activity theory still understands learning as dialectical. The metaphor of learning as ascension, used by Vygotsky (1962) and Ilyenkov (1982) to describe the "accretion of experience," persists. Their assumption is that a unitary, stable self develops continually, even across discontinuous contexts, like an astronaut who orbits through and learns from worlds while remaining insulated from them (but see Nardi et al., 2002). Consequently, activity theory has a hard time dealing with indeterminacies in these areas: when the orbit is broken, the learning spiral is an incomplete eddy, we have difficulty applying it. And these eddies are quite common in a net work environment, in which work fragmentation and "continuous partial attention" (McCarthy & Boyd, 2005; Stone, 2006) are prevalent features of the work.

THEORIZING TRAINING FOR NET WORK: ACTOR–NETWORK THEORY'S CONTRIBUTION

But although activity theory may have difficulty with these discontinuities, that's not to say that actor–network theory provides any real solutions to the problem. How can it? It has very little to say about training or learning. In fact, as we saw in Chapter 3, its stance makes these topics almost impossible to discuss. Its primary contribution is to highlight critiques of these topics.

So let's start with a relevant concept from actor–network theory that does get a lot of play: *competence.* As we saw in Chapter 2, competence in actor–network theory is seen as a property of the assemblage of humans and nonhumans. As Callon argues, a description of competence involves reconstructing the network in which it is deployed. In this actor–network, humans and nonhumans collectively assign roles; competence emerges from the interaction among these elements (1991, pp. 138–139). That is, competence – and expertise – cannot be ascribed to individuals, only to assemblages.

Latour's writings abound with examples. One is that of the food processor whose safety feature prevents people from accidentally slicing off their fingers; certainly my Cuisinart has kept me from becoming a nine-fingered man! Another is the chain of circulating rerepresentations deployed during any extended scientific inquiry, without which science would be impossible (1987, 1990, 1999b). In fact, Latour argues that these nonhumans impart not just competence but also morality (1999b, 2002). Speed bumps and seatbelts compel us to comply with moral dictates; good fences make good neighbors.

This general understanding of competence is certainly not unique to actor–network theory: it resonates with distributed cognition (Hutchins, 1995) and ecological understandings of mind (Bateson, 1972). Activity theorists have also flirted with this understanding of competence (e.g., Cole & Engeström, 1993), but the difference is that activity theorists still argue that individuals are the final stop: individual and collective human agency is what asymmetrically drives the activity; even though mediational means increase and develop human abilities, those developing human abilities are at the core of expertise. In contrast, actor–network theorists understand expertise symmetrically, as emerging from the assemblage rather than being driven by human action. Without her lab, the scientist is not a scientist; without the food processor's safety features, the sous chef becomes a nine-fingered fumbler; without fences, we are not such good neighbors.

This view presents an interesting perspective on some things we have seen at Telecorp. Fred, the NOC worker whose considerable expertise led him to develop an innovative spreadsheet to track his work and contacts, was described by a CLEC provisioner as a "fuck-up" (see Chapter 5). Jean in Accounts Payable barely understood her new job dealing with schools and libraries discounts, having been briefly apprenticed at short notice, but her spreadsheets and collaborative genres enabled her to perform competently (see Chapter 4). Similarly, Angelina in Computer Services transformed her brief apprenticeship into a range of forms and runsheets for mediating her billing cycle – and thereby extended her competence and the competence of anyone who might replace her. These and many, many others were able to perform competently (and usually confidently) as they performed boundary-spanning work, thanks to the ecologies of genres and tools they deployed and the interconnections they fostered with others. Like Yochai Benkler's networked individual (2006), Gilles Deleuze's dividual (1995), and especially Donna Haraway's cyborg (1991), these workers found "their" competencies fluctuating as a function of the assemblages in which they acted. Rather than astronauts, developing without being touched by the boundaries they crossed, these workers were cyborgs: whole only in combination with their many artifacts, practices, and activities, always in flux given the flux in these heterogeneous network elements. And that's the main point: actor–network theory doesn't draw the vertical–horizontal distinction that activity theory does, instead using assemblages or networks to frame and evaluate competence. This approach avoids the rigidity of the vertical–horizontal distinction, but it also loses the analytical power of that distinction.

This is not to say that individual development is nonexistent or meaningless – but it is certainly not central in the view of actor–network theory, which tracks movements and assemblages rather than individuals' learning.

NET WORK, NET LEARNING

Throughout this book, I've been trying to theorize net work through the dialogue between activity theory and actor–network theory. But we have a real conundrum here: the two theoretical perspectives we've been using seem to be miles apart on the issue of learning. How can they be reconciled?

Well, they probably can't. But that's fine, since reconciliation is not the point of this book. As I said in Chapter 1, I'm not planning to resolve or synthesize this dialogue, but I am exploiting points of agreement between the two and using these to develop my account of net work. So a better question might be: At what points do these two perspectives agree, and how can we use this agreement to come to a conclusion about how networks learn?

Let's go back to the four characteristics of networks that were discussed in Chapter 2 – four points of agreement between activity theory and actor–network theory – and apply them to what we've seen in this chapter. Networks are heterogeneous, multiply linked, black-boxed, and transformative.

Heterogeneous

Networks are heterogeneous and juxtaposing different things – humans and nonhumans, individuals and groups, tools and infrastructure, rules and beliefs – into assemblages that collectively perform activities. Certainly that is the case with net learning: workers at Telecorp were heterogeneous as individuals, worked in heterogeneous groupings (functional groups, disciplines, fields, trades), used heterogeneous contacts to learn, and mediated their activities with heterogeneous genres and tools. They opportunistically drew in new sources for learning, including optional corporate training, documentation, and informal contacts with workers inside and outside the company. Sometimes they developed their own mediatory genres, such as Angelina's runsheets and the manual that emerged from the notebook at the front desk.

Multiply Linked

These heterogeneous components were multiply linked: they could come together at almost any point, generating new sorts of expertise and, arguably, new realities (Law, 2004a; for a very different take, see Gonzalez & Mark, 2004, on "working spheres"). Every worker could contact every other worker directly by phone or e-mail, most could contact workers from other companies, and most could be contacted directly by customers; most workers could read each other's F1 notes or other circulated texts; most workers came in contact with different functional groups, disciplines, fields, and trades through formal training, apprenticeship, and trial-and-error. This fact, combined with the contingent nature of most learning at Telecorp and the rapid changes in the company and its industry, meant that no worker had the same learning experience. Predictably, evaluations of information sources, such as "If [a BigTel worker is] a manager, she's not a good one," or "You have no idea of what [the F1 notes from before 1989] are saying," or "Fred is a fuck-up," became vital for determining which linkages to pursue. Similarly, heterogeneous nonhumans could be brought into contact at any point: as we saw in Chapters 4 and 5, legislation, regulations, infrastructure, and circulating rerepresentations of these could meet and become articulated at various points in the network.

Black-Boxed

Combined, heterogeneity and multiple links pose real problems for net learning. Without relatively stable assemblages and relatively stable interfaces between them, learning becomes too contingent to be generalized and too idiosyncratic to be reproduced; competence, which activity theory and actor–network theory agree to some extent is related to an assemblage (or constellation of mediational means), becomes unpredictable and impossible to sustain across linkages; vertical learning becomes difficult to support and horizontal learning is too irregular to teach. This was the situation at Telecorp. As I implied in Chapter 2, every worker was on the border and hidden passes were everywhere. No wonder the most common learning techniques at Telecorp emphasized contingency: the pace of change was so rapid that workers had trouble identifying stable practices. Consequently, they developed a healthy focus on reactive, tactically oriented learning that emphasized finding and exploiting informal contacts, as we saw above.

What Telecorp was missing here was not *modularization* per se. Modular work leads to silos, organizationally separate units, and as we saw in Chapter 5, such silos are not sustainable in net work, which favors interconnected, rhizomatic organization. Particularly at Telecorp, the industry was changing far too quickly to develop and sustain silos. In this sense, Telecorp's interconnectedness was a tactical strength. But that tactical strength became a strategic problem, because Telecorp lacked standard avenues for learning. Workers attempted to provide some of these standard avenues through importing and stabilizing genres, learning and switching social languages – and becoming boundary workers (Engeström et al., 2005) or networked individuals (Benkler, 2006) or dividuals (Deleuze, 1995) in the process. Yet their efforts were stymied by the lack of stable interfaces across functional groups. The sorts of "boundary practices" that Etienne Wenger discusses (1998, p. 114), stable brokering practices that provide interfaces between different functional groups, were not widespread at Telecorp. The vital rhetorical skills that were needed to support them in a networked environment – skills such as confidence-building and negotiation – were developed and supported only informally through opportunistic volunteer mentoring. These skills were sorely needed in a net work environment but were also some of the most difficult skills to teach. As Sheila in Sales told me:

> It's amazing because a lot of people at Provisioning have problems with BigTel. And I know part of it is that BigTel is angry. But I think a lot of it is this is new to them too. And I wish that CLEC [Provisioning] would kinda grasp that too. Where – whenever it was resale, I could get anything I wanted. Anything! We're not supposed to turn numbers on after 3:00. I called in, we were supposed to have this number turned on, and because it was a flow through, and because I had always been nice to this person before, and I went to their manager and told him how wonderful they were – and they were like, looked through it, "Oh, it's just a flow through – I can have that on by 5:00."

Sheila encouraged others to build these trust-building skills, primarily through her informal mentoring, just as she had learned them.

Furthermore, in this rapidly changing environment, experiences were aggregated primarily through F1 notes and not easily generalized beyond a particular customer's history. Because Telecorp's black boxes could not be closed, workers were faced with a startling array of contingencies and not enough options for managing them in their learning. Some localized, informal arrangements did develop – for instance, Anita at the Internet Help Desk became the de facto point of contact between that group and Rosalind in Billing Administration – but these were not sufficient to black-box the interfaces among functional groups.

Transformative

Telecorp's strategic problem with black-boxing affected its transformative work. Networks are transformative, as we saw in Chapters 2 and 5, and so is learning in a net work environment. Ideally, networks provide enough relative stability to sustain regular sets of transformations, regular sets of rerepresentations that allow networks to work. Those regular sets of transformations occurred at Telecorp: as I said in Chapter 1, the company worked well and provided good service to its customers. But orders were not the only thing that Telecorp transformed. In a net work environment in which workers had to continually learn, these workers were constantly transformed as well. And here Telecorp had failed to erect a regular set of transformations: there was no regular progression or set of resources for supporting the learning transformations of workers. Consequently, transformations – of workers but also of orders and service and information – were often unstable and unpredictable, veering into unexpected parts of the company.

CONCLUSION

So Telecorp, although it performed net work well, had not achieved net *learning* to the extent necessary. Formally, it was trying to address a networked environment with learning and training measures that were better suited to modular work, measures that emphasized vertical learning but did not address horizontal learning. That is, modular silos were formally supported, but boundary work was not. Informally, Telecorp's learning and training measures were better suited to a smaller organization with less turnover and consequently stressed contingencies rather than principles.

The result was an organization whose learning was tactical rather than strategic and reactive rather than proactive.

Yet – and I emphasize this again, because it's easy to forget – *Telecorp still worked.* The network still learned. What's more, the entire industry was beset by these same problems or worse: as high as turnover was at Telecorp, at BigTel it was "unreal" (Gwendolyn, Human Resources). Even though learning for net work was unevenly supported and characterized as "thrown to the wolves," "trial and error," "sink or swim," somehow it worked. And that brings us back to the question I asked at the beginning of this book: How on earth does Telecorp function when the right hand doesn't know what the left hand is doing?

7

Conclusion: How Does Net Work *Work*?

The psalmist laments: "If I forget thee, O Jerusalem, let my right hand forget her cunning." As has become clear throughout this book, Telecorp's right hand did not know what the left hand was doing. Yet neither hand lost its cunning: Telecorp was a successful company with generally satisfied customers and employees. How? How did this organization bear up, even thrive, despite the multiple disruptions, the lack of guarded borders, the influx and fluxing of genres and social languages, the lack of modularity in work, the turnover, and the spotty support for training and learning?

Or to put it differently: What do we *do* about net work? What must we learn – or not forget – if the right hand is to remember its cunning? How do we go about examining, investigating, theorizing – and organizing, supporting, managing, and coordinating – such work? How do we retain the dynamism, cultivate the necessary interconnections, and put together a vocabulary to describe it while introducing the stability necessary for people to thrive in their net work?

Let's return to the dialogue we've had throughout the book, the one between activity theory and actor–network theory – or if you prefer, between dialectics and rhizomatics, weaving and splicing, development and alliance, modernism and amodernism. Because that's what this study and this book boil down to – how to retain and extend the insights of each as we continue to deal with rapidly changing work organization. How to take the two perspectives and put together a reasonable settlement, a synchretism rather than a synthesis.

Why? Because without a synchretism, a dialogue, we won't be able to address the many difficulties faced in net work. With a strictly developmental view, we won't be able to address the inferences and crosstalk that characterize net work, we won't be prepared to examine "dividuals" or dialogic individuals, and we won't adequately deal with the political–rhetorical alliances that must and do form to enable net work. And with a strictly political–rhetorical view, we won't be able to sense or support the developmental movements that continually happen in net work, and we'll be stuck in the constant, unproductive critique of which Latour warns (1995), the kind of critique that is best described by the euphemism "ankle-biting."

We don't want to bite ankles *or* hands; we want to strengthen hands and keep them from losing their cunning. So let's concentrate on a constructive path by reviewing and extending agreement between our two theoretical approaches. Let's start with what net work is.

WHAT DO WE KNOW ABOUT NET WORK?

What has emerged from this dialogue, begun in Chapter 1, that we've forced between activity theory and actor–network theory?

As we saw in Chapter 1, both approaches agree that networks are relatively stable, material assemblages of humans and nonhumans that collectively form standing sets of transformations. And in both approaches, as we saw in Chapter 2, networks are understood as heterogeneous, multiply linked, transformative, and black-boxed.

Heterogeneous

Networks are *heterogeneous*, constituted through relationships or associations among elements. These relationships change constantly – although networks achieve relative stability, they also acquire and shed associations with elements. The network's assemblage proliferates; the network tends to become more intricate, linking to and incorporating more groups, disciplines, fields, and trades as well as more technologies, regulations, legislation, and customers.

Multiply Linked

This heterogeneity is achieved through weaving and splicing. In weaving, a relatively stable part of the network develops over time. A functional group develops and refines practices, a discipline consolidates and extends social languages, a field develops certifications and genres. In splicing, interconnections are established among historically and developmentally unrelated parts of the network. Functional groups that have historically been kept separate must suddenly interoperate; genres and social languages from one field or discipline are deployed in another; tools and approaches from divergent activities are juxtaposed to yield hybrids. Splicing work is political and rhetorical, in flux, in need of new settlements and agreements. As we saw throughout the book, weaving and splicing happen constantly. But weaving is highlighted in modular work, in which disciplines and fields are generally kept in organizationally separate "silos." Splicing is highlighted in net work, in which organizational connections among assemblages, hidden passes, have proliferated at all levels. In net work, heterogeneity and its resulting multiple linkages are made visible through increased multiplicity, increased influxes of genres and resulting genre hybrids, and increased deployment of varying social languages.

Transformative

Due to these multiple links among heterogeneous elements, a network must represent and rerepresent phenomena in various ways, often conflicting ways. These circulating rerepresentations include not just information coming into the network but also parts of the network itself. In Chapter 1, Anita represented Geraldine in the F1 notes, while Darrel and Gil offered competing representations of a customer in their e-mail correspondence. In Chapter 5, we saw a cascade of rerepresentations that collectively constituted an order. Such transformations are part of even the simplest division of labor, but they proliferate in net work organizations, which are both highly heterogeneous and highly interlinked. These circulating texts *textere*, or weave together, the net work.

Black-Boxed

Finally, networks that develop over time develop "black boxes" to manage complexities: simple interfaces that filter out, limit, and manage complexity. Although black boxes come from actor–network theory, they are quintessentially woven: they emerge from historically developing activities that are kept separate enough for stable interfaces to develop. But they are also settlements that take a lot of work to achieve and maintain, and they can unravel at any time. In a rapidly developing, heavily spliced net work environment, such as Telecorp's, they can be very difficult to achieve.

At the same time, this dialogue between activity theory and actor–network theory has certainly not yielded total agreement. As discussed in Chapter 3, the two approaches have several fundamental disagreements (Table 7.1).

As I promised in Chapter 3, we have had a real dialogue – a real *argument*, in fact – between these two approaches, one in which actual agreements have

TABLE 7.1. *Remaining disagreements between activity theory and actor–network theory*

Activity theory	Actor–network theory
The first stroke is a weave	The first stroke is a splice
Developmental	Political–rhetorical
Competence, cognition	Negotiation
Dialectic	Rhizomatic
Genealogical	Antigenealogical
Asymmetrical	Symmetrical
Structural	Relational
Irreversible	Reversible
Contradictions	Translations

been acknowledged and actual differences have been aired. I've applied each approach's claims to the Telecorp case to examine how well they explain what we've seen and what insights they add. We have discovered advantages posed by each framework for understanding work in technologically mediated organizations. And as promised, I am not going to declare a reconciliation – or a winner – in this argument.

That being said, I see much potential for developing activity theory in particular through this dialogue. So let's move from description to prescription, drawing on this synchretism to better address the shift from modular work. Again: What do we *do* about net work? And how can we best develop activity theory in order to do it?

WHAT DO WE *DO* ABOUT NET WORK?

Net work poses particular challenges for at least three groups of people. *Workers* must constantly coordinate, negotiate, build trust and alliances, learn, and cross boundaries. *Managers* can no longer rely on hierarchical work organization to provide topsight (if they ever could) and must figure out how to support net work. And *researchers* must learn how to trace and conceptualize the constant boundary crossing that characterizes this work.

Implications for Workers

Relatively speaking, researchers (and, to a lesser extent, managers) have it easy: they can investigate, observe, and describe net work. But workers have to actually *live* it. Knowledge workers have been getting a lot of advice lately about how to do this from sources as diverse as popular time management books and online communities of "lifehackers." But let me summarize the implications that follow from what we've learned about Telecorp.

Rhetoric

Net workers need to become *strong rhetors*. Rhetoric, which is too often glossed as "lying," is the study of argumentation and persuasion (Aristotle, 1991) – and net workers sorely need to understand how to make arguments, how to persuade, how to build trust and stable alliances, how to negotiate and bargain and horse-trade across boundaries. In net work, which is intricately and unpredictably connected with everyone on the border, workers could find themselves doing this rhetorical work with nearly anyone. Like Machiavelli, they must persuade locals to show them the hidden passes that allow them to accomplish their work.

Time Management

Because everyone is at the border, because black boxes are in short supply and of short duration, anyone can potentially lay claim to another's time. Networks overlap and can be reconstituted unexpectedly, and the result is heavy work fragmentation. Workers must be able to adopt or adapt ways to deal with work fragmentation, including genres and rules that allow them to create their own stable transformations, their own black boxes, for prioritizing, organizing, and achieving work. That might involve learning popular time management techniques (Allen, 2003) or participating in online communities that face similar problems; it certainly will involve examining, evaluating, adapting, and adopting the local innovations that co-workers have developed.

Project Management

Similarly, when everyone is at the border, border crossing is constant and collaboration across functional groups becomes more pervasive. Consequently, workers must take on more of the work that used to be done by managers: planning projects, developing strategic and tactical understandings of their projects, becoming aware of the other projects in which their collaborators are embroiled. They need to become aware of and manage the "working spheres" (Gonzalez & Mark, 2004) in which they operate, the overlapping work activities that largely share the same tools but different rules, communities, and divisions of labor.

Adaptability

Finally, workers must be ever more adaptable. Being on the border means having to learn horizontally as well as vertically, having to understand others' work and social languages and genres, having to forage expertly for information. It also means learning how to assess sources and arguments, learning how to determine who to trust and when, learning how to persuade others to lead one through the hidden passes of the organization. It means opportunistically adapting technologies for one's own use and purposes (Sumner & Stolze, 1997) and discarding them when they no longer fit. Adaptability, to put it in a nutshell, means being agile enough to splice new components into a relatively stable, woven system.

In providing these implications, I don't want to sound like a new economy cheerleader, something that critics of knowledge work tend to accuse others of being (Gee, Hull, & Lankshear, 1996). Let's be less like cheerleaders and more like Machiavelli here. Or to put it differently, let's take a *postcritical* stance (Selber, 2004), acknowledging that net work is hard work, perhaps even *unfair* work, and then figuring out how to cope with and excel at it.

Implications for Managers

Workers have to live net work but so do managers. Managers, in fact, have a tough time with net work as opposed to modular work. Familiar managerial genres (such as organizational charts) no longer accurately represent or demarcate actual relationships. Sensible rules (such as strictly regulated contact points across organizational sections) are – necessarily – ignored. Trying to force net work into a modular work configuration tends to sharply reduce agility; once you put a phone or a networked computer on workers' desks, a modular work configuration will rapidly decay. Furthermore, trying to force a modular work configuration by limiting these channels will, in many cases, sharply limit the ability to interact and prosper in industries characterized by net work. So what do managers do about net work, based on what we saw at Telecorp?

Black-Boxing

As we've seen, black-boxing is a vital but often neglected part of net work. The most convenient black boxes – divisions depicted in organizational charts, teams assembled by managers, communication systems, and knowledge bases – are constantly being opened in net work, as we saw in Chapter 2. If managers try to "lock" these black boxes, the boxes will leak and connect to each other via hidden passes – or work will grind to a halt.

Instead, managers need to encourage stabilizing regimes. Let's call these sorts of black boxes "liaisons," "APIs," and "aggregations."

Liaisons are workers or positions that develop to provide stable connections across groups. For instance, as we saw in Chapter 6, Anita at the Internet Help Desk developed a stable, collegial relationship with Rosalind in Billing Administration, and this relationship allowed the two to reliably coordinate work between the two functional groups. Of course, other connections between the groups could happen at any moment, but they didn't. Team members trusted the two and deferred most of their communication to this channel. Managers can look for, cultivate, and support such relationships.

APIs, like the application program interfaces used in programming, consist of routines, protocols, and tools that allow simple interactions to generate complex effects. APIs in net work might include genres and other boundary objects. For instance, in Chapter 5 we saw that FOCs circulated through several functional groups. As they circulated, they allowed workers in each group to understand what they needed to understand about the order without placing follow-up calls. When managers see APIs fail – for instance, when CLEC Provisioning abandoned the AS/400 for a homegrown Access database – they should concentrate on either improving or substituting the API. That is, managers should learn to trace the genres, the regular information flows, and see if they are being transformed easily and well.

Aggregations are bottom-up characterizations of large sets of information enabled by "applications that aggregate individual work practices in order to depict relations among the work of group members" (Hart-Davidson, Spinuzzi, & Zachry, 2006). They are enabled through infrastructure that might include "tagging," in which individuals characterize parts of a large data set for their own use. Tags start out as idiosyncratic, but a "folksonomy" or emergent set of shared categories typically emerges as a second-order effect (Hart-Davidson et al., 2006). At the time of the study, Telecorp did not have the infrastructure to support folksonomies. But managers could consider deploying this sort of infrastructure, which trades control over characterization for insight into emergent understandings of work.

Strategic Thinking
I advocated project management skills for workers. Managers should support these skills, providing "topsight" for workers, recognizing that without resources for strategic thinking, workers can become bogged down in a reactive tactical stance. Because workers are forging their own unpredictable and

largely uncontrollable connections, managers who control strategic information too tightly can find that workers have routed around them and left them behind. More than ever, managers must provide a persuasive vision for each project and sufficient feedback for workers to see – and take ownership of – that project.

Training

That brings us to training. As we saw in Chapter 6, Telecorp's workers received support for *vertical* learning through multiple channels, but support for *horizontal* learning was restricted to informal, contingency-oriented channels. Managers should find ways to support horizontal learning across boundaries through formal as well as informal training and materials. They should particularly focus on supporting the sorts of skills that I mentioned above: rhetoric, time management, project management, and adaptability.

Implications for Researchers

Like workers and managers, researchers face important challenges from net work. These center around bounding the case.

As we saw in Chapter 3, actor–network theorists repeat Machiavelli's criticism of those who have "dreamed up republics and principalities which have never in truth been known to exist" (Machiavelli, 2003b, p. 50), and they apply it to researchers. Let's not make that mistake.

It's standard practice to bound research cases within a context defined in time and space, such as an organization, locale, or activity (Creswell, 1997; Yin, 2003). But as we've seen, net work is characterized by unpredictable and intermittent connections among widely distributed points: workers could at any moment find themselves talking with people in the next cubicle or the next state, people who could be co-workers, competitors, customers, or even former co-workers, friends, or relatives. Net work is not neatly segmentable into contexts or activities. Like the workers that Gonzales and Mark studied, net workers find themselves constantly shifting among multiple overlapping "working spheres" (2004). Instead of bounding the case, then, I repeat the advice I gave in Chapter 1: follow the actors and texts, the contradictions, the disruptions, and especially the genres.

In addition, researchers might consider what net work – and in particular multiplicity – might mean for characterizing the data collected in a case study. It is hardly revolutionary to suggest that we should compare participants' accounts with our own. But I suggest, along with actor–network theorists, that this comparison should happen at an ontological level as well.

As my colleagues and I have argued, research participants should be allowed to define the events and genres involved in their own work, to collectively construe the units and boundaries involved in their work. We argue that participants "should collectively make the call about what constitutes their work, what is a tool, and what is an action. Furthermore, they should be able to determine how to locally adapt their work," and they should be able to "tell their own stories with their own definitions and scales" (Spinuzzi, Hart-Davidson, & Zachry, 2006, p. 47). In fact, this is a rearticulation of the notion of aggregation discussed earlier. Researchers, workers, and managers all have much to gain by providing workers the infrastructure to describe, construe, and analyze their own work. As I've argued elsewhere (Spinuzzi, in press), increased connectivity will tend to have this effect anyway; we might as well leverage it.

These implications for workers, managers, and researchers are fairly concrete. As we'll see in the next section, there are also implications for theorists – activity theorists.

HOW DO WE DEVELOP ACTIVITY THEORY FOR NET WORK?

Although I've fostered a dialogue between activity theory and actor–network theory throughout, we've nearly reached the end of that discussion. As I said in Chapter 1, my end point is the further development of activity theory to address net work. Activity theory is better suited for this task, I believe, because it has a coherent, developmental account of learning and competence (see Chapter 6), and at the same time it has already begun developing accounts of splicing, such as knotworking and netWORKing. In contrast, actor–network theory is simply not designed to account for development. That's not a mortal failing, just a limitation in how it can be applied as a tool for investigating net work; we're not separating sheep from goats, but hammers from spatulas.

That doesn't mean that activity theory gets off the hook. Activity theory has historically emphasized development over political–rhetorical issues and weaving over splicing, as we saw in Chapters 2 and 3. And that has led to a degree of inflexibility when applied to net work, a tendency to focus on development and to interpret all phenomena in those terms: to bound and contain activities within those triangles, heuristics that depict work activities modularly. As we saw in Chapter 3, this tendency can be traced back to activity theory's core: dialectic.

Some of activity theory's more forward-looking theorists have begun to leverage nondialectical ways of describing interactions in networks. The most important development in this direction, although currently under-developed, is activity theory's adoption of M. M. Bakhtin's dialogism. As we saw in Chapters 1 and 5, for instance, Yrjö Engeström and his colleagues have started to use dialogism to characterize how activities interact without dialectical synthesis, although they do not draw a clean line between dialectics and dialogism. This seems to be a vital development if activity theory is going to address splicing, alliances, multiplicity, and rhetoric in much detail. As we saw in Chapter 3, dialectic by itself leads to arborescent, structural explanations of activity. Any thoroughgoing theorization of net work also has to include an account of the constant splicing that goes on, splicing that does not involve the synthesis and merging, the reconciliation of contradictions that dialectic leads us to expect.

As we've seen, rhetoric is a vital part of net work: net workers have to build trust and alliances, persuade others, negotiate, compromise, and haggle to build shared settlements. Rhetoric, as I argued in Chapter 2, has been a weak spot for activity theory due to its reliance on dialectic, so bringing in dialogism provides a way to better acknowledge and deal with rhetoric in net work. It provides a way to build in, rather than implicitly squeeze out, the multiplicity of perspectives and n-dimensional articulations among activities. It also allows us to sidestep dialectic's one-way motion, time's arrow, by reminding us that activities are political–rhetorical *settlements*. In doing so, it allows us to examine and discuss the alliances that actor–network theory describes. Dialogism potentially lets us integrate political–rhetorical concerns into activity theory without sacrificing its focus on development. This is a line of inquiry that has barely begun, particularly by rhetoricians (Russell, 1997b), and that must be continued if activity theory is to address net work adequately.

As we saw in Chapter 5, net work involves circulating rerepresentations – boundary objects, typically cast as genres – and as these rerepresentations cross boundaries, they perform in different activities. They work in ecologies in which they serve as compound mediators, assemblages that function differently from their components. In such assemblages, associative reasoning – rhizomatic reasoning – is no longer childish (as Vygotsky saw it) but central for understanding and performing net work.

So although I recommend activity theory as a primary framework, it should be used cautiously, with full knowledge of its limitations and with reconsiderations of these points. We need a more flexible, more associational activity theory with a stronger splicing account if we're going to analyze net work properly. We need activity theory to be more dialogical and more rhetorical. We need a synchretism.

HOW DO WE COPE WITH NET WORK?

At the beginning of this chapter, I asked how to ensure that the right hand doesn't forget its cunning: how to retain the dynamism and flexibility necessary for net work while introducing the stability that workers need in order to thrive. Net work poses several challenges to the way we perform, manage, research, and theorize work. It's tempting to be purely reactive by trying to enforce and maintain a modular work organization or purely critical by focusing on the negative effects of net work and the sometimes utopian claims that surround knowledge work. But both stances are essentially conservative ones, reacting to changes in work organization by retreating to past solutions and ready criticisms. Throughout this book, I've taken a different stance, a postcritical, strategic stance – surveying the ground for possibilities rather than dreaming up republics and principalities. Only by taking a strategic stance will we be able to identify objectives, set goals, take action, and retain the dynamism and flexibility necessary to cope with net work – whether we're workers, managers, researchers, or theorists. Others can bite ankles; let's concentrate on strengthening hands, making the right and left equally dextrous, and teaching them the cunning they need for performing net work.

Notes on Methodology

Telecorp presented some methodological challenges that are familiar to qualitative researchers. On the one hand, I wanted to develop a thick description of workers' communicative practices at the organization. On the other hand, I also wanted to develop a general overview of how the organization communicated. Telecorp's management wanted this as well, since management had become concerned about perceived communication issues across the organization. Compounding these issues was the goal of intruding as little as possible on the organization's work.

In the interest of satisfying these objectives, I designed a case study that would allow me to observe and interview approximately a third of the workers in each functional unit in Midsize City, where Telecorp's corporate offices and the majority of its workforce were located. This study design yielded a less thick description for individual workers than a more bounded case study would have (e.g., a case bounded by a functional group; see Wenger, 1998, for an example). However, it allowed me to examine routine communicative interactions from multiple perspectives. When workers from the NOC and CLEC Provisioning collaborated, for instance, I was able to draw on multiple interviews and observations from both sets of workers – and from third parties – to interpret the collaboration.

DATA COLLECTION

I observed 89 individuals and interviewed 84 of them (the other 5 either left Telecorp before the second observation or were not available for interviews). In addition, I observed five group training sessions. I collected the following data:

Observations of Individual Work
I performed two two-hour observations of each worker. These observations were recorded in exhaustive field notes, collected primarily through a handheld device with an attached keyboard (Spinuzzi, 2003c).

Observations of Training
In addition, I performed six observations of training sessions, each lasting from one to four hours. Again, these observations were recorded in exhaustive field notes.

Interviews
I performed one semistructured postobservational interview after the second observation of each participant. These interviews tended to be short (15–30 minutes) and were structured around the components of an activity system: subject, object, mediational means, community, rules, division of labor, and outcome.

Textual Artifacts
During observations and interviews, I collected texts from each functional group. Texts were both communicative (passed among workers) and mediational (meant for the worker alone, such as checklists). I also took photos of workspaces, particularly focusing on how artifacts were arranged in those workspaces. These artifacts had been observed in use and were triangulated with the observations and interviews. Some artifacts were redacted before they were turned over to me.

DATA ANALYSIS

For an overview of the data, I transcribed all observational notes and portions of each interview, placed them in a database, then applied descriptive codes based on a starter list of activity theory-related concepts (see Miles & Huberman, 1994). The large number of participants meant that I could triangulate within and across observations, interviews, and artifacts.

In addition, I wrote analytical memos at the end of most observations to reflect on emerging connections (Miles & Huberman, 1994).

For specific events and functional groups, I used more specific analyses:

Flow Diagrams
To examine ways in which texts circulated through Customer Service, I identified specific worker roles and the ways that they communicated,

particularly the genres that circulated among them. Flow diagrams are described by Beyer and Holtzblatt (1998, Chapter 6) and are based on network diagrams (Miles & Huberman, 1994, Chapters 5 and 6).

Genre Ecology Modeling
To examine genre assemblages in Credit & Collections and Cash Posting, I identified and examined genres being used in each functional group, then coded interactions among them (see Spinuzzi, 2002a, for a detailed methodological discussion).

Sociotechnical Graphs
To examine substitutions among genres in the NOC, I mapped articulations of humans and nonhumans as "statements" and the substitutions among them (Latour, Mauguin, & Teil, 1992; cf. Spinuzzi, Hart-Davidson, & Zachry, 2006).

Role-Ordered Matrices
To develop general descriptions of functional groups and their objectives, I examined descriptions that workers provided of their own work, comparing these within and across functional groups and to official descriptions provided by Telecorp.

WORKS CITED

Akrich, M. (1992). The de-scription of technical objects. In W. Bijker & J. Law (Eds.), *Shaping technology, building society: Studies in sociotechnical change* (pp. 205–224). Cambridge, MA: MIT Press.

Akrich, M. (1993). A gazogene in Costa Rica: An experiment in techno-sociology. In P. Lemonnier (Ed.), *Technological choices: Transformation in material cultures since the Neolithic* (pp. 289–337). New York: Routledge.

Akrich, M., Callon, M., & Latour, B. (2002a). The key to success in innovation part I: The art of interessement. *International Journal of Innovation Management*, 6(2), 187–206.

Akrich, M., Callon, M., & Latour, B. (2002b). The key to success in innovation part II: The art of choosing good spokespersons. *International Journal of Innovation Management*, 6(2), 207–255.

Alberts, D. S., & Hayes, R. E. (2003). *Power to the edge*. Available from: http://www.dodccrp.org/files/Alberts_Power.pdf.

Allen, D. (2003). *Getting things done: The art of stress-free productivity*. New York: Penguin.

Alliance for Telecommunications Industry Solutions (2004). *Network*. Available from: http://www.atis.org/glossary/definition.aspx?id=3457.

Amidon, S. R. (2005). Writing the learning organization: A framework for teaching and research. *Business Communication Quarterly*, 68(4), 406–428.

Antunes, P., & Costa, C. J. (2003). From genre analysis to the design of meetingware. *Proceedings of the 2003 International ACM SIGGROUP Conference on Supporting Group Work* (pp. 302–310). New York: ACM Press.

Aristotle (1991). *The art of rhetoric*. New York: Penguin.

Aristotle (1992). *The politics*. New York: Penguin.

Arquilla, J., & Ronfeldt, D. (2001a). The advent of netwar (revisited). In J. Arquilla & D. Ronfeldt (Eds.), *Networks and netwars: The future of terror, crime, and militancy* (pp. 1–28). Santa Monica, CA: RAND.

Arquilla, J., & Ronfeldt, D. (2001b). *Networks and netwars: The future of terror, crime, and militancy*. Santa Monica, CA: RAND.

Atkinson, S. R., & Moffat, J. (2005). *The agile organization: From informal networks to complex effects and agility*. Available from: http://www.dodccrp.org/files/Atkinson_Agile.pdf.

Aufderheide, P. (1999). *Communications policy and the public interest: The Telecommunications Act of 1996.* New York: Guilford Press.

Bakhtin, M. M. (1981). *The dialogic imagination: Four essays.* Austin: University of Texas Press.

Bakhtin, M. M. (1984). *Problems of Dostoevsky's poetics.* Minneapolis: University of Minnesota Press.

Bakhtin, M. M. (1986). *Speech genres and other late essays.* Austin: University of Texas Press.

Bateson, G. (1972). *Steps to an ecology of mind.* New York: Ballantine Books.

Bateson, G. (1979). *Mind and nature: A necessary unity.* New York: E. P. Dutton.

Bazerman, C. (1988). *Shaping written knowledge: The genre and activity of the experimental article in science.* Madison: University of Wisconsin Press.

Bazerman, C. (1999). *The languages of Edison's light.* Cambridge, MA: MIT Press.

Bazerman, C. (2003). *What is not institutionally visible does not count: The problem of making activity assessable, accountable, and plannable.* Available from: http://wac.colostate.edu/books/selves_societies.

Beniger, J. (1989). *The control revolution: Technological and economic origins of the information society* (reprint ed.). Cambridge, MA: Harvard University Press.

Benkler, Y. (2006). *The wealth of networks: How social production transforms markets and freedom.* New Haven, CT: Yale University Press.

Berg, M. (1996). The fruitful a-modernism of a lingering modernist: Commentary on Bruno Latour's "On Interobjectivity." *Mind, Culture, and Activity, 3*(4), 252–258.

Berg, M. (1997). *Rationalizing medical work: Decision-support techniques and medical practices.* Cambridge, MA: MIT Press.

Berg, M. (1998). The politics of technology: On bringing social theory into technological design. *Science, Technology, & Human Values, 23*(4), 456–490.

Berg, M. (1999). Accumulating and coordinating: Occasions for information technologies in medical work. *Computer Supported Cooperative Work, 8*(4), 373–401.

Berg, M. (2000). Lessons from a dinosaur: Mediating is research through an analysis of the medical record. *HOIT '00: Proceedings of the IFIP TC9 WG9.3 International Conference on Home Oriented Informatics and Telematics: IF at home: Virtual influences on everyday life* (pp. 487–506). Deventer, The Netherlands: Kluwer.

Beyer, H., & Holtzblatt, K. (1998). *Contextual design: Defining customer-centered systems.* San Francisco: Morgan Kaufmann.

Blackler, F., Crump, N., & McDonald, S. (2003). Organizing processes in complex activity networks. In D. Nicolini, S. Gherardi, & D. Yanow (Eds.), *Knowing in organizations: A practice-based approach* (pp. 126–150). Armonk, NY: Sharpe.

Blackler, F., & McDonald, S. (2000). Power, mastery and organizational learning. *Journal of Management Studies, 37*(6), 833–851.

Boczkowski, P. J. (2005). *Digitizing the news: Innovation in online newspapers.* Cambridge, MA: MIT Press.

Bødker, S. (1991). *Through the interface: A human activity approach to user interface design.* Hillsdale, NJ: Erlbaum.

Bødker, S., & Andersen, P. B. (2005). Complex mediation. *Human-Computer Interaction, 20*, 353–402.

Boot, M. (2007). *War made new: Weapons, warriors, and the making of the modern world.* New York: Gotham.

Bowker, G. (1987). A well ordered reality: Aspects of the development of Schlumberger, 1920–39. *Social Studies of Science, 17,* 611–655.

Bowker, G., & Star, S. L. (1999). *Sorting things out: Classification and its consequences.* Cambridge, MA: MIT Press.

Bowker, G. C. (1994). *Science on the run: Information management and industrial geophysics at Schlumberger, 1920–1940.* Cambridge, MA: MIT Press.

Braverman, H. (1974). *Labor and monopoly capital.* New York: Monthly Review Press.

Brull, S. V., & Elstrom, P. (1997, December). At 7 1/2 cents a minute, who cares if you can't hear a pin drop? *Business Week, 46.*

Callon, M. (1986a). The sociology of an actor–network: The case of the electric vehicle. In M. Callon, J. Law, & A. Rip (Eds.), *Mapping the dynamics of science and technology: Sociology of science in the real world* (pp. 19–34). London: Macmillan.

Callon, M. (1986b). Some elements of a sociology of translation: Domestication of the scallops and the fishermen of Saint Brieuc Bay. In J. Law (Ed.), *Power, action and belief: A new sociology of knowledge?* (pp. 196–233). Boston: Routledge.

Callon, M. (1991). Techno-economic networks and irreversibility. In J. Law (Ed.), *A sociology of monsters? Essays on power, technology and domination* (pp. 132–161). London: Routledge.

Callon, M. (1992). The dynamics of techno-economic networks. In R. Coombs, P. Saviotti, & V. Walsh (Eds.), *Technological change and company strategies: Economic and sociological perspectives* (pp. 72–102). New York: Harcourt Brace Jovanovich.

Callon, M. (2002). Writing and (re)writing devices as tools for managing complexity. In J. Law & A. Mol (Eds.), *Complexities: Social studies of knowledge practices* (pp. 191–217). Durham, NC: Duke University Press.

Callon, M. (2004). The role of hybrid communities and socio-technical arrangements in the participatory design. *Journal of the Center for Information Studies,* 5(3), 3–10. Available from: http://www.yc.musashi-tech.ac.jp/~cisj/05/5_01.pdf.

Callon, M., & Law, J. (1982). On interests and their transformation: Enrolment and counter-enrolment. *Social Studies of Science, 12*(4), 615–625.

Callon, M., Law, J., & Rip, A. (1986). How to study the force of science. In M. Callon, J. Law, & A. Rip (Eds.), *Mapping the dynamics of science and technology: Sociology of science in the real world* (pp. 3–15). London: Macmillan.

Callon, M., & Rabeharisoa, V. (2003). Research "in the wild" and the shaping of social identities. *Technology in Society, 25,* 193–204.

Carlson, W. B., & Gorman, M. E. (1992). Socio-technical graphs and cognitive maps: A response to Latour, Mauguin and Teil. *Social Studies of Science, 22,* 81–89.

Carroll, L. (2003). *Alice in Wonderland.* Buffalo, NY: Firefly Books.

Carter, L. (Ed.). (2005). *Market matters: Applied rhetoric studies and free market competition.* Creskill, NJ: Hampton Press.

Castells, M. (1996). *The rise of the network society.* Malden, MA: Blackwell.

Charlton, B. G. (2006). The rise of the boy-genius: Psychological neoteny, science and modern life. *Medical Hypotheses, 67*(4), 679–681.

Clark, D. (2007). Rhetoric of empowerment: Genre, activity, and the distribution of capital. In M. Zachry & C. Thralls (Eds.), *Communicative practices in workplaces and the professions: Cultural perspectives on the regulation of discourse and organizations* (pp. 155–180). Farmingdale, NY: Baywood Publishing.

Cole, M. (1996). *Cultural psychology: A once and future discipline.* Cambridge, MA: Harvard University Press.

Cole, M., & Engeström, Y. (1993). A cultural-historical approach to distributed cognition. In G. Salomon (Ed.), *Distributed cognitions: Psychological and educational considerations* (pp. 1–46). Cambridge: Cambridge University Press.

Covey, S. R. (1990). *The seven habits of highly effective people.* New York: Free Press.

Crandall, R. W. (1991). *After the breakup: U.S. telecommunications in a more competitive era.* Washington, DC: Brookings Institution.

Creswell, J. W. (1997). *Qualitative inquiry and research design: Choosing among five traditions.* Thousand Oaks, CA: Sage.

Czerwinski, M., Horvitz, E., & Wilhite, S. (2004). A diary study of task switching and interruptions. *CHI '04: Proceedings of the SIGCHI Conference on Human Factors in Computing Systems* (pp. 175–182). New York: ACM Press.

Davis, D. D. (2000). *Breaking up (at) totality: A rhetoric of laughter.* Carbondale: Southern Illinois University Press.

de Armond, P. (2001). Netwar in the Emerald City: WTO protest strategy and tactics. In J. Arquilla & D. Ronfeldt (Eds.), *Networks and netwars: The future of terror, crime, and militancy* (pp. 201–238). Santa Monica, CA: RAND.

de Laet, M., & Mol, A. (2000). The Zimbabwe Bush Pump: Mechanics of a fluid technology. *Social Studies of Science, 30*(2), 225–263.

Deleuze, G. (1995). *Negotiations, 1972–1990.* New York: Columbia University Press.

Deleuze, G., & Guattari, F. (1987). *A thousand plateaus: Capitalism and schizophrenia.* Minneapolis: University of Minnesota Press.

Devitt, A. J. (1991). Intertextuality in tax accounting: Generic, referential, and functional. In C. Bazerman & J. G. Paradis (Eds.), *Textual dynamics of the professions: Historical and contemporary studies of writing in professional communities* (pp. 336–357). Madison: University of Wisconsin Press.

Drucker, P. F. (2003). *The essential Drucker: The best of sixty years of Peter Drucker's essential writings on management* (reprint ed.). New York: Collins.

Duesterberg, T., & Gordon, K. (1997). *Competition and deregulation in telecommunications: The case for a new paradigm.* Indianapolis, IN: Hudson Institute.

Edwards, S. J. A. (2000). *Swarming on the battlefield: Past, present, and future.* Santa Monica, CA: RAND.

Ehn, P. (1989). *Work-oriented design of computer artifacts.* Hillsdale, NJ: Erlbaum.

Engels, F. (1954). *Dialectics of nature.* Moscow: Foreign Languages Publishing House.

Engels, F. (1975). *Socialism: Utopian and scientific.* New York: International Publishers.

Engeström, R. (1995). Voice as communicative action. *Mind, Culture, and Activity, 2*(3), 192–214.

Engeström, Y. (1987). *Learning by expanding: An activity-theoretical approach to developmental research.* Helsinki: Orienta-Konsultit Oy.

Engeström, Y. (1990). *Learning, working, and imagining: Twelve studies in activity theory.* Helsinki: Orienta-Konsultit Oy.

Engeström, Y. (1992). *Interactive expertise: Studies in distributed working intelligence.* University of Helsinki.

Engeström, Y. (1996a). Developmental work research as educational research: Looking ten years back and into the zone of proximal development. *Nordisk Pedagogik, 16*(3), 131–143.

Engeström, Y. (1996b). Interobjectivity, ideality, and dialectics. *Mind, Culture, and Activity, 3*(4), 259–265.

Engeström, Y. (1999). Expansive visibilization of work: An activity-theoretical perspective. *Computer Supported Cooperative Work, 8,* 63–93.

Engeström, Y. (2001). Expansive learning at work: Toward an activity theoretical reconceptualization. *Journal of Education and Work, 14*(1), 133–156.

Engeström, Y. (2004). *New forms of learning in co-configuration work.* Available from: http://is2.lse.ac.uk/events/ESRCseminars/engestrom.pdf.

Engeström, Y., Engeström, R., & Kärkkäinen, M. (1995). Polycontextuality and boundary crossing in expert cognition: Learning and problem solving in complex work activities. *Learning and Instruction, 5,* 319–336.

Engeström, Y., Engeström, R., & Vähääho, T. (1999). When the center does not hold: The importance of knotworking. In S. Chaiklin, M. Hedegaard, & U. J. Jensen (Eds.), *Activity theory and social practice* (pp. 345–374). Denmark: Aarhus University Press.

Engeström, Y., & Escalante, V. (1996). Mundane tool or object of affection? The rise and fall of the Postal Buddy. In B. A. Nardi (Ed.), *Context and consciousness: Activity theory and human-computer interaction* (pp. 325–374). Cambridge, MA: MIT Press.

Engeström, Y., Puonti, A., & Seppänen, L. (2003). Spatial and temporal expansion of the object as a challenge for reorganizing work. In D. Nicolini, S. Gherardi, & D. Yanow (Eds.), *Knowing in organizations: A practice-based approach* (pp. 151–186). Armonk, NY: Sharpe.

Fitzpatrick, G. (2000). Centres, peripheries, and electronic communication: Changing work practice boundaries. *Scandinavian Journal of Information Systems, 12,* 115–148.

Gay, G., & Hembrooke, H. (2004). *Activity-centered design: An ecological approach to designing smart tools and usable systems.* Cambridge, MA: MIT Press.

Gee, J. P., Hull, G., & Lankshear, C. (1996). *The new work order: Behind the language of the new capitalism.* New York: Westview Press.

Geisler, C. (2001). Textual objects: Accounting for the role of texts in the everyday life of complex organizations. *Written Communication, 18*(3), 296–325.

Geisler, C. (2003). *When management becomes personal: An activity-theoretic analysis of Palm technologies.* Available from: http://wac.colostate.edu/books/selves_societies

Gerlach, L. P. (2001). The structure of social movements: Environmental activism and its opponents. In J. Arquilla & D. Ronfeldt (Eds.), *Networks and netwars: The future of terror, crime, and militancy* (pp. 289–310). Santa Monica, CA: RAND.

Gonzalez, V., & Mark, G. (2005). Managing currents of work: Multi-tasking among multiple collaborations. *European Conference in Computer Supported Cooperative Work.* Paris: Springer-Verlag.

Gonzalez, V. M., & Mark, G. (2004). "Constant, constant, multi-tasking craziness": Managing multiple working spheres. *CHI '04: Proceedings of the SIGCHI Conference on Human Factors in Computing Systems* (pp. 113–120). New York: ACM Press.

Hakkarainen, K. (2003). Can cognitive explanations be eliminated? *Science & Education, 12*, 671–689.

Handbook of Texas Online (2005). *s.v. "Telephone Service."* Available from: http://www.tsha.utexas.edu/handbook/online/articles/view/TT/egt2.html.

Haraway, D. J. (1991). *Simians, cyborgs, and women: The reinvention of nature.* New York: Routledge.

Haraway, D. J. (1996). *Modest_witness@second_millenium.femaleman_meets_oncomouse: Feminism and technoscience.* New York: Routledge.

Hart-Davidson, W., Spinuzzi, C., & Zachry, M. (2006). Visualizing writing activity as knowledge work: Challenges and opportunities. *SIGDOC '06: Proceedings of the 24th Annual International Conference on Design of Communication* (pp. 70–77). New York: ACM Press.

Häyrynen, Y.-P. (1999). Collapse, creation, and continuity in Europe: How do people change? In Y. Engeström, R. Miettinen, & R.-L. Punamäki (Eds.), *Perspectives on activity theory* (pp. 115–132). New York: Cambridge University Press.

Heldman, P. K., Heldman, R., & Bystrzycki, T. A. (1997). *Competitive telecommunications: How to thrive under the Telecommunications Act.* New York: McGraw-Hill.

Helle, M. (2000). Disturbances and contradictions as tools for understanding work in the newsroom. *Scandinavian Journal of Information Systems, 12*, 81–114.

Hewitt, H. (2005). *Blog: Understanding the information reformation that's changing your world.* Nashville, TN: Nelson Business.

Holland, D., & Reeves, J. (1996). Activity theory and the view from somewhere: Team perspectives on the intellectual work of programming. In *Context and consciousness: Activity theory and human-computer interaction* (pp. 257–282). Cambridge, MA: MIT Press.

Hughes, M. W. (1996). Telecommunications reform and the death of the local exchange monopoly. *Florida State University Law Review, 24*, 179–217.

Hughes, T. P. (1993). *Networks of power: Electrification in Western society, 1880–1930.* Baltimore, MD: Johns Hopkins University Press.

Hutchings, D. R., Smith, G., Meyers, B., Czerwinski, M., & Robertson, G. (2004). Display space usage and window management operation comparisons between single monitor and multiple monitor users. *AVI '04: Proceedings of the Working Conference on Advanced Visual Interfaces* (pp. 32–39). New York: ACM Press.

Hutchins, E. (1995). *Cognition in the wild.* Cambridge, MA: MIT Press.

Hyysalo, S. (2005). Objects and motives in a product design process. *Mind, Culture, and Activity, 12*(1), 19–36.

Ilyenkov, E. (1977). *Dialectical logic: Essays on its history and theory.* Moscow: Progress.

Ilyenkov, E. (1982). *The dialectics of the abstract and the concrete in Marx's Capital.* Moscow: Progress.

Johnson-Eilola, J. (1998). Living on the surface: Learning in the age of global communication networks. In *Page to screen: Taking literacy into the electronic era* (pp. 185–210). New York: Routledge.

Johnson-Eilola, J. (2001). Datacloud: Expanding the roles and locations of information. *Proceedings of the 19th Annual International Conference on Computer Documentation* (pp. 47–54). New York: ACM Press.

Johnson-Eilola, J. (2005). *Datacloud: Toward a new theory of online work.* Cresskill, NJ: Hampton Press.

Kaptelinin, V. (1996). Computer-mediated activity: Functional organs in social and developmental contexts. In B. Nardi (Ed.), *Context and consciousness: Activity theory and human-computer interaction* (pp. 45–68). Cambridge, MA: MIT Press.

Kaptelinin, V. (2005). The object of activity: Making sense of the sense-maker. *Mind, Culture, and Activity, 12*(1), 4–18.

Kaptelinin, V., & Nardi, B. A. (2006). *Acting with technology: Activity theory and interaction design.* Cambridge, MA: MIT Press.

King, J. L., & Frost, R. L. (2002). Managing distance over time: The evolution of technologies of dis/ambiguation. In P. J. Hinds & S. Kiesler (Eds.), *Distributed work* (pp. 3–26). Cambridge, MA: MIT Press.

Korpela, M., Mursu, A., & Soriyan, H. (2002). Information systems development as an activity. *Computer Supported Cooperative Work, 11,* 111–128.

Korpela, M., Soriyan, H., & Olifokunbi, H. (2000). Disturbances and contradictions as tools for understanding work in the newsroom. *Scandinavian Journal of Information Systems, 12,* 191–210.

Latour, B. (1986). The powers of association. In J. Law (Ed.), *Power, action and belief: A new sociology of knowledge?* (pp. 264–280). London: Routledge.

Latour, B. (1987). *Science in action: How to follow scientists and engineers through society.* Philadelphia: Open University Press.

Latour, B. (1988a). *The Pasteurization of France.* Cambridge, MA: Harvard University Press.

Latour, B. (1988b). The politics of explanation: An alternative. In S. Woolgar (Ed.), *Knowledge and reflexivity: New frontiers in the sociology of knowledge* (pp. 155–176). London: Sage.

Latour, B. (1988c). *The Prince* for machines as well as machinations. In B. Elliott (Ed.), *Technology and social processes* (pp. 20–43). Edinburgh: Edinburgh University Press.

Latour, B. (1990). Drawing things together. In M. Lynch & S. Woolgar (Eds.), *Representation in scientific practice* (pp. 19–68). Cambridge, MA: MIT Press.

Latour, B. (1991). Technology is society made durable. In J. Law (Ed.), *A sociology of monsters? Essays on power, technology and domination* (pp. 103–131). London: Routledge.

Latour, B. (1992a). A reply to Carlson and Gorman. *Social Studies of Science, 22,* 91–95.

Latour, B. (1992b). Where are the missing masses? The sociology of a few mundane artefacts. In W. Bijker & J. Law (Eds.), *Shaping technology, building society: Studies in sociotechnical change* (pp. 225–258). Cambridge, MA: MIT Press.

Latour, B. (1993a). Ethnography of a "high-tech" case: About Aramis. In P. Lemonnier (Ed.), *Technological choices: Transformation in material cultures since the Neolithic* (pp. 372–398). New York: Routledge.

Latour, B. (1993b). *We have never been modern.* Cambridge, MA: Harvard University Press.

Latour, B. (1995). Social theory and the study of computerized work sites. In W. Orlikowski, G. Walsham, M. Jones, & J. DeGross (Eds.), *Information technology and changes in organizational work* (pp. 285–307). London: Chapman & Hall.

Latour, B. (1996a). *Aramis, or the love of technology*. Cambridge, MA: Harvard University Press.

Latour, B. (1996b). On interobjectivity. *Mind, Culture, and Activity, 3*(4), 228–251.

Latour, B. (1996c). Pursuing the discussion of interobjectivity with a few friends. *Mind, Culture, and Activity, 3*(4), 266–289.

Latour, B. (1999a). On recalling ANT. In J. Law & J. Hassard (Eds.), *Actor-network theory and after* (pp. 15–25). Oxford: Blackwell.

Latour, B. (1999b). *Pandora's hope: Essays on the reality of science studies*. Cambridge, MA: Harvard University Press.

Latour, B. (2002). Morality and technology: The end of the means. *Theory, Culture & Society, 19*(5), 247–260.

Latour, B. (2004). *Politics of nature: How to bring the sciences into democracy*. Cambridge, MA: Harvard University Press.

Latour, B. (2006). *Reassembling the social: An introduction to actor-network theory*. New York: Oxford University Press.

Latour, B., Mauguin, P., & Teil, G. (1992). A note on socio-technical graphs. *Social Studies of Science, 22*, 33–57.

Latour, B., & Woolgar, S. (1979). *Laboratory life: The social construction of scientific facts*. Beverly Hills, CA: Sage.

Lave, J., & Wenger, E. (1991). *Situated learning: Legitimate peripheral participation*. New York: Cambridge University Press.

Law, J. (1986a). The heterogeneity of texts. In M. Callon, J. Law, & A. Rip (Eds.), *Mapping the dynamics of science and technology: Sociology of science in the real world* (pp. 67–83). London: Macmillan.

Law, J. (1986b). On the methods of long distance control: Vessels, navigation and the Portuguese route to India. In J. Law (Ed.), *Power, action and belief: A new sociology of knowledge?* (pp. 234–263). Boston: Routledge.

Law, J. (1992). Notes on the theory of the actor-network: Ordering, strategy, and heterogeneity. *Systems Practice, 5*(4), 379–393.

Law, J. (1999). After ANT: Complexity, naming and topology. In J. Law & J. Hassard (Eds.), *Actor-network theory and after* (pp. 1–14). Oxford: Blackwell.

Law, J. (2002a). *Aircraft stories: Decentering the object in technoscience*. Durham, NC: Duke University Press.

Law, J. (2002b). On hidden heterogeneities: Complexity, formalism, and aircraft design. In *Complexities: Social studies of knowledge practices* (pp. 116–141). Durham, NC: Duke University Press.

Law, J. (2004a). *After method: Mess in social science research*. New York: Routledge.

Law, J. (2004b). And if the global were small and noncoherent? Method, complexity, and the baroque. *Environment and Planning, 22*(1), 13–26.

Law, J., & Callon, M. (1992). The life and death of an aircraft: A network analysis of technical change. In W. Bijker & J. Law (Eds.), *Shaping technology, building society: Studies in sociotechnical change* (pp. 21–52). Cambridge, MA: MIT Press.

Law, J., & Mol, A. (Eds.). (2002). *Complexities: Social studies of knowledge practices*. Durham, NC: Duke University Press.

Law, J., & Singleton, V. (2005). Object lessons. *Organization, 12*(3), 331–355.

Lektorsky, V. A. (1999). Activity theory in a new era. In Y. Engeström, R. Miettinen, & R.-L. Punamäki (Eds.), *Perspectives on activity theory* (pp. 65–69). New York: Cambridge University Press.

Lenert, E. M. (1998). A communication theory perspective on telecommunications policy. *Journal of Communication, 48*(4), 3–23.

Leont'ev, A. (1974). The problem of activity in psychology. *Soviet Psychology, 13*(2), 4–33.

Leont'ev, A. N. (1978). *Activity, consciousness, and personality.* Englewood Cliffs, NJ: Prentice-Hall.

Lipnack, J., & Stamps, J. (1994). *The age of the network: Organizing principles for the 21st century.* Essex Junction, VT: Omneo.

Locke, C., Levine, R., Searls, D., & Weinberger, D. (2001). *The cluetrain manifesto: The end of business as usual.* New York: Perseus Books.

Longaker, M. G. (2006). Back to basics: An apology for economism in technical writing scholarship. *Technical Communication Quarterly, 15*(1), 9–29.

Ludvigsen, S. R., Havnes, A., & Chr. Lahn, L. (2003). Workplace learning across activity systems: A case study of sales engineers. In *Between school and work: New perspectives on transfer and boundary-crossing* (pp. 291–310). Boston: Pergamon.

Luria, A. R. (1976). *Cognitive development, its cultural and social foundations.* Cambridge, MA: Harvard University Press.

Machiavelli, N. (2001). *The art of war* (2nd ed.). Cambridge, MA: Da Capo Press.

Machiavelli, N. (2003a). *The discourses.* New York: Penguin Books.

Machiavelli, N. (2003b). *The prince.* New York: Penguin Books.

Malone, T. W. (2004). *The future of work: How the new order of business will shape your organization, your management style and your life.* Boston: Harvard Business School Press.

Mark, G., Gonzalez, V. M., & Harris, J. (2005). No task left behind? Examining the nature of fragmented work. *CHI '05: Proceedings of the SIGCHI Conference on Human Factors in Computing Systems* (pp. 321–330). New York: ACM Press.

Marx, K. (1990). *Capital: Volume 1.* New York: Penguin Books.

McCarthy, J. F., & boyd, danah m. (2005). Digital backchannels in shared physical spaces: Experiences at an academic conference. *CHI '05: CHI '05 extended abstracts on human factors in computing systems* (pp. 1641–1644). New York: ACM Press.

McMaster, S. (2002). *The telecommunications industry.* Westport, CT: Greenwood Press.

Miettinen, R. (1998). Object construction and networks in research work: The case of research on cellulose-degrading enzymes. *Social Studies of Science, 28*(3), 423–463.

Miettinen, R. (1999). The riddle of things: Activity theory and actor-network theory as approaches to studying innovations. *Mind, Culture, and Activity, 6*(3), 170–195.

Miettinen, R. (2005). Object of activity and individual motivation. *Mind, Culture, and Activity, 12*(1), 52–69.

Miettinen, R., & Hasu, M. (2002). Articulating user needs in collaborative design: Towards an activity-theoretical approach. *Computer Supported Cooperative Work, 11*, 129–151.

Miles, M. B., & Huberman, A. M. (1994). *Qualitative data analysis: An expanded sourcebook* (2nd ed.). Thousand Oaks, CA: Sage.

Miller, C. R. (1984). Genre as social action. *Quarterly Journal of Speech, 70*, 157–178.

Mol, A. (2002). *The body multiple: Ontology in medical practice.* Durham, NC: Duke University Press.

Mol, A., & Law, J. (1994). Regions, networks and fluids: Anaemia and social topology. *Social Studies of Science, 24*(1), 641–671.

Mueller, M. L. (1997). *Universal service: Competition, interconnection, and monopoly in the making of the American telephone system.* Cambridge, MA: MIT Press.

Nardi, B. A. (Ed.). (1996a). *Context and consciousness: Activity theory and human-computer interaction.* Cambridge, MA: MIT Press.

Nardi, B. A. (1996b). Studying context: A comparison of activity theory, situated action models, and distributed cognition. In B. A. Nardi (Ed.), *Context and consciousness: Activity theory and human-computer interaction* (pp. 69–102). Cambridge, MA: MIT Press.

Nardi, B. A. (2005). Objects of desire: Power and passion in collaborative activity. *Mind, Culture, and Activity, 12*(1), 37–51.

Nardi, B. A., & O'Day, V. L. (1999). *Information ecologies: Using technology with heart.* Cambridge, MA: MIT Press.

Nardi, B. A., Whittaker, S., & Schwarz, H. (2002). NetWORKers and their activity in intensional networks. *Computer Supported Cooperative Work, 11*, 205–242.

Orlikowski, W. J., & Yates, J. (1994). Genre repertoire: The structuring of communicative practices in organizations. *Administrative Science Quarterly, 39*, 541–574.

Paltridge, S. (1995). *Telecommunication infrastructure: The benefits of competition.* Paris: Organisation for Economic Co-operation and Development.

Paretti, M. C., McNair, L. D., & Holloway-Attaway, L. (2007). Teaching technical communication in an era of distributed work: A case study of collaboration between U.S. and Swedish students. *Technical Communication Quarterly, 16*(3), 327–352.

Pickering, A. (1995). *The mangle of practice.* Chicago: University of Chicago Press.

Polodny, J. M., & Page, K. L. (1998). Network forms of organization. *Annual Review of Sociology, 24*, 57–76.

Public Utilities Commission of Texas. (1999, April). *Meeting new challenges: Fiscal year 1999 annual report.* Austin: Public Utilities Commission of Texas.

Reynolds, G. (2006). *An army of Davids: How markets and technology empower ordinary people to beat big media, big government, and other goliaths.* Nashville, TN: Nelson Current.

Ronfeldt, D. (2007). *In search of how societies work: Tribes – the first and forever form.* Available from: http://www.rand.org/pubs/working_papers/2007/RAND_WR433.pdf.

Ronfeldt, D., & Arquilla, J. (2007, August). *The promise of noöpolitik.* Available from: http://www.firstmonday.org/issues/issue12_8/ronfeldt/index.html.

Rhodes, L., & Hadden, S. G. (1995). *The evolution of universal service in Texas: A report.* Austin, TX: Lyndon B. Johnson School of Public Affairs.

Russell, D. R. (1995). Activity theory and its implications for writing instruction. In J. Petraglia (Ed.), *Reconceiving writing, rethinking writing instruction* (pp. 51–77). Mahwah, NJ: Erlbaum.

Russell, D. R. (1997a). Rethinking genre in school and society: An activity theory analysis. *Written Communication, 14*(4), 504–554.

Russell, D. R. (1997b). Writing and genre in higher education and workplaces: A review of studies that use cultural-historical activity theory. *Mind, Culture, and Activity, 4*(4), 224–237.

Russell, D. R., & Yañez, A. (2003, February). *"Big picture people rarely become historians"*: *Genre systems and the contradictions of general education.* Available from: http://wac.colostate.edu/books/selves_societies/

Saarelma, O. (1993). Descriptions of subjective networks as a mediator of developmental dialogue. *The quarterly newsletter of the Laboratory of Comparative Human Cognition, 15*, 102–112.

Schryer, C. F. (1993). Records as genre. *Written Communication, 10*(2), 200–234.

Schryer, C. F., Lingard, L., & Spafford, M. (2007). Regularized practices: Genres, improvisation, and identity formation in health-care professions. In M. Zachry & C. Thralls (Eds.), *Communicative practices in workplaces and the professions: Cultural perspectives on the regulation of discourse and organizations* (pp. 21–44). Farmingdale, NY: Baywood Publishing.

Scott, J. K. (1992). Exploring socio-technical analysis: Monsieur Latour is not joking! *Social Studies of Science, 22*, 59–80.

Selber, S. A. (2004). *Multiliteracies for a digital age.* Carbondale: Southern Illinois University Press.

Senge, P. M. (1994). *The fifth discipline.* New York: Doubleday.

Serres, M. (1982). *The parasite.* Baltimore, MD: Johns Hopkins University Press.

Serres, M. (1983). *Hermes: Literature, science, philosophy.* Baltimore, MD: Johns Hopkins University Press.

Serres, M. (1995). *The natural contract.* Ann Arbor: University of Michigan Press.

Serres, M., & Latour, B. (1995). *Conversations on science, culture, and time.* Ann Arbor: University of Michigan Press.

Shapin, S., & Schaffer, S. (1985). *Leviathan and the air-pump: Hobbes, Boyle, and the experimental life.* Princeton, NJ: Princeton University Press.

Sheller, M. (2004). Mobile publics: Beyond the network perspective. *Environment and Planning, 22*, 39–52.

Slattery, S. (2005). Technical writing as textual coordination: An argument for the value of writers' skill with information technology. *Technical Communication, 52*(3), 353–360.

Sless, D. (1994). The telecomm bill: Redesigning a computer generated report. In R. Penman & D. Sless (Eds.), *Designing information for people: Proceedings from the symposium* (2nd ed., pp. 77–97). Fyshwick, Australia: Goanna Print.

Spasser, M. A. (2000). Articulating collaborative activity: Design-in-use of collaborative publishing services in the flora of North America project. *Scandinavian Journal of Information Systems, 12*, 140–172.

Spasser, M. A. (2002). Realist activity theory for digital library evaluation: Conceptual framework and case study. *Computer Supported Cooperative Work, 11*, 81–110.

Spinuzzi, C. (2002a). Modeling genre ecologies. *Proceedings of the 20th Annual International Conference on Computer Documentation* (pp. 200–207). New York: ACM Press.

Spinuzzi, C. (2002b). Toward a hermeneutic understanding of programming languages. *Currents in Electronic Literacy, 6.* Available from: http://currents.cwrl.utexas.edu/spring02/spinuzzi.html.

Spinuzzi, C. (2003a). Knowledge circulation in a telecommunications company: A preliminary survey. *Proceedings of the 21st Annual International Conference on Documentation* (pp. 178–183). New York: ACM Press.

Spinuzzi, C. (2003b). *Tracing genres through organizations: A sociocultural approach to information design.* Cambridge, MA: MIT Press.

Spinuzzi, C. (2003c). Using a handheld PC to collect and analyze observational data. *Proceedings of the 21st Annual International Conference on Documentation* (pp. 73–79). New York: ACM Press.

Spinuzzi, C. (2004). Four ways to investigate assemblages of texts: Genre sets, systems, repertoires, and ecologies. *SIGDOC '04: Proceedings of the 22nd Annual International Conference on Design of Communication* (pp. 110–116). New York: ACM Press.

Spinuzzi, C. (2005). Lost in the translation: Shifting claims in the migration of a research technique. *Technical Communication Quarterly, 14*(4), 411–446.

Spinuzzi, C. (2007a). Introduction to *TCQ* special issue: Technical communication in the age of distributed work. *Technical Communication Quarterly, 16*(3), 265–277.

Spinuzzi, C. (2007b). Who killed Rex? Tracing a message through three kinds of networks. In M. Zachry & C. Thralls (Eds.), *Communicative practices in workplaces and the professions: Cultural perspectives on the regulation of discourse and organizations* (pp. 45–66). Farmingdale, NY: Baywood Publishing.

Spinuzzi, C. (in press). The genie's out of the bottle: Leveraging mobile and wireless technologies in qualitative research. In A. Kimme Hea (Ed.), *Going wireless: A critical exploration of wireless & mobile technologies for composition teachers and scholars.* Cresskill, NJ: Hampton Press.

Spinuzzi, C., Hart-Davidson, W., & Zachry, M. (2006). Chains and ecologies: Methodological notes toward a communicative-mediational model of technologically mediated writing. *SIGDOC '06: Proceedings of the 24th Annual International Conference on Design of Communication* (pp. 43–50). New York: ACM Press.

Star, S. L. (1995). Introduction. In S. L. Star (Ed.), *Ecologies of knowledge: Work and politics in science and technology* (pp. 1–35). Albany, NY: SUNY Press.

Star, S. L., & Griesemer, J. R. (1989). Institutional ecology, "translations" and boundary objects: Amateurs and professionals in Berkeley's Museum of Vertebrate Zoology, 1907–39. *Social Studies of Science, 19,* 387–420.

Stone, L. (2006). *Continuous partial attention.* Available from: http://continuouspartialattention.jot.com/WikiHome.

Suchman, L. (2003). Organizing alignment: The case of bridge-building. In D. Nicolini, S. Gherardi, & D. Yanow (Eds.), *Knowing in organizations: A practice-based approach* (pp. 187–203). Armonk, NY: Sharpe.

Sumner, T., & Stolze, M. (1997). Evolution, not revolution: Participatory design in the toolbelt era. In M. Kyng & I. Mathiassen (Eds.), *Computers and design in context* (pp. 1–26). Cambridge, MA: MIT Press.

Sun, H. (2004). *Expanding the scope of localization: A cultural usability perspective on mobile text messaging use in American and Chinese contexts.* Unpublished doctoral dissertation, Rensselaer Polytechnic Institute, Troy, NY.

Sun, H. (2006). The triumph of users: Achieving cultural usability goals. *Technical Communication Quarterly, 15*(4), 483–504.

Swarts, J. (2004). Textual grounding: How people turn texts into tools. *Journal of Technical Writing and Communication, 34*(1&2), 67–89.

Tapscott, D., & Williams, A. D. (2006). *Wikinomics: How mass collaboration changes everything.* New York: Portfolio.

Temin, P. (1987). *The fall of the Bell system: A study in prices and politics.* New York: Cambridge University Press.

Thévenot, L. (2002). Which road to follow? The moral complexity of an "equipped" humanity. In J. Law & A. Mol (Eds.), *Complexities: Social studies of knowledge practices* (pp. 53–87). Durham, NC: Duke University Press.

Tuomi-Gröhn, T. (2003). Developmental transfer as a goal of internship in practical nursing. In T. Tuomi-Gröhn & Y. Engeström (Eds.), *Between school and work: New perspectives on transfer and boundary-crossing* (pp. 199–232). Boston: Pergamon.

Tuomi-Gröhn, T., & Engeström, Y. (Eds.). (2003). *Between school and work: New perspectives on transfer and boundary crossing.* Boston: Pergamon.

Tuomi-Gröhn, T., Engeström, Y., & Young, M. (2003). From transfer to boundary-crossing between school and work as a tool for developing vocational education: An introduction. In T. Tuomi-Gröhn & Y. Engeström (Eds.), *Between school and work: New perspectives on transfer and boundary-crossing* (pp. 1–15). Boston: Pergamon.

Tzu, S. (2002). *The art of war.* New York: Penguin.

Victor, B., & Boynton, A. C. (1998). *Invented here: Maximizing your organization's internal growth and profitability.* Boston: Harvard Business School Press.

Voloshinov, V. N. (1973). *Marxism and the philosophy of language.* New York: Seminar Press.

Vygotsky, L. S. (1962). *Thought and language.* Cambridge, MA: MIT Press.

Vygotsky, L. S. (1978). *Mind in society: The development of higher psychological processes.* Cambridge, MA: Harvard University Press.

Wells, G. (2001). *Dialogic inquiry: Towards a socio-cultural practice and theory of education.* New York: Cambridge University Press.

Wenger, E. (1998). *Communities of practice: Learning, meaning, and identity.* New York: Cambridge University Press.

Wenger, E. (2003). Communities of practice and social learning systems. In D. Nicolini, S. Gherardi, & D. Yanow (Eds.), *Knowing in organizations: A practice-based approach* (pp. 76–99). Armonk, NY: Sharpe.

Wertsch, J. V. (1991). *Voices of the mind: A sociocultural approach to mediated action.* Cambridge, MA: Harvard University Press.

Wertsch, J. V. (1998). *Mind as action.* New York: Oxford University Press.

Wilde, L. (1991). Logic: Dialectic and contradiction. In *The Cambridge companion to Marx* (pp. 275–295). New York: Cambridge University Press.

Wilson, C. (1971). *A consumer viewpoint on Texas telephone utilities: Report of the chairman.* Texas Senate.

Witte, S. P. (2005). Research in activity: An analysis of speed bumps as mediational means. *Written Communication, 22*(2), 127–165.

Wolfe, J. (2002). Annotation technologies: A software and research review. *Computers and Composition, 19,* 471–497.

Xavier, P. (1995). *Universal service obligations in a competitive telecommunications environment.* Paris: Organisation for Economic Co-operation and Development.

Yates, J. (1989). *Control through communication: The rise of system in American management.* Baltimore, MD: Johns Hopkins University Press.

Yates, J., & Orlikowski, W. (2002). Genre systems: Structuring interaction through communicative norms. *Journal of Business Communication, 39*(1), 13–35.

Yin, R. K. (2003). *Case study research: Design and methods* (3rd ed.). Thousand Oaks, CA: Sage.

Zachry, M. (1999). Constructing usable documentation: A study of communicative practices and the early uses of mainframe computing in industry. *Proceedings of the 17th Annual International Conference on Computer Documentation* (pp. 22–25). New York: ACM Press.

Zachry, M. (2000). The ecology of an online education site in professional communication. *Proceedings of IEEE Professional Communication Society International Professional Communication Conference and proceedings of the 18th Annual ACM International Conference on Computer Documentation* (pp. 433–442). New York: IEEE Educational Activities Department.

Zinchenko, V. P. (1996). Developing activity theory: The zone of proximal development and beyond. In B. A. Nardi (Ed.), *Context and consciousness: Activity theory and human-computer interaction* (pp. 283–324). Cambridge, MA: MIT Press.

Zuboff, S. (1988). *In the age of the smart machine: The future of work and power.* New York: Basic Books.

Zuboff, S., & Maxmin, J. (2004). *The support economy: Why corporations are failing individuals and the next episode of capitalism.* New York: Penguin Books.

INDEX

Made in the USA
Coppell, TX
06 March 2021